Reflections on Pediatric Medicine from 1943 to 2010

One Man's Odyssey through the Golden Years of Medicine— A True Dual Love Story

Byron B. Oberst, MD, FAAP

iUniverse, Inc.
New York   Bloomington

Reflections on Pediatric Medicine from 1943 to 2010
One Man's Odyssey through the Golden Years
of Medicine—A True Dual Love Story

Copyright © 2010 by Byron B. Oberst, MD, FAAP

All rights reserved. No part of this book may be used or reproduced by any means, graphic, electronic, or mechanical, including photocopying, recording, taping or by any information storage retrieval system without the written permission of the publisher except in the case of brief quotations embodied in critical articles and reviews.

The views expressed in this work are solely those of the author and do not necessarily reflect the views of the publisher, and the publisher hereby disclaims any responsibility for them.

iUniverse books may be ordered through booksellers or by contacting:

iUniverse
1663 Liberty Drive
Bloomington, IN 47403
www.iuniverse.com
1-800-Authors (1-800-288-4677)

Because of the dynamic nature of the Internet, any Web addresses or links contained in this book may have changed since publication and may no longer be valid.

ISBN: 978-1-4502-5520-2 (sc)
ISBN: 978-1-4502-5522-6 (dj)
ISBN: 978-1-4502-5521-9 (ebk)

Printed in the United States of America

iUniverse rev. date: 9/13/2010

DEDICATION

To my Beautiful and Wonderful Wife - Mary

And

Sons: Byron – Terrance - Matthew

And

Grandsons: Matthew – Justin - Conor

And

Great Grandchildren: John - Annabelle – Sam

Contents

Preface. XIII

Part I 1
From High School through the First
Year of Pediatric Residency
   Chapter 1 3
   Chapter 2 9
   Chapter 3 15
   Chapter 4 25
   Chapter 5 31

Part II. 37
The Years from 1947 to 1951
San Antonio-Japan-Detroit
   Chapter 6 39
   Chapter 7 42
   Chapter 8 45
   Chapter 9 50
   Chapter 10 56
   Chapter 11 60
   Chapter 12 67
   Chapter 13 76

Part III 79
Back to Omaha 1950 to 1959
Establishing Our Practice
   Chapter 14 82
   Chapter 15 84
   Chapter 16 86
   Chapter 17 89
   Chapter 18 91

Chapter 19 93
Chapter 20 95
Chapter 21 98
Chapter 22 100
Chapter 23 103
Chapter 24 105
Chapter 25 106
Chapter 26 107
Chapter 27 110
Chapter 28 112
Chapter 29 114
Chapter 30 117
Chapter 31 119
Chapter 32 122
Chapter 33 125
Chapter 34 128

PART IV 133
THE DECADE OF THE 1960'S
DISCOVERING MANY AREAS OF INTEREST

Chapter 35 136
Chapter 36 138
Chapter 37 140
Chapter 38 145
Chapter 39 147
Chapter 40 149
Chapter 41 153
Chapter 42 158
Chapter 43 163
Chapter 44 166
Chapter 45 167
Chapter 46 169
Chapter 47 171
Chapter 48 174
Chapter 49 176
Chapter 50 178
Chapter 51 180

Chapter 52 181
Chapter 53 188
Chapter 54 191
Chapter 55 195
Chapter 56 201
Chapter 57 203
Chapter 58 205
Chapter 59 209
Chapter 60 210

PART V 213
THE DECADE OF THE 1970'S
OUR FIRST LONG RANGE PRACTICE PLAN

Chapter 61 217
Chapter 62 219
Chapter 63 220
Chapter 64 225
Chapter 65 228
Chapter 66 232
Chapter 67 236
Chapter 68 241
Chapter 69 243
Chapter 70 245
Chapter 71 248
Chapter 72 250
Chapter 73 259
Chapter 74 264
Chapter 75 266
Chapter 76 268
Chapter 77 270
Chapter 78 275
Chapter 79 277

Part VI 279
Our New Office and the New Long Range Plan
The 1980's

Chapter 80 281
Chapter 81 288
Chapter 82 292
Chapter 83 296
Chapter 84 298
Chapter 85 300
Chapter 86 304
Chapter 87 306
Chapter 88 310
Chapter 89 311
Chapter 90 313
Chapter 91 316
Chapter 92 317
Chapter 93 319
Chapter 94 322
Chapter 95 325
Chapter 96 335

Part VII 337
The Years 1988 to 2009
The Retirement Years and New Adventures
and
New Fields to Conquer

Chapter 97 342
Chapter 98 344
Chapter 99 346
Chapter 100 351
Chapter 101 354
Chapter 102 360
Chapter 103 362
Chapter 104 365

Part VIII 369
Major Changes in 2009
A Catastrophe Happened
Chapter 105 372
Chapter 106 373
Chapter 107 374
Chapter 108 377
Chapter 109 378
Chapter 110 381

Epilogue 385

Curriculum Vitae 389
EDUCATIONAL BACKGROUND 389
MEMBER OF THE FOLLOWING SOCIETIES 390
ACTIVITIES 391
CIVIC DUTIES 396
PUBLICATIONS 397
PAPERS PRESENTED TO VARIOUS AUDIENCES. . .401
HONORS RECEIVED 408

Preface

**Reflections on Pediatric Medicine from
1943 to 2010
This story traces the Odyssey of One Man's Journey through the
Golden Years of Medicine in the Pursuit
Of his Passion of Medicine to the Present Time**

Come take this fascinating journey with me and enjoy a trip through time the likes of which you will not experience again. As I stand here at the tender age of eighty-seven looking backwards, never did I envision the many highways and byways that I would travel during my medical lifetime and afterwards. Life for me has always been an interesting and challenging adventure with the exploring of different venues and the poking into new crevasses just to see what might be hidden in there.

I will begin, not at the very beginning, but will start with my high school years where the first glimmerings of an interest in medicine began. Within a short space of time, this interest burst into a major conflagration and became my Holy Grail from thence forth.

This story has been bouncing around in my mind like a billiard ball trying to find a way to break out of its mold and to be told. My beloved Mary and I were born, raised, lived, and educated in Omaha, Nebraska except for our time spent in the Army Medical Corps and Detroit, Michigan. We traveled a great deal with and without our family. Mary and I did not meet until my final years in medical school. This meeting is a tender love story all by itself and bears telling later in this book.

In addition to graduating from the University Of Nebraska College Of Medicine, I was certified by the American Board of Medical Examiners and became a Fellow of the American Academy of Pediatrics. As this story unfolds, it will describe some of the many honors and awards that I received unsolicited from many different venues.

This tale paints with a word brush, beginning with the high school years and continues to the present day, an interesting story. It tells of the intense struggle that as a dedicated Pediatrician I endured from being torn between the seductive siren wiles and embraces of medicine versus the love and demands of a wonderful family. This story has the magic of romance, love, pathos, achievements, disappointments, and extreme happiness. This tome entails, in addition to the romance, the intricate twists of intrigue, memoirs, autobiography, and the early moments of medical history details of which are interwoven together and desire to be told. I have seen medicine change as few current living persons have. Many of these changes will be visited and explained.

This story teller begins with the early years of medicine when there were few specific therapies with which to treat patients except for the application of intense supportive care until the body could either conquer the disease process or succumb to it. In the beginning, the discovery of a method to produce Penicillin in quantities occurred somewhere in 1942-1943 and ushered in a revolution in the treatment of acute infectious diseases. As a Junior Medical Student, I observed the very early use of penicillin when it cost $25 for a million units and was used in five thousand unit doses. Over time, I watched the miracle of the effect of the many different antibiotics had on innumerable acute infectious disease states.

I will take you, the reader, from the introduction of immunizations and their effects upon the various childhood diseases, to the almost total eradication of polio, measles, mumps, and, now, chicken pox. The Whooping Cough Vaccine has had a mixed acceptance amongst the public. This was due to the untoward reporting of some overly zealous and exploiting reporter writing in an erroneous manner of the hazards of this vaccine. Because of this malicious reporting, children have died because the parents believed these reports and withheld the vaccine from their children. Unfortunately, deaths have continued to the most recent days due to this misguided information. The ever present worry of tetanus has been severely muted starting with the universal use of the tetanus toxoid vaccine amongst the troops during the WWII years. I will describe the early problems of laboratory testing due to the large volumes of blood which were required and the very difficult task of obtaining it. There was the total lack of therapeutic testing and treatment facilities such as renal dialysis, cardiac imaging, and other modalities which are now available in abundance in these more modern times. The needs for all of these critical areas had to be addressed, in the early days, in a crude, improvised, and makeshift manner. These different improvisations will be visited and explained.

Interestingly, I was a very early pioneer in the use of the exchange transfusion for the rH problem infants, in exploring the adolescent years, in studying the attention deficit child (ADD with/without Hyperactivity), in applying modern management techniques to my private practice, in exploring computer applications to healthcare and healthcare delivery, in working on an electronic medical record, and in delving into other interesting pediatric problem areas as they were uncovered. These and many other medical entities will be visited and explained.

Coupled with endeavoring to handle the wiles and seductions of medicine, I describe my growth as a husband and as a father including the many different activities our family enjoyed throughout the years from time of our boys' births through their various interests while growing up and on into their world of adulthood. I have had a fascinating life juggling my family needs versus the demands of a very large and diverse pediatric practice.

Once again, this is a recurring story of romance, intrigue, adventure, and includes the exploration of many fascinating avenues which took many twists and turns during my medical lifetime. The book is written in eight parts and is divided by the decades of time. Enjoy a trip down memory lane the likes of which will probably never be seen again. B B Oberst M.D., FAAP

Acknowledgements

To my wonderful and beloved Mary, who has been a lifelong inspiration and who has managed to keep my feet on solid ground!

To my three sons who taught me much and made life full of pleasant experiences, adventures, and some headaches.

To my main editor, Terrance Oberst, who wielded his red pen without regard for his father's feelings, likes, or dislikes.

And

To Penny Albers for her Final Proof Reading of this Novel.

Books by B. B. Oberst M.D., FAAP
Practical Guidance for Pediatric and Adolescent Practice

Computer Applications to Private Practice-A Primer
Co-Editor: R. Reid M.D.

Computers in Private Practice Management
Co-Author: J. Long

My beloved Mary   *Dr. Obie as an Intern*

Part I

From High School through the First Year of Pediatric Residency

Chapter 1

As I stand here in this moment in time looking backward in a reflective manner to the early days of medicine and gazing forward to the present and near future, I must tell this tale of the unscientific early days in medicine less this information and the advances of this unbelievable period might be lost into the grey walls of time. This Reflection will be a narrative on my various adventures and my intense passion for Medicine as it evolved over the past sixty-nine years. It started with my North High School years from January 1935 to June 1940. This was a span of three and one half years. I was always a dedicated student and enjoyed learning, especially, in new fields to conquer.

North High School Front View – East

Because my Father had been in World War I and had been a LT. Col. in the Army Reserves, I, naturally, participated in the ROTC Unit at North High. I loved football, but I was rather small and feisty. Freshman and Junior Varsity years were filled with the usual bumps and bruises plus being totally ignored by the coaches due to my size of 145 pounds soaking wet. I hurt my shoulder while playing junior varsity football as a sophomore. Dr. Sucha, an Orthopedist, treated me gratis. My glimmering interest in Medicine began with Dr. Sucha.

In those days, we wore leather helmets and had built in hip pads. I played Guard going both ways. Needless to say, my clock was cleaned at regular intervals; but I lettered in my junior year by playing in at least nine different quarters. It was unusual in those days for someone to be in both ROTC and play a major sport. My academics were excellent even though I carried five to five and one half credits each semester rather than the required four. Because my necessary requirements to graduate had been completed in three and one half years, I was eligible to graduate in June of 1940 instead of the following January 1941; which I did.

During these depression years, my Mother and I were almost destitute. Her husband left her when I was ten years old. She had no skills, but she worked on a WPA job helping poverty stricken families. Over time, she honed skills in working with youth. She became the Director of the South Omaha Social Settlement. Later on, she ran the West Side Christ Child Society Recreation Center. She was like a Pied Piper with children and could relate to them in an unbelievable manner. These jobs kept a roof over our head and food on the table.

At times when she was temporarily laid off from her WPA job, all the money we had was the $5 per week that I earned at the grocery store driving a delivery truck.

For my part at age thirteen, I burned trash papers daily for a neighborhood hamburger stand for $.25 per week. Later, I peddled my bike delivering prescriptions at $.10 per hour for the Carter Lake Pharmacy. During the summer months, I would earn $8-9 per week mostly riding my bike. I could manage the soda fountain with a flourish and could whip up a mean malted milk. There were no child labor laws at that time.

Finally, when I got my driver's license, I drove a grocery delivery truck for the Laurel Avenue Grocery. I learned how to stock shelves and to take grocery orders over the phone. This was a small personal service grocery store and catered to its customers. The customers frequently left their backdoor unlocked so that I could put the perishables in the icebox. There were very few refrigerators in those days. There were some fringe benefits connected with this job. If I could plan to arrive at Mrs. M.'s house around 10:00 AM on Saturday mornings, the bakery would be coming out of the oven. She would insist that I have some goodies with a glass of milk or cocoa. The Barker sisters made the best peanut brittle that one could imagine.

This job lasted through my first year in college. Most of my friends were in a similar financial situation. If you wanted to do such things as date or buy anything, you worked somewhere at something to earn the money.

Less someone thinks that there was all work and no play, think again. In our freshman year, a number of we boys and girls met at Bill Shook's house on Friday nights, and we rolled up the rugs for dancing space. The girls taught us to dance using different dance steps. Smooth ballroom dancing was the "In Dancing".

In my sophomore year, my first big dance was the Sea Scout Ball at Krug Park's Ballroom with Janet M. Krug Park was an Amusement Park with rides and a big swimming pool. When I was ten and eleven, I would peddle my bike from near twenty-fourth and Ames to fifty-second and Bedford, which was a long way and mostly uphill, in order to go swimming. There were no neighborhood pools. This Park has long since gone into oblivion. I dated Janet for awhile until she resumed her relationship with Ralf S., whom she ultimately married.

In my junior and senior years, it was every Friday night dancing at the Downtown Music Box Ballroom with a different date each week. This Ballroom has long been gone into dust from the destruction ball. Dancing was a wonderful pastime. You were able to hold a girl in your arms and glide around the floor. There was none of the dance by yourself hop and jump antics of today which is called dancing. After the dance, we would have a snack at the Blackstone Hotel's – now gone - Golden Spur Coffee Shop consisting of a Chocolate Éclair and a coke.

I began my relationship at this time with Don Erickson, a classmate, which deepened into a special friendship. He was a cheerleader at North High. I was never sure whether he was cheering for the team or because I was getting my clock cleaned. He was never brave enough to tell me. This friendship lasted seventy years until he left me forever. He was as close as a brother could be. We had wonderful times together cruising in my mother's little blue Willis car. I taught several friends to drive a car as cars were scare in those days. Don is the only one I ever regretted teaching as he became a terrible driver.

Don Erickson – A Friend for 70 Years

These were great clean fun years without any alcohol or sex being considered. In my senior year, there was the ROTC Military Ball. I was a Second Lieutenant. Carol H. and I participated in the Grand March. This was a very thrilling experience.

While in High School, I worked in the School Cafeteria scraping dishes at noon for all three luncheon shifts. This job took one of my study halls, and the grocery job took the last hour of school. This loss meant that with five and one half credits there was much, much night studying including Sundays. I was elected to be the Secretary of the Senior Class and made the National Honor Society.

Because of my accumulated credits and the opportunity to obtain a scholarship to the University of Omaha through the help of my Brother-in-Law, Howard Sorensen, I elected to graduate early and to start College in the fall of 1940. My position football coach made me feel really good when he said, "Oberst, if I'd known you were going to leave early you would not have been on the team". Oh well! It was my life. It worked out for the best in the long run.

Obie's Graduation Picture

Our Senior Picnic was held at Peony Park in the Royal Grove Outdoor Ballroom. The floor was as smooth as glass. Peony Park was a beautiful place. As its name implied, there were hundreds of peonies and other flowers all around the Park. The outdoor ballroom was so romantic with dancing under the stars in the cool night air. With a lovely girl in your arms, who was a great dancer, what else would you ask for? I won the prize for the best Waltz with Janet M. During the summer, as a group, we had many enjoyable Sunday picnics or went dancing at the outdoor Royal Grove Ballroom with different dates. All the "Big Bands" toured through Peony Park at one time or another. When I worked there, it was a free treat to watch and listen to different bands.

Chapter 2

I entered into Pre-Med Studies in the fall of 1940 at the University of Omaha, "OU" (now the University of Nebraska at Omaha-"UNO"), as a wide eyed naive teenager wanting to become a doctor; who thought that he wanted to take care of children. This early desire began in my junior year of High School and gradually evolved into a firm goal. My Mother's work with children certainly influenced my interest in pediatrics.

I joined the "Theta Phi Delta" social fraternity and was elected Pledge President. Over time, I was the secretary and, finally, the president of the fraternity. I was also the president of the Intra-Greek Council. I abhorred "Hell Week" so that I lobbied to abolish it and was successful. I enjoyed my years and study at the University of Omaha, except for German and Physics which were very difficult for me. I had never encountered difficulty in school subjects before. This experience was very unnerving to me.

I met a great fellow, Glenn Gustafson, who became a wonderful, but short lived friend due to the War. Glenn, Don Erickson, and I became almost inseparable. We triple dated constantly. One of us would try to obtain a date with a girl, whom was new to the three of us, every three weeks. This will sound mighty chauvinistic; but if the date was not a good dancer, she was never invited again. Glen was a "Golden Glove Champion" boxer at his weight class. I would spar with him and get my block knocked off at regular intervals. We, three, were almost inseparable until Glenn went into the Air Force. Friends used to label us as the "Grew Some-Three Some". We would sign birthday cards and other items to each other with our name and a 1/3 insignia. He was lost over the English Channel flying fighter escort for the early bombers going over Germany. I still miss him for he was such a great guy.

Glenn Gustafson in Flight Uniform

During my second year of college (1941), it became obvious that World War II was just over the horizon; then, Pearl Harbor happened. Dean Pointer of the University Of Nebraska College Of Medicine suggested to those of us who were in Pre-Med programs to apply for a Reserve Officer's Commission. The Services desired this action so we could complete our necessary classes for Medical School. We became Reserve Second Lieutenants. This action was deemed necessary by the government to ensure a continuous supply of physicians for the Armed Services.

By the end of 1941, most of the male students had left for the Service in one branch or another. There was such a shortage of male bodies that the Administration cancelled the 1942 football program. We, students, had a great three days of fun striking against this ruling and skipping classes. This activity was all for no avail. Anyway, there were not enough able bodied males to field a decent team. Ha!

Those of us in Pre-Med were informed that our education needed to be speeded up. We were to complete all of the three year requirements in two and one half years. Wow! The University of Omaha had an excellent Pre-Med Program. Mary Ward PhD, the head of the Chemistry Department, was the Counselor for the pre-med students.

Reflections on Pediatric Medicine from 1943 to 2010

Medical School entrance time had been advanced. We would start classes in March 1943 instead of the following September. This entailed a frantic and frenzied push to complete all of the required credit hours. We had to utilize both of the 1942 summer school sessions in order to obtain a full semester of the necessary credit hours. As a result, I was only able to take the required four hours of Organic Chemistry rather the desired eight hours. This loss of basic knowledge became acutely apparent to me when taking Pharmacology and Biochemistry during the second year of Medical School.

At this time, I had made the acquaintance with a fellow Pre-Med student, Bill Boelter. This friendship lasted for a many years and well into our practice years.

I had a four year Delphian Society Scholarship to the University of Omaha which was worth $50 per semester. This scholarship covered credit hours and lab fees but not books. As I lived at home and went to school using public transportation, this itinerary saved expenses. I worked afternoons from 12:30 PM to 5:00 pm at the Northwest Bell Telephone Revenue Accounting Department arranging, sorting, and moving government required records. I had to design and make new storage vaults which were located in substations around the city. This vault work comprised measuring and ordering the necessary metal shelving for these records and supervising its assembly. The records had to be placed in order and an index made so that others could locate a necessary record. This endeavor was a big job. This temporary job lasted until I went to Medical School. For some reason or another, my telephone superiors liked both me and my work. When it seemed as though my current job was about to run out, they would find new tasks for me. I ended up working for the Disbursement Accounting Department and the Statisticians Office in addition to my primary job at Revenue Accounting. This temporary job lasted for as long as I needed it. My superiors treated me very well. I even received a salary raise to $.55 per hour.

On weekends, Don Erickson and I worked at the Peony Park Ballroom taking tickets and keeping order. Chuck Malec, son of the owner, was a fraternity brother at OU and obtained the jobs for us. I, frequently, watched a beautiful girl come to the Park with various handsome escorts. She was a very graceful dancer. She had shoulder length raven black hair parted in the middle with a widow's peak. She was petite. She was about five foot four and was very slender. I doubt if she weighed more than one hundred and five pounds soaking wet. She had a beautiful Celtic complexion. It was years before I was able to find a way to meet her. I ended up marrying her. More about this real life love story at a later date.

Mary at Age 18

Because of needing to use so much public transportation, I decided to purchase a cheap used car. The John Opitz Chevrolet Dealer was just a block from the Phone Company on 19th and Dodge Street in Omaha. I bought a 1930 Huppmobile for $80 and paid for it at $5 per month. This car lasted through my Pre-Med years until gas rationing came into play. Four friends living near my grocery store in North Omaha paid for the gas in order to ride to school. The car had a cloth roof which would leak when it rained. I would past a piece of black oilcloth, which I obtained at the Woolworth Dime Store, onto the roof about every six months. I kept a small umbrella in the rear seat where most of the leaks occurred. This old car used to blow a head gasket about every four to six months. Because of the cost for replacement, I quickly learned how to put in a new one. Before I went to Med School, I sold the car to a fraternity brother, Bob E., for $50.

Until this point, I had not paid a great deal of attention to the tenants of my Catholic religion. I did not have a Catholic education as my father was against it. Through my Mother, I made the acquaintance of Father Schneider, who was Superintendent of the Omaha Parochial Schools. I would tutor with him on Sunday afternoons on various aspects of Catholicism until I was comfortable with my faith.

During this time, I began going with a lovely Lutheran young lady, Lorraine R. We dated exclusively for the next three years. When her folks began to get serious thoughts about us, we decided to go our separate ways due to our major religious differences. In those days, religion was a very essential part of life. Differences were critical. This situation was not nearly as important today.

The job at the phone company at $.50 per hour handled most of my textbook costs. By working at the grocery store on Saturdays from 6:30 am to 7:00 pm for $5 and, later on, with a raise to $7, this money paid for my other living expenses. Once again, these two jobs really cut into study time as all my classes and labs at Omaha U had to be scheduled in the mornings between 8:00 am until 12 noon. Frequently, I worked alone in the lab without much teacher assistance. This solo work hurt me in Qualitative Analysis Chemistry.

During the summer of 1942, my classes were every weekday morning and Tuesday and Thursday afternoons. This schedule was essential in order to complete the Pre-Med requirements. Work at the phone company was curtailed to Monday, Wednesday, and Friday afternoons. I worked taking tickets at Peony Park Ballroom from 7:00 pm to midnight on Tuesday, Thursday, and Saturday nights for a few extra dollars. This money was in addition to my grocery store salary. The college budget was tight but manageable. My scholarship did not pay for summer school sessions. I tried to add a job at the downtown Omaha Public Library working in the reference department from 5:00 pm to 9:00 pm. After three weeks, this addition proved to be too much to handle and still be able to study.

I finished all my Pre-Med requirements by December 1942. I was elected to the Who's Who of American Colleges and Universities, which honor was similar to being a "Phi Beta Kappa" Honoree. In those days, it was permissible to transfer the first year Medical School Credit Hours back to the University. I was able to graduate in June 1944 by transferring my medical school credits to Omaha University for my BS Degree.

My scholarship was for four years. With my leaving for Medical School early, this move left one and one half years of the scholarship available for someone else to use. I lobbied the Delphian Society that the remainder of this scholarship be given to my dear friend, Don Erickson. This transfer was made. This situation helped Don leave his job and begin to attend college until he went into the Navy Officer Training Program.

Study hours usually lasted until 1 or 2 am. There were six in my Pre-Med Class who were accepted to University of Nebraska College of Medicine. Our entrance into the school was to be in March 1943.

There were about eight weeks between the end of Pre-Med and the start of Medical School. My good Pre-Med friend, Bill Boelter, and I headed off to the Packing Houses for a job to earn our tuition money. We ended up stevedoring on the loading docks of Armour's Packing House. We loaded 80 pound boxes of canned meat into freight boxcars to go to Russia for the War effort. Over time, the two of us could outwork most of the other older and more experienced workers on the docks; so we were able to put in considerable overtime. This extra money helped to provide the dollars that we needed for our tuition. Most nights, we were hard pressed to drag ourselves home because of the fatigue factor. We earned $500 during this period. During these days, I heard more filthy language than I knew existed; and I was no angel.

Chapter 3

Bill and I had never had this much money in our lifetime. After we paid our tuition costs and bought our first semester books the money was gone, gone, gone. There was no time in the near future to earn more. Talk about anxiety!!!

Our early classes covered embryology, histology, pathology, anatomy, and similar basic science medical courses. The volume of material to cover was tremendous. We had a whole new language to learn and assimilate. In those days, a medical degree program was handled as a standard Doctorate Degree program with a major paper at the end of the first year and a dissertation prior to graduation. My first year paper was on the function of the female Fallopian Tubes. A bound research project paper was due at the end of the senior year. I wrote on Tetanus (Lockjaw) and the Tetanus Toxoid Vaccine.

My dear friend, Don Erickson, was home on leave from the Navy and came to my house for a visit. Before Don arrived, my study partner, Bill Boelter, and I opened all of our textbooks, which were many, and placed them all around the living room. When Don came in, we went from one book to another pretending to read and recite something. As he left, he said, "Boy, you fellows really have a huge amount of material to learn". We laughed and laughed at our little joke.

Dr. Latta was the supreme determiner on whether or not you passed the first year of medicine. He taught Embryology and Hematology. This was the study of blood formation and its disease states. During his first lecture, he said, "Look at the student on either side of you as one of you will NOT be there after the end of the first semester". As

I looked around, there were classmates who were Pharmacists, PhD's in Physiology, Teachers, Insurance Salesmen, and many older people. Some of whom had taken Comparative Anatomy and other direct premedical courses.

How was I going to able to compete with all of this talent while being one of the youngest members of this class? Ugh! Think about being scared spit less! Our class started with one hundred and eight and graduated eighty-six. Wow!! There was one girl in our class, Verla W. We teased her unmercifully. If anyone else outside of our class so much as looked cross eyed at her, we, all, would come down on whoever it was like a plague of locusts or a ton of bricks.

My first two embryology exams were a disaster. I was so nervous that I hurried too much to answer the four essay questions. Dr. Latta called me into his office to review the exam questions. He wondered why I failed to answer one of the four questions on each exam. I almost fell off the chair. I didn't even see them. Dr. Latta suggested that I should read the exam questions through twice before I began to answer any of them. He encouraged me by saying, "Oberst, I have studied your records; and you are able to do much better". I settled down and did much better. By the end of the first semester, all advantages the other students had previously acquired were gone. We were all on the same footing. What a relief. Now, I could compete on a level playing field.

We had one week of vacation at the end of the first semester. I spent this time studying hematology blood slides in Dr. Latta's office. This interest in blood states remained with me during my early years of practice in the 1950's.

Because of the pressures, I decided that I needed some outside spiritual help. I lived near thirtieth and Ruggles Street in North Omaha. I took the bus and transferred to the streetcar to get to school. I needed to transfer again at fortieth and Cumings street. This corner was just a block from the Cathedral. I would stop for 7:00 am Mass; then, I would pop back onto another streetcar and go on to the medical school. This action I did each weekday morning during my medical school years. This faith reinforcement helped keep my feet on the ground and addressed my need for self confidence. Today, it still is the corner stone of my life.

Half way through our first year, the Army took over the Medical Schools. We had to resign our reserve commissions. We were placed in uniform as first class privates. The Army paid our tuition and lab fees, gave us uniforms, furnished our books and lab items, and paid us $30 per month. This action happened just in the nick of time. There was no way that any money could be earned to pay for the next semester fees.

We were inducted into the Army at Fort Leavenworth, Kansas for a two week basic training program. What a Godsend and at such a crucial time when money was non-existent and no way to earn any funds. When back in school, we had to make roll call formation at 7:45 am. Classes started at 9:00 am. We had to stand for inspection each Saturday morning behind the University Hospital with shoes shined and our hair cut.

I loved Gross Anatomy, which was the main and central course, during the entire first year. I ranked tenth in my class at the end of the freshman year. This outcome was not too bad for being one of the younger whipper snappers in the group. Due to my grades, I was excused from taking the final "Four Star Chamber" examination. Most students had to suffer through this oral evaluation conducted by four examiners. Anatomy had never ceased to amaze and fascinate me about the wonders of the human body. This knowledge helped me in my future consultative practice to be able to mentally visualize what was happening within a patient.

Bill Boelter and I were anatomy partners for our cadaver. We frequently worked late in the lab. Sometimes we played dumb and childish stunts on our classmates by putting paper in all the light sockets so there was no light available at the next anatomy lab period. On another occasion, we shifted all of the dissection clothes from one locker to another wily nilly. What chaos this caused the next day when people came to change into their dissecting clothes. What a mess and anger! For fear of detection and reprisals, we stopped this nonsense. The cadaver was kept in a formaldehyde solution, which really had a distinctively bad odor; when on the bus going home, people tried to avoid sitting near us.

The two basic science years were taught by full time paid faculty. Physiology was my favorite subject in my second year and remained so throughout my medical life. How the body functioned and repaired itself was a source of total fascination for me. My paucity of Organic Chemistry knowledge took its toll in grades in Pharmacology and Biochemistry during this second year.

The Clinical Years were basically taught by Volunteer Faculty. There were only two full time paid Teachers on the faculty in the Clinical Years. One physician was a pediatrician and the other one was an obstetrician. They were paid through Maternal and Child Health Funds not Medical School funds. The junior year was divided into small groups called "Clerkships"; and we rotated though the different aspects or services of Medicine. An attending Volunteer Faculty member in that particular specialty would meet us for ward rounds each morning. The individual faculty member changed from day to day. We had large accompanying classroom lectures. Dr. E. J. Kirk, Internist, was noted as an authority on Anthrax because of his position as Company Physician for Armours' Packing House. Dr. Beber was an Internist with a PhD in Biochemistry. His questions on Pharmacology were frightening. We feared "Beber Days".

I loved my clerkship on Pediatrics. Dr. Gedgoud's rounds were marvelous. We were assigned a case to study, research, and have an oral exam by him. I had a fascinating case with Thyroid Disease. This case prompted a later interest in children with Thyroid Disease and related hormone dysfunctions. This interest occurred long before there were Subspecialists available in Endocrinology. Later on, I became sort of a pseudo Endocrinologist Subspecialist by default. These clinical years really flew bye.

I had parted from my lovely Lorraine over major religious differences during my freshman year. We had gone together for three years. We were both very strong in our different faiths. It was very traumatic for me, but this situation ended up being a blessing in disguise. Later on, I met my beloved Mary with the help of a mutual friend, Bob Stitt. My grades had suffered. I had fallen from tenth in my class to around fifty. I gradually recovered to twenty-fifth by graduation

There were almost no Residents in those early days of Medical Training. A few of the major teaching hospitals around the country offered some specialty training programs, but these were few and far between. During our Clinical Years, only one Faculty member, Dr. Frank Conlin, an Internist specializing in Diabetes, ever mentioned anything remotely resembling an ethical obligation towards our patients. To offset this lack and need, I went to Creighton University night school and tutored with Father Noonan SJ who previously had been President of Creighton and was the retired head of the Philosophy Department. He tutored me in Medical Ethics, Logic, and Theology. We, Catholic med students with the help of Father Vincent Decker SJ, formed a "Neuman Club" to help us satisfy our ethical needs.

My friend, Eugene Rutherford, was leaving for the service; so I bought his 1938 Studebaker sedan for $100. This action took care of my meager transportation needs until I went on active duty in 1947.

I discovered that I had a very great interest in Pediatrics as a vocation after my Junior Year on the Pediatric Service. Dr. Gedgoud was one of the two full time professors in the Clinical Years. He gave all of the Pediatric Lectures and conducted most of the Pediatric Ward Rounds. Later, he became my mentor, counselor, confidant, and was my practice associate for about twelve years. He was a marvelous teacher and a shrewd diagnostician of sick children. I decided that I really loved Pediatrics and wanted to go into this field.

During my Junior Year, I saw the early days of antibiotics with some of the first usage of Penicillin and Sulfa drugs at the University Hospital. The results were spectacular. During this year, I watched a forty year old mother die from Tetanus contaminated by a compound fracture of her leg. She had dragged herself through the barnyard to obtain help. She died ten days later of Lockjaw or Tetanus. This problem left a huge impression upon me. This scenario would be very unlikely to happen today because of the Tetanus Toxoid Vaccine.

Because of my past experience with Tetanus, I wrote my senior thesis on Tetanus and the emerging use of the Tetanus Toxoid Vaccine. World War II had proven the effectiveness of this biological material through its being given to personnel in a preventive manner prior to being in combat and receiving any wound. This vaccine worked preventive miracles. With several different nation's troops, who were averse to receiving the beef prepared vaccine, there was over a fifty percent death rate amidst their wounded from Tetanus.

During the summer of our senior year, Dick Kalmonsohn and I were partners on the home delivery service under the supervision of Miss Braun, a licensed midwife. We would go to the low income patient's home with the proper sterile supplies for the home delivery. Most of the homes that we were in were dirty and unkempt. This experience was quite an eye opener. We decided to take a repeat on this service, as it was available. This experience was so enlightening. It was a great teaching lesson. I was left with a feeling of charity towards the indigent which lasted throughout my practice years.

Now for a true love story, in early February 1945, my friend, Bob Stitt was home on leave from the Marine Air Corps and the South Pacific. I prevailed upon him to get a date with a young lady, Mary Nadolny, whom I had admired for a long time from afar when I worked at Peony Park. I was never able to meet her. He had worked with her at the Orpheum Theatre where she had been an Usherette. We double dated and went to the lovely indoor Peony Park Ballroom to dance.

Mary at Age 19
Usherette Uniform
Orpheum Theatre

Finally, my dream was realized. At last, I was able to meet her. It took me until March 11, 1945 to obtain a date with her. She was so popular. Naturally, we went to Peony Park to dance. Dancing with her was like having a feather in your arms. She was so easy to talk to that I am afraid that I babbled like a brook. She was such an attentive listener. I was smitten and enthralled. At the end of the first dance set, she took my hand as we walked off the floor. Her taking my hand felt just like "magic". I wanted to marry her by May, but she told me, "Forget it".

Mary and Obie First Date and Courtship at Peony Park

As her house was only a few blocks from Creighton University, I thought that I would drop in one evening and say hello. I was a gone goose when it came to my thoughts about Mary. Well, her three sisters kept me company, but not Mary. She stayed upstairs until I got the not too subtle a message and left. I never tried that caper again. I had to keep plugging away to convince her that she was meant for me. It took me until December 27, 1945 that she was convinced enough that she should marry me. I was in heaven and have been walking on air from that magic moment of her taking my hand ever after. The magic is still present in full force sixty-five years later.

Her sister, Therese, became exposed to diphtheria through a friend; so the family had to have nose and throat cultures. This was due to Quarantine on diphtheria being mandated in those days. Her sisters, Josephine and Therese, had positive Nasal Cultures and were confined to the contagious ward at the Douglas County Hospital for ten days. I was so surprised to find them at this hospital when on Junior Clerk Contagious Disease Ward Rounds. The family was very distressed at having the stigma of being a "Pest House" inhabitant. They were a very proud people. Over time and because of immunizations, the Contagious Disease Hospitals and Wards became a thing of the past.

I was not a favored person within the Nadolny family at this time as I had just begun to date Mary. Her mother was very suspicious of medical students and their supposed reputations. Pre-Med students were looked on favorably, but not med students. They were unwelcomed.

The following December 27, 1945 we were married at her parish, St. John's Church. The Church was beautiful with all of the Christmas decorations. Father Wilwerding SJ performed the marriage ceremony. When he talked to me at our Premarital Conference, he stressed the importance of keeping the romance in our relationship alive and ongoing. I endeavored to do this very thing by remembering to give my beloved Mary an Anniversary Card every March 11, which was the day that we had our first date. I would bring her flowers for no real reason; and when I had to go out of town, I would leave love notes under her pillow, inside the medicine cabinet, and by the coffee pot. I would call her every night to say good night. These simple items I still do 65 years later.

Father told Mary to always look nice when it was time for me to come home from work as there were a number of good looking girls out in the working world. She always looked wonderful to me. When I would finally arrive home after an exhausting day, she would look so pretty with her hair fixed and her make-up on. She was a frugal person and did not spend money foolishly even when we were better off. She has always taken pride in her appearance. She was and is a very "Lady, Lady Type" of person. Father was a wise man and gave us sound and useful advice. My patients enjoyed speaking with her on the phone. She had such a soothing way about her. Sometimes, I thought they would call after hours just to hear her voice.

December 27, 1945 was an amazing day. Our marriage occurred near the end of my senior year. My sister, Annabelle said, "That my face lighted up like a beacon while Mary walked down the aisle". I had to pinch myself to believe that it was really true that I was marrying her. She was so beautiful inside and out. The wedding party consisted of her three sisters, her cousin, Pat Mulvihill, Bill Boelter, and Chuck McDonald. As of this writing, the three men and Jennie, Mary's sister, have gone. It was very snowy at the time of our wedding.

Papa Joe Nadolny
Four Daughters
Tree-Mary-Jenny and Jo

We had a one day honeymoon at the Lincoln Hotel in Lincoln, Nebraska. As our apartment would not be available for ten days, my good friend, Bill Boelter and his wife, Eileen, stayed with her mother so that we could use their place. Talk about true friendship!

We had our first apartment near forty-eighth and Capitol Avenue until Mary found one closer to her parents. We ate at her parents frequently, especially on Sundays. These actions saved us money and gave us her family to enjoy. My family was scattered to both coasts and not available.

Many of my acquaintances knew that I was in Omaha. At the last minute, I would be called upon to usher at various weddings. I ended up ushering seventeen times and being a best man twice. Obviously, most of my friends were in the service and came on short leaves to get married.

I had to take the State Basic Science Tests at the end of the first two years of med school. Naturally, the exams were planned right after a week of vacation. The week was spent studying for these tests. Ho-hum! The State Licensure Examination came at the end of the senior year. In addition to these State tests, I used the option of taking the National Board of Medical Examinations and paid the $100 fee. These tests were similar in kind to the two Nebraska State tests. However, these latter tests included an additional oral examination at the end of one's internship. This certification had greater acceptance by many more states in the place of using the state reciprocity for a medical licensure. I used these exams for my Michigan license when I went to the Henry Ford Hospital in Detroit after leaving the service.

With graduation coming over the horizon in March of 1946, the decision as to where to intern became a priority. I elected to apply to the University of Nebraska Teaching Hospital and was accepted. This was a prime and prized teaching place. We did not need to move out of town. This action was very convenient for us at the time. The War had just ended. The Medical Schools wanted to resume the July to June school year. All the interns' classes before us had had a nine month internship due to the accelerated WW II program. Our class was selected to help with the desired correction. We ended up with a fifteen month internship. We received $25 per month with room, board, and laundry. We had to wear white uniforms and clean white shoes.

Obie in Intern Whites

Mary worked at the World Insurance Company for $100 per month. We were able to have a small apartment near her Mother's place. Because of our limited financial situation, we ate many meals at Mary's home which helped our budget. In addition to her salary and my $25 salary including board and room, and by me selling of a pint of blood for $25 every six to eight weeks, we were able to make ends meet.

Chapter 4

If I thought the Medical School years were grueling, boy was I wrong? There were only eight interns to cover the entire hospital. There was only one internal medical resident, an amputee, on the staff. In those days, you were supposed to dedicate your body and soul to the hospital regardless of anything else, including your marriage.

As a result, none of us were able to go outside of the hospital walls for the first six weeks we were there. We were almost stir crazy and extremely fatigued. Our wives were ready to give us our walking papers. Amongst ourselves, the interns decided to cover for each other. We were able to be off two nights during the week and one of the weekend days, I ended up being off Tuesday and Thursday nights and Sunday afternoon and evenings. Mary would come to the Hospital on Saturday evenings, which usually was quiet. We would spend it in the Intern Quarters visiting while I took calls; but at least we were together. She would take the bus home about 10:30 pm. This was not a good solution, but one we could live with. I would call her each night to say goodnight about 10:30 pm from the dark and silent surgical area.

Most of the time, the Volunteer Faculty members assigned to a service only came when you called them for assistance. Because of the War and the shortage of Physicians for the civilians, the Attendants had very little time to make charity rounds. We were on our own for the most part. We learned by the "Hands On and by Seat of Your Pants" method and a lot of time spent in the Library. When a new patient was admitted to any Ward, you were expected to do a complete Medical History, Physical Examination, Complete Blood Count, and

Urinalysis before the next day. These results had to be on the patient's chart by morning. This created quite a press if there was more than one admission on your service. During the night, if a patient needed an X-ray, you were elected to do it. It wasn't until near the end of our internship that an X-ray Technician was on call and available for emergencies. What a contrast with today's factory output on multiple procedures and fancy machines?

I discovered early on that it was quite a transition to go from books to the bedside. There was a great Nurse, Mrs. Mason, on the Men's Medical Ward who taught me how to write "Orders" on a patient's chart. On one occasion, an elderly man had a sinus infection; and I glibly wrote nose drops and hot packs four times a day. Well!!! Many times we, Interns, were up a good share of the night working on new admissions. We would endeavor to catch a nap right after lunch as this was a rather quiet time in the hospital. Because of her longevity at the hospital, "Mother Mason" was very familiar with the Interns' habits and practices. She would patiently wait until we were just dropping off to sleep. The doorbell buzzer in our room would suddenly go off waking us with a jump. This startle reflex still bothers me today when I am asleep and the phone rings. Boy, do I jump! We would have to run down the hall to reach the phone. There was not the luxury of a phone in each of our rooms. Mrs. Mason's sweet voice would say, "Doctor, you wrote an order for hot packs for patient so and so. Would you please come down to the ward and explicitly write where you want the hot packs. Do you want them on the patient's feet, abdomen, or wherever"? You would grumble all the way to the Ward; but ever after, you would pay closer attention to how and what orders were written. This lesson was not wasted on me. I made a great effort to write clear and precise orders for ever more.

In the very beginning, I knew that I did not care for surgery. However, I ended up doing more surgery than any of my fellow interns to the marked dismay of Dr. Cochran. He was just back from the War, had been a Colonel in a field hospital, and was the chief surgical resident. In those early days, he was a real pain in you know where! He was determined that I would not be rewarded with many surgical experiences during my time on the surgical service. Later on, I came to greatly admire him and his ability. We, interns, were taught routinely on how to do tonsillectomies, appendectomies, hernia repairs, and similar common surgical procedures.

In those days, most doctors were trained to be family practitioners. They would be expected to practice in outstate Nebraska, and needed to know how to do these procedures.

In addition to these operations, I was the only Intern in years at the University Hospital to do a hysterectomy under supervision by Dr. David F., Gynecologist, or to complete a nephrectomy. The Attending Urologist, Dr. Payson A., was called away for a major emergency in the middle of the operation; so I was left to complete the nephrectomy. Boy, did I feel alone and really did sweat. Due to circumstances beyond Dr. Cochran's control, I ended up doing six appendectomies; whereas my contemporaries rarely did more the three. Dr. Cochran was fit to be tied at my successes. Ha!

In pediatrics, we saw a disease entity called Nephrosis. This condition involved the child's kidneys being affected with a marked loss of blood proteins which caused huge amounts of body swelling due to stored up abdominal fluid (ascites). The fluid would accumulate in the abdomen to such a point that it would interfere with the child's breathing. The fluid had to be siphoned off by a paracentesis. A large needle was inserted through the abdominal wall. Dicky B. received this approach frequently for almost a year before he finally had a worthwhile remission. I quickly learned how to do this procedure, how to drain fluids out of the chest cavity, and many other procedures, which are seldom necessary in today's medical world.

There was Willy S. who was about three years old. Willy went next door to Grandma's house; saw a pop bottle with some liquid, which he drank. Unfortunately, the content of the bottle was a lye cleaning solution. This contact with lye corroded his esophagus. He could not swallow any liquids or food. To endeavor to correct this problem, a tube was surgically placed into his stomach through the abdominal wall. Each week when he went to surgery, an Urologist put a cystoscope into the stomach hole, and an ENT Physician sat at his head and put an esophagoscope down his throat. The physicians endeavored to dilate the esophagus from above and below. It took almost a year before this was accomplished; then a string was passed so dilatations could be more easily accomplished. What different experiences I had encountered during my internship. Wow!

One evening about 9:00 PM, I was making Chart Rounds on the Pediatric Ward. It was very quiet. Wards were big rooms with curtains between beds. There was one room on each Ward for special uses such as isolating an infectious patient.

The lights were dim; everyone was quiet and supposedly asleep when I heard some giggling sounds out on the Ward. I went to investigate when lo and behold I saw Bobby R. hanging by his knees from the back of the bed. Well! The main problem was that Bobby had had his appendix out that morning. It had been a real red hot one almost ready to burst. I almost lost my teeth thinking of all the horrible complications that might occur.

Old Bobby really received a major tongue lashing from you know who. Fortunately, nothing untoward resulted from his foolishness; but I had a big lesson in how resilient children are.

Drawing blood out of infants was a major procedure. There were no micro techniques so a large volume of blood was required for any laboratory test. I became very proficient in obtaining blood from the internal and external carotid veins in the neck, femoral veins in the upper leg, and from an infant's anterior fontanel (Soft Spot).

There was a small laboratory off the entrance to the Pediatric Ward. Every Monday morning, I had to perform a urinalysis test on each child and a quantified sugar determination on any child with diabetes.

My experiences in this teaching hospital were a series of major learning experiences which stood me in good stead for the rest of my medical years. Many of the tasks we, personally, had to do were done by paid employees in private hospitals. This occurrence was a major different between a teaching hospital and the private hospital.

My first service as an intern was Pediatrics. I was called to the Emergency Room to see an infant who confused the admitting intern. Tom Viner was on that service. I made a cursory examination of this infant, who was filthy, rigid, and had an unpleasant grimace to its face. My tentative diagnosis was Tetanus, and I called Dr. Gedgoud. The infant was critical. He confirmed my impression. Now, the fun began. The infant was tube fed a special formula. My job was to test the resistance of the baby's abdominal rigidity and to administer rectal

Avertin to relax the abdomen every three hours day and night. This regime went on for ten days before the infant recovered. My reputation was made amongst my fellow interns as one who knew his Pediatrics. I tried hard to perpetuate this illusion.

The University Hospital was a secular place and did not provide much spiritual support to the patients. When a Catholic patient desired some help, I was called to arrange for a Priest to come from a nearby parish. As there were no guidelines for the house staff to follow with Catholic patients, I wrote, with Father Decker's help from our Neuman Club days, a short brochure regarding how to provide for these patients' critical needs. This brochure included what to do with demise. This information was incorporated into the "Interns' Manual. My hospital associates teased me by referring to me as "Father Oberst". Many times over lunch, they would have fun teasing my about some Catholic Teaching as it would relate to medicine. Thanks to Father Noonan SJ I could hold my own and give back as well as I received.

About two thirds of the way through the internship, the Army sent out notices that a limited number of the current intern crop could take a year of specialty training before satisfying their mandatory two year army commitment. This mandatory payback was required because our medical training had been subsidized. I went to Dr. Gedgoud for advice about where I should apply for a Pediatric Residency.

About this time, most of the medical schools were developing many different types of residency programs to meet the demands of the returning WWII physicians. This need was created by the Physicians desiring many different types of specialty training. This demand was occurring in unprecedented numbers.

Dr. Gedgoud suggested that I stay here at Nebraska as the new Children's' Hospital was being built. It was located just behind the University Hospital. The first shovel of dirt had just been turned over. He said that he would discuss this possibility with Dr. Henske, who was the perpetual and perennial Volunteer (unpaid) Chairman of the Pediatric Department. When Dr. Henske interviewed me, he asked, "Oberst, do you want to work"? I said, "Yes" little dreaming of what all that would entail. The Army approved my Pediatric Residency for one year.

Because we had a fifteen month internship rather than the previous nine months or the standard twelve, my last three months were spent, by my design, on the OB-GYN Service. This additional time stood me in good stead during my time in the service and, later on, when moonlighting in Detroit. Dr. Willis Taylor was the Resident on this service. His Father was a popular OB-GYN Specialist. He had had a major heart attack. Bill spent most of his time holding his Father's practice together while trying to be the OB-GYN resident. For all practical purposes, I ended up running this service. What an experience for a young "still wet behind the ears" intern.

Chapter 5

As I was entitled to a week vacation during my residency, I naively asked Dr. Moser, the hospital administrator, for my week to be taken before I started my year's training so as not to break up my year. He approved. Well!!! Mary and I came to the hospital to get my mail one day and heard Dr. Henske screaming at Dr. Moser at the top of his voice. He said, "Whoever takes a vacation before they start a job. Oberst better be on the ward by 8:00 am Monday or else". Mary heard his bellowing clear down the hallway, and her eyes got as big as saucers. The following Monday I was on the ward at 7:00 am. At precisely 8:00 am, Dr. Henske came, took one look at me, and turned around and left without a word. Whew!

What a wonderful year this one turned out to be. Talk about work! Little did I know what this term would really mean? Because there was an intern on the Pediatric Service, I did not have to live in the hospital any longer. I had to be "On Call" every twenty-four hours, seven days a week. This situation worked out well as I seldom had to be called into the hospital for an emergency. I could handle most of the situations with the intern by telephone.

I learned a big, big lesson from one of the rotating interns who came onto the Pediatric service. We were discussing something about a child's behavior when he turned to me and asked, "How many children do you have"? I replied, "None". With a snide look at me, he went on to say," I thought so. You don't know a damn thing about what makes children tick. I have four little ones and I know what I am talking about". Boy! Did that remark ever give me something to think about? I spent the next forty years trying to learn about children, how they would act, and why?

As I was the first ever Pediatric Resident at the med center, I was the "Fair Haired Boy" and pet of the entire Volunteer Faculty. My tasks were many and varied. It seemed as though every faculty member had a special pet job for me. Each 7:00 am, I made rounds on every Pediatric Patient and every infant in the nursery. At precisely 8:00 am, Dr. Gedgoud would walk from his office onto the Ward. We would make rounds on all the patients together. He would try to find something I had missed. He felt great when he did, and I felt great if he didn't. On Wednesdays, I went to the Pediatric Outpatient Clinic and worked with Dr. Klok, a Volunteer Faculty Pediatrician from Council Bluffs. On Saturday morning, I was part of the Nebraska Crippled Children's Program for child heart problems, especially, rheumatic heart disease.

Afternoons from 1-3:00 pm, I went to the Child Savings Institute and performed physical examinations on the infants, who were involved in a special meat study. Dr. Clark, a General Practitioner who emphasized the care of children, and Dr. Ruth Leverton, a noted Nutritionist at the University of Nebraska at Lincoln, were conducting a Swift's Baby Meat feeding program and study. There was a nutrititionist-in-residence as an intern from the Lincoln Campus at the Institute. The lab work was done by a pathology resident. To me, the main thing we learned from this study was that very young babies could tolerate meat early in life.

Each Tuesday afternoon, I went to the Hattie B. Monroe Rehabilitation Home to check on our rheumatic heart patients. I was on call for the Creche Society Home for Court Children. Amidst these various duties, I taught student nurses on the Pediatric Ward and Medical Students, when the Volunteer Attending failed to show up. This absence was rather frequent.

During this same year, I became acquainted with a Dr. Tompkins, who had just returned from the South Pacific. He was one of the most progressive and innovative pediatricians I had ever known before or since that time. He had spent a great amount of time while he was in the South Pacific deciding as to the method of pediatric practice he desired. He was a master at interpreting "Clues" demonstrated by the infant or child as to what to expect and/or need at any particular age period. He would use these clues to give parental advice. He held parent classes on

Saturday afternoons on infant and child emotional and psychological growth and development. I attended these sessions with a passion. I was like a sponge thirsting for knowledge.

Dr. Tompkins, Dr. Ralph Moore-Radiologist at the University and, later, at Children's Hospital, used volunteer medical students' newborns, and performed a series of X-ray studies on the infants' stomach. They demonstrated different causes for infant colic. These studies evaluated faulty techniques in the feeding of infants, which could affect the infants' stomach emptying time. There were about six different faulty feeding techniques that could lead to "Colic" in an infant. With improved feeding techniques by the mother, many infants would avoid the headaches of "Colic". These studies became the basis for a series of eight published papers which I wrote in collaboration with Drs. Tompkins, Moore, and Gedgoud. The papers were published in medical journals after I returned to Omaha to practice. Later on, the Similac Company, which was an infant formula company, published a brochure with the stomach studies for their salesmen; which was to be handed out to doctors. These studies later evolved into a defined child growth and development philosophy, which I labeled "Guided Growth". This growth philosophy was promoted and highlighted during my entire practice years.

Dr. Gedgoud instituted a Mother-Infant lying-in room arrangement in the University Hospital where the infant stayed with the mother twenty-four hours a day. He had me plot on graph paper the infant's eating and sleeping pattern times, which were kept by the mother. This exercise was the basis for another paper to be published. To me, the main item we learned from this study was that first baby mothers liked the arrangement; whereas, repeat mothers declined the opportunity as they wanted to rest while in the hospital before taking their infant home. At this time, mothers and babies stayed in the hospital for ten days after childbirth. Obviously, this stay is not possible today with the extreme hospital costs. This observation was not unique to me during my practice years.

The new Children's Hospital opened its door to patients in March of 1948. Just prior to its opening, the nurses and I had to manually put together rubber tubing and glass adapter IV sets, clysis sets, sterile surgical packets, cut down sets, spinal puncture trays, and similar necessary treatment and procedure items. There were no ready made sterile packets on the shelf to open as there is today. Everything had to be placed in an autoclave sterilizer before it could be used.

I admitted the first patient to Children's Hospital in March 1948. He was a child, who was cared for by Dr. Henske. He came in for a hernia repair to be performed by Dr. Charles McLaughlin. He was a marvelous general surgeon, who became an excellent Pediatric Surgeon through repeated staff use. This acquired skill was long prior to any surgeons being available with subspecialty training in pediatrics surgery.

Original Childrens' Hospital – 1948

An intern from the University Hospital was assigned to sleep in Childrens' Hospital at night. Here again, I was "On Call" for any needs day and night in addition to the University needs. My plate was really overflowing. The roof fell in on me this same March 1948 when Dr. Gedgoud decided to leave the University and to go into practice with Dr. Tompkins. Well! I ended up running the day to day aspects of the Pediatric Department under Dr. Henske's supervision. Earlier in my interview for the residency, when Dr. Henske had said "Oberst do you want to work?" Little did I know how true those words would be and that so much would happen. This one year covered more activities for me than any two or more years in other program. All of these responsibilities stood me in good stead during my years in the Army Medical Corps.

About this same time, Dr. Henske decided to have me do some special projects for him related to costs of care. There was a lovely thirteen year old girl who had a perpetually draining osteomyelitis infection in her leg. She was in and out of the hospital frequently for surgical procedures such as scraping her bone marrow cavity to clean up the draining sites. She needed frequent blood transfusions until she reacted to them and became markedly jaundiced. This reaction took place before much of anything was known about rH Factors and other blood subtype interactions.

My job was to determine what the medical costs were. They were horrendous. Another cost study entailed a six year old girl with chronic draining ears needing multiple mastoidectomies (ear operations). With a regime of daily nosedrops, sulfanilamide, and ear drops, her ears did not drain. Stop any one of the three medications, and the drainage would begin again. The costs had mounted to well over $30,000, which in 1948 was a terrific amount.

Another milestone during my residency year was the first open heart procedure done in the state. Dr. Dewey Bisgard, the first chest surgeon in Nebraska and in this general region, studied the recently reported Taussig-Blalock and Potts Procedures for the correction of the heart malformation, "Blue Baby Syndrome – Tetralogy of Fallot". He worked for a year in the animal lab to perfect his skills. He operated on a five month infant utilizing a Potts Procedure. The operation went well, but the baby's pulmonary vessels were too small to handle the physical strain and tension of the procedure, itself. The infant died.

The erythroblastosis Rh factor had just been determined as being the cause of marked Yellow Jaundice in many newborns. The exchange transfusion, as the treatment of choice for this condition, was in its very early infancy. A baby was born with this condition at the University Hospital. Dr. Gedgoud and I performed this procedure for the first time in the state of Nebraska. In those days, it was recommended that 50 cc's of blood be used back and forth and in and out of the infant during the exchange of blood. This 50 cc volume of blood was much too much for the infant's small heart to handle. The baby died from right heart failure. Little did I know that this experience would project me into almost a subspecialty situation when I returned home to Omaha? This would be after completing my time in the service and at the Henry Ford Hospital in Detroit.

This one year of Pediatric Residency packed more and so many different types of learning experiences that anyone could ever possibly conceive. My future time in the Service utilized all of these skills and experiences that I had acquired. This year went by so fast that July 1947 came before I was mentally prepared to go into the Service for my mandatory two years. My passion for Pediatrics had received a huge enhancement during these past years.

Part II to follow
San Antonio – Japan – Detroit

Part II

The Years from 1947 to 1951
San Antonio-Japan-Detroit

Chapter 6

July 1947 came with a rush, and before I was ready for the changes. I had to report to Fort Sam Houston in San Antonio, Texas and the Brook Army Medical Center for my Officer Medical Corps Training July 1. My orders stated that I was now a First Lieutenant in the US Army Medical Corps.

We sold the Studebaker Sedan for $100 and borrowed $200 from my Mother in order to handle our travel expenses. This money had to sustain us until the Army began to issue us our paychecks. My Mother went with me to the Nebraska Clothing Company in Omaha to be fitted for my dress uniform consisting of a dark brown blouse type of office dress blouse uniform and light pink trousers. My fatigue uniform was still the fatigues from the Medical School first class private uniforms including the high top shoes, which we had been issued in our freshman year.

We took the Missouri Pacific Railroad and traveled by coach. It was very interesting in that when we left Kansas City to precede south that the coach cars became segregated. This was a new and strange experience for us. This situation became even more marked the further south we traveled.

We previously, had made reservations for the night at the old and famous Menger Hotel in San Antonio. We checked into our motel unit the next day. This was to be our home for the next six weeks. The motel was about two miles from Fort Sam. It had a small kitchenette which we utilized.

My medical and intern schoolmate, John Barmore and his wife, Dorothy, stayed at the same motel. I was able to ride to the Post in his car. We were being introduced to Medical Officer Responsibilities and Duties which were extensive. We had to start early each day with major physical exercises to get in shape. This was badly needed as we were all grossly out of condition.

John and Dorothy Barmore

We learned about food handling, food safety, and the importance of cleanliness, barrack health, immunizations for the troops. We learned why there were sanitation rules, public health matters, venereal diseases, and many other community health measures pertaining to troop health. This period of time was well spent and was very useful to me in the coming days, weeks, months, and years. Little did I realize how important this training would become?

We took a car trip with the Barmores to the Gulf of Mexico and Corpus Christie, Texas. We went out on the bay in a deep sea fishing boat. Poor John Barmore became so sea sick that he just sat holding his head while we were fishing. Mary was the best fisherwoman and caught the biggest "Drum Fish"

When we returned to shore, we went for a dip in the ocean. This dip was very refreshing and enjoyable until the tide came in about 4:00 pm. All of a sudden we were being stung by multiple floating jelly fish,

Man-o-Wars. How unpleasant this experience was. We quickly got out of the water.

San Antonio was a very interesting and lovely city. We spent our free time exploring its many different sights. We rode the bus everywhere. We encountered a major segregation experience on the bus while we were enjoying the city. Previously, we had noticed the separate rest rooms. We took a local bus and, after boarding, walked to the back of the bus. The bus didn't move. We did not know why it did not move. Finally, the bus driver hollered out, "You cannot ride in the back of the bus. Please move to the front." Embarrassed, we followed his directive and proceeded on our journey.

We went to the end of the bus line and walked the mile to the restored San Jose Mission. This Mission was fascinating and historical. However, we were disappointed in the Alamo. It was so small and not preserved very well. It could use a major reconditioning. There were the beautiful Chinese Sunken Gardens which were located in an old abandoned rock quarry. This city had one of the first open pit zoos which was amazing to us. Many years later, we returned to San Antonio for a Pediatric Meeting. The city was even more beautiful with the developed "River Walk" and the new surroundings.

Chapter 7

When our training came to a close, I was assigned to be a Ship Surgeon out of San Francisco. What a blow! Fortunately, this assignment had occurred because I did not have a listed certified residency. Once this error was rectified, I was sent to the First Army Headquarters on Govenours Island off the tip of Manhatten. The First Army headquarters had command of the entire New England States and surrounding area.

I intensely studied the train tables for sights to see and relish along the way. We took the train to Chicago and spent a day enjoying and building memories. We visited the Shedd Aquarium, The Field Museum, and saw the Buckingham Fountain. We took the New York Central Train over night in a lower berth, for an added $5, through Canada to Niagra Falls, New York. We arrived early in the morning. We spent a wonderful honeymoon day at the falls. We went below the falls wearing rain gear, walked across the bridge to the Canadian side, and had dinner there while watching the nightly colored lights on the falls from the Canadian side. The falls were beautiful with the illumination.

We returned to the train about 10:00 pm, still had the berth, and traveled down the Hudson Valley to Albany, New York. At Albany, we left the train and took the "Hudson Day Line Boat" down the River. We passed many important and historical places including West Point. We arrived at the New York City Thirty-sixth Street Pier about 6:00 pm. With the help of the "Tourist Desk", we obtained a room at the "Tudor Hotel" as we did not know anything about a Guest House being available at the Army Headquarters.

I reported to the Post on Monday morning. It was necessary to take a ferry boat to Govenours Island. There were no accommodations for dependents on the Island. We had to find a place to live. In a very naïve way, we consulted one of many "Hole in the Wall" Real Estate offices which were found everywhere. We paid a price for our naivety. We located an apartment in a Brownstone building by paying a "Finder's Fee". This apartment was just west of Central Park near seventy-sixth Street. It was one large room with a small kitchenette. There was an Opera Singer, who practiced scales all day on the top floor. There was a man on the third floor with two huge Great Dane dogs. He took them for walks several times a day. It was a strange introduction to our new life style.

Shortly after reporting for duty, I learned that there were "NO" dependents on the Island. Govenours Island needed a Pediatrician like it needed a hole in the head. The Officer's Mess was something to behold because it was the First Army Headquarters. There was a great variety and many different types of food. Cost seemed to be no problem. At noon, I would sit on the sea wall and watch the steam ships come and go. The Queen Mary and Queen Elizabeth Ocean Liners came and went past the island alternating every other week.

To get to the tip of Manhatten, I had to take the subway to Battery Park and, then, tip toe through the drunks lying there in order to board the ferry. It seemed I was like going to Alcatraz Island. When I was the Office of the Day for the weekend, I would go to the post on Saturday am. I would not come home until Monday evening when my duty time was over. Mary was scared to death to stay alone in such a strange place.

We found out that Mary was expecting our firstborn after our romantic times under the Texas moon. She had a big problem with morning sickness. On my time off, we spent a considerable amount of effort exploring New York City. We visited the Metropolitan Museum of Art, the Museum of Natural History, most of the other major Museums, the Empire State Building, the Rockefeller Center, and the Statue of Liberty. We went to Coney Island, the Bronx Zoo, Central Park, and visited many other memorable sights.

As there were no dependents on the Island, I lobbied to be transferred to a different Post. It became apparent to the Commanding Officer that there was nothing for me to do with my Pediatric Training. After awhile, I was transferred to Fort Dix, New Jersey. This was a post of about thirty thousand men with many dependents. The current Pediatrician was to be discharged soon. I was to replace him. Fort Dix was the induction center for the First Army area and was the embarkation point for Europe. Troops returning from Europe were discharged from here. It was a very busy place.

Chapter 8

As soon as I had orders for this new station, we took the train to Bordentown, New Jersey, which was close to Fort Dix. The famous boys' Bordentown Military Academy was located here. We found a place to stay in a rooming house and ate our meals at either the Bordentown Diner or the local "Greasy Spoon". We eventually, bought a very old used Chevrolet Coupe from a retiring Army Sergeant.

I took the bus to and from Fort Dix until we were able to move into the little cabin, which Dr. Allen, the previous Post Pediatrician, rented from its Philadelphia owner. The cabin was located on a dammed up lake in a resort type of area, Brown's Mills. It was located about five miles from Fort Dix. It had four rooms provided with heat from a small furnace in a hole in the ground and a propane space heater for the living room. Winters were rather chilly in our house. We fell in love with our little love nest. There was no phone, but the friendly neighbors across the road did have one and were very accommodating to our few needs. There was a drug store in Pemberton about five miles from us. We did our grocery shopping at a big store in Mount Holly about twenty miles from our house. We did our Christmas shopping at Gimbles in Philadelphia. We so enjoyed our little house and the surrounding area. The fall colors were beautiful all around the lake. It was extremely pleasurable sitting on a bench by the lake. Mary went home for the month of November for her sister, Josephine's, wedding. Now, two of the four sisters were married.

Mary on Bench by Brown's Mills Lake

During the winter, deer walked around our cabin. We cut our own Christmas tree in the nearby pine forest. With our little coupe, we traveled all around central New Jersey. This car drank oil like it was gasoline. I bought oil by the gallon at the Sears store in Trenton. We enjoyed traveling to Princeton, the Jersey Shore, and Atlantic City. One of our favorite drives was up the New Jersey side of the Delaware River for about fifty miles, cross over to the Pennsylvania side, come back along the river to the Washington Crossing area, and back home. We found a delightful place to eat on the Pennsylvania side overlooking the river named "The Cat and the Fiddle". Mary was a real trooper and enjoyed our adventurous rides.

Brown's Mills House in Winter

With the help of the Administrator of the Trenton Women's Hospital, I was able to locate an excellent Obstetrician for Mary. He was Doctor Preiss. I wanted a private Obstetrician for Mary rather than the army doctors. Our old car served us well going to and from Trenton for her prenatal checks. Cars were still very hard to come by even though War II had been over since 1945. It was now 1948.

The Post Surgeon was Colonel Threadgill, who had been trained at the University Of Nebraska College Of Medicine. Because of this fact, we had much in common. As it was a month before Dr. Allen left the Post, I was assigned to a troop dispensary. What an education! Morning "Sick Call" would average about one hundred and fifty to two hundred men. Without the experience provided by the Dispensary Master Sergeant, this task would have been impossible to handle. It was necessary to evaluate all the men on "Sick Call" within the required two hour framework. There were a number of the troops who attempted to avoid the twenty mile hikes and similar major training activities. When I was the "Officer of the Day", it was necessary to spend the night at the Post Dispensary caring for emergencies which were brought in at all hours. Added to this job, the "Officer of the Day" had to check each prisoner in solitary confinement as only one full meal in three days was allowed. In those other days, bread and water was the only food available for those prisoners in solitary confinement. There were about nine doctors assigned to Fort Dix. Most of whom were from this surrounding area.

My colleagues were from diverse medical schools such as in Bangor Maine, Philadelphia, Louisiana, Michigan and Minnesota. I found that my training might be a bit short during discussions relating to medical theory, but it was very strong on the important practical applications. Once again, I was quizzed, harassed, and teased about my Catholic faith. Father Noonan SJ came to my defense time and time again.

Fort Dix was the induction center for the New England States, New York State, and the surrounding area. As an Induction Center, it required a detailed impersonal physical examination line without any regard for privacy. It was, also the Embarkation Post for the European Theatre, and the Discharge Station for those troops leaving the service. There were plenty of bodies to be examined.

When Dr. Allen left the service to finish his Pediatric training in Cincinnati, Ohio, I assumed the Dependent Pediatric Care. Dr. Elmer Mueller had had some Internal Medical Training. He cared for the female dependents. We made a good combination. I held a "Sick Call" for children in the morning and had "Well Baby Checks" in the afternoon. There was a plentiful supply of patients available from the Fort Dix families, from a nearby major Army Hospital, from the McGuire Airbase which was adjacent to Fort Dix, and from the Lakehurst Navel Air Base, which was up the road about twenty-five miles. This was the air field where the dirigible, "Hindenburg" crashed and burned.

If I had a problem which needed a consultation and with the Colonel's permission, I would use either Dr. Joseph Stokes of Philadelphia Children's Hospital, who was world famous; or I would use Dr. Waldo Nelson of Philadelphia's St. Christopher's Hospital and author of the universally used, '"Nelson's Textbook of Pediatrics". With permission, I attended clinical conferences by these two men every other Tuesday. One conference was conveniently held in the morning and the other in the afternoon.

I tried out a few ideas to enhance my own thoughts about children's care and my future practice. I began a series of Parenting Lectures one evening a week. These talks were similar to the ones Dr. Tompkins gave to his practice on Saturday Afternoons. This action was well received. I was happy as a lark with what I was doing, and so was Colonel Threadgill. I tried out several other ideas which were used after I went into practice in Omaha in 1951.

This year, 1948, the American Academy of Pediatrics held its annual October meeting in Atlantic City. I was authorized to attend. We saw a number of useful items among the various vendors' exhibits for our coming family addition. Our baby boy came into the world on April 12, 1949. We were elated. Mary's Mother came to be with us for a month until Mary was back on her feet. Grandmother Nadolny was very experienced by having had four daughters and having previously worked at the Child Savings Institute. This institution was an infant adoptive agency. One day, I heard a sudden outburst from the bedroom; Grandma came out of the room dripping from eyes to chin. Bull's Eye! Male infants had been scarce in her life.

In May, our happy little world was shattered by receiving orders for me to proceed to Sendai, Japan, wherever that was. I quickly went to Colonel Threadgill as I wanted to stay and enjoy what I had built up in the dependent care area. He felt the same way. The Colonel was very satisfied with the current dependent care and had had very few, if any, complaints.

He moved heaven and earth utilizing all types of reasons including the Red Cross Crisis Office to change the Surgeon General's Office ruling. The last reason we used for this crisis was the fact that our infant son had developed skin eczema, needed special medical care, and utilized a specialized formula, "Nutramigen". This formula would be impossible to obtain overseas. All of this fervor was for no avail. I was heartbroken thinking of missing the watching of our boy's growth and development during his first year of life.

Between the Colonel and the Red Cross hardship documentation, the Surgeon General's office finally threw in the sponge and said, "You are a Pediatrician so take him with you and "YOU" care for his eczema". Wow! Our prayers were answered.

Chapter 9

We left Brown's Mill and Fort Dix the last of June 1949 with many feelings of nostalgia and fond memories and traveled to Omaha to Mary's folks. I took a quick "Look and See" trip to the Mayo Clinic in Rochester, Minnesota. This trip was to check out a possible residency to complete my training. A Dr. Kennedy was the Chairman of the Pediatric Department and interviewed me for the position. After a few general questions, he asked me, "What I had been doing?" I glibly and proudly explained, "I had been the Post Pediatrician at Fort Dix, New Jersey. I saw about twenty to twenty-five children in the morning "Sick Call" and about fifteen to twenty babies in the well child clinic in the afternoons". I was very pleased with my work and self. Well! Dr. Kennedy said, "Oberst, you haven't been practicing Pediatrics. You have been looking at bodies." Boy! Was I ever deflated?

Mary and Obie's Picture

Our time in Omaha was chaotic as Mary's youngest sister, Therese, was to be married the two days after we were to report to Camp Stoneman in Pittsburgh, California. This was not a very happy time for us. We flew to California and checked into a hotel for the night with our two month old baby. As our son, Byron, had skin eczema, we had tried several formulas without much success. We decided on "Nutramigen" as the one of choice. This formula was an aminoacid formulation and was very hard to obtain.

To expedite our baby's personal needs, we carried an extra suitcase which contained a small hot plate, a saucepan, several cans of Nutramigen, special plastic bottles, and a number of the new, but very crude, paper diapers which we had discovered at the Atlantic City Meeting. We could set up housekeeping wherever we landed. Remember, this was 1949. Travel with infants was neither encouraged, common, nor was it very popular. We, both, became adept at changing diapers in strange places and under unusual circumstances

When I reported to the Embarkation Post on July 1, 1949, we encountered another Army snafu. I was scheduled to sail from San Francisco, and Mary and the baby were to leave from Seattle. This arrangement was totally unacceptable to us. After waving my telegraph orders in front of many faces, we were assigned together and were to sail on July 10, 1949. We moved to San Francisco and stayed at the Hotel California until we sailed. We had carried a wicker bassinette for Byron to sleep in with us from New Jersey. Our room was on the 17th floor and had a very large closet. By was able to sleep well in the closet due to the quiet.

Knowing that Nutramigen would be impossible to obtain in Japan, I scoured all of the drug stores in downtown San Francisco for this formula. I was able to find several cans which would last for the time at sea. In desperation, I contacted the Mead Johnson Sales Representative in San Francisco and explained my dilemma. He said, "No problem. I'll make arrangements for your needs". We calculated that I would need one hundred pounds of one pound cans to last for the next year. He planned to ship the "Nutramigen" on a boat leaving before us. When we returned home to the states, we had used all but ten pounds of the formula. As the San Francisco Docks were on strike before we were to sail, he had the material trucked from Los Angeles and put it on another ship bound for Japan before we left. In this manner, a supply of the formula would be available as soon as we arrived in Japan. All this service was gratis. I looked very kindly for years on all Mead Johnson products thereafter.

While staying in San Francisco waiting for our boat, we took in many sights via the Grey Line Tours. These included the Golden Gate Bridge, the Cliff House, Seal Rock, and a tour of the nearby Muir Redwood Woods. In the woods, I had to carry By in my arms all the way. After awhile, my arms felt like they were going to fall off because of fatigue and pain. In those days, there were no "Baby Carriers" or slings on the US market. When we arrived in Japan, we found that the Japanese mothers had solved this problem centuries before. The mothers carried their infant in a papoose like carryall on their back while they worked in the rice paddies.

We took the Cable Car to Fisherman's wharf, saw China Town, viewed Nob Hill, enjoyed the Japanese Gardens and many other sights before we sailed. It was a most enjoyable time. Even though it was July, it was cold in San Francisco. Mary needed to buy a light coat.

We left San Francisco from Treasure Island on the SS Buchner, which had previously been the Queen of the Pacific Princess Cruise Line. I was the temporary Ship Surgeon to take the ship to Japan. Another physician would bring it back to the states. I found out that the Ship Surgeon was the third commanding officer aboard the vessel under the Ship's Captain and the permanent Ship Troop Commander.

We carried many dependents and troop replacements to different overseas stations. There were about two thousand passengers aboard. The Buchner traveled the "Milk Route" to Japan with stops at Honolulu, Guam, Manila, Okinawa, and, finally, Yokohama. My tasks consisted of holding a morning "Sick Call" for the troops, then, one for dependents; and, finally, an inspection of various aspects of the ship where medical oversight was critical.

The inspection of the cleanliness of the kitchen and the safety of the kitchen food preparation were very important duties. My tasks were over before noon. My time became my own. Mary, By, and myself would be together for the rest of the day.

I had a wonderful Master Sergeant in the ship hospital, who knew the Army Regulations forward and backward and all the items in between. He was in charge of the medical personnel except for the nurses. He was of great help when I was bothered by a passenger Colonel about his mistress's complaints. The Colonel had the choice to cease and desist bothering me or face being put ashore at the next port. He decided to stay aboard ship.

I was clued in to be especially particular in the kitchen area. This area was the place to head off food poisoning. This catastrophe could be devastating aboard with a shipload of people. Thank heavens for the Fort Sam Houston Training. I insisted that all pots, pans, and dishes be spotless by using a "White Glove" type inspection technique. I insisted that all food handlers had to wear white jackets, not bare torsos, when preparing food. This need was apparent even though it was very hot below decks when in tropical waters. My name was mud amongst many of these contract foreign crew members.

Our stop at Honolulu was very enjoyable as another close classmate, Elton Newman and his family, was stationed at the Army Trippler General Hospital. We had attended their wedding. We enjoyed a great weekend with them seeing the island of Oahu.

Whenever the ship came into a port or sailed away to sea, an Army Band played "Far Away Places", "Harbor Lights" and similar songs. It was very touching to see the dependents departing from the ship, meeting family members, or others having to leave their spouses behind. In those days, army personnel had to spend a year on an overseas assignment before they were eligible to have their family join them. We were very fortunate to be able go together with coordinated travel.

We passed Wake Island and Midway Island and saluted the fallen as we sailed by. We saw considerable disposable surplus army equipment lying all around on Guam. We encountered the tail end of a Typhoon off Guam which had wrecked Okinawa. We picked up several hundred Engineer Troops to take them to this island. The typhoon waves were huge. We had cold meals for three days. We tied By's Bassinette to an anchored bunk to hold it steady. He slept through the storm. What an experience! During the typhoon, I had my only major medical accident aboard ship. A boy fell off of the top bunk and broke his arm. I set it, and sent him ashore to the hospital at Manila for follow up care. My service on the orthopedic ward at Nebraska came into use with this accident.

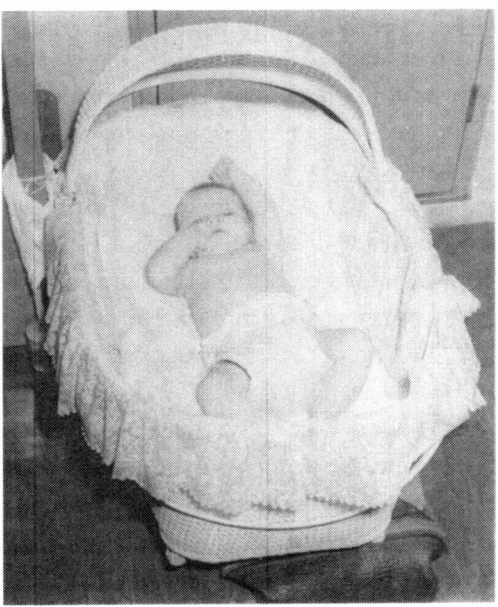

By in Bassinette – Japan 1950

When we landed at Manila, the Port Surgeon lent us his jeep and driver. The Port Officer's Club was having a fancy party that evening while we were in port. There was a tall graceful and skilled couple who demonstrated many different exotic dance steps. They put on a great floor show. The ship nurses looked after By for us and had fun spoiling him. I would usually obtain a bottle of formula from the hospital refrigerator before going to bed. By letting it sit out, it was warm enough for By when he awakened during the night. This action hit a big road block when we arrived in tropical waters. Nothing smells worse than rancid "Nutramigen". Ugh!

The War had ended in 1945. Manila was still one great big mess in 1949. There had been very little effort by the population to repair the War damage. The city had been devastated by bombs. There would be a small water faucet in an intersection which would service a three block area for all of the population's needs. People lived in squalor. They made homes in bombed out buildings using corrugated sheets for walls. We were told that there were still bodies in the Old Walled City of Manila from the War years. There must have been fifty sunken Japanese ships in the harbor. One could see parts of vessels sticking out of the water.

These vessels were caught as sitting ducks as we had been at Pearl Harbor. The communists were trying to create havoc in the Philippines. It was not safe to travel from Manila to Clark Air Base, about fifty miles away, unless one was in a convoy. The Philippine folks did not seem to have any initiative to better themselves.

After Manila, we landed at Okinawa and left the Engineer Troops to repair the typhoon damage. As Okinawa was not considered a "Secured Island", we were told to take Small Arms with us if we went ashore. Being "very brave" Ha! we elected to stay aboard the ship and be safe.

Our last stop was Yokohama after twenty-one plus days at sea. We felt that we had just concluded a "Honeymoon Cruise". We arrived in the early afternoon. While at sea, my first year in the service ended. I was automatically promoted to the rank of Captain.

Chapter 10

After we embarked from the SS Buchner, we had accommodations on the overnight train to Sendai, Japan, which had a population of about two hundred and fifty thousand people. This town was two hundred miles north of Tokyo. The bunks in the train were very short and narrow due to the small stature of the Japanese people. This small bunk made sleep very uncomfortable and next to impossible. By was in the lower bunk with Mary. There were a number of very noisy soldiers in our car making sleep difficult for me until I "Pulled Rank" and told them to, "Be quiet and watch the foul language".

We arrived in Sendai about 7:00 am. There was no one to meet us. I asked the Army Ambulance parked at the railroad station to take us to the 172nd Station Hospital. When we arrived, the chief nurse told us that we were expected the next day. She let us use her room to freshen up and care for By. We were so tired that we took a nap. We were awakened by the sound of many little click clacks. These noises were made by many wooden platform shoes walking down the street. It was an eye opener that we were going to be exposed to a very different culture and way of life.

172nd Station Hospital = Sendai Japan

Colonel Naimark was the Hospital Commandant and a long time regular army person. He had us go to the Guest House in the Kawachi Dependent Housing area, which we did. We had a lovely room and stayed there for about five days until Mrs. Naimark prevailed upon her husband to assign us housing because of our baby. This move was instituted early instead of having to wait in line for housing to become available. We were assigned a lovely two story duplex (Townhouse) which came complete with a Japanese servant, Takayama. She worked sixty hours per week at our convenience. If we wanted a cook or house boy in addition, it would cost about $7 per month for each one. We decided to have no others.

Our food was obtained at the Commissary. The vegetables were grown on a chemical hydroponic farm. The milk was reconstituted from dried powdered milk. We were constantly warned NOT to obtain or eat any food on the Japanese market regardless how good it looked. Japanese fruits and vegetables were fertilized with "Night Soil", which was human feces. There were no other forms of fertilizers available due to the size of the country and the lack of sufficient cattle. This unsanitary situation could lead to any number of severe medical problems. Fresh meat was delivered to the meat markets in open air wagons or carts and was covered with swarms of flies. There was no refrigeration in the meat markets.

As I was usually free from duties after 3:00 pm, Mary and I took long walks around Sendai while Takayama cared for By. I bought a small German Kodak "Retina II" camera at the Post Exchange and became interested in photography. I established a make-shift dark room in a closet under the stairs in our duplex. This interest became a lifelong major hobby. Later on, I bought a used Keystone 8 mm movie camera from my classmate, John Barmore. This purchase enhanced my interest in another branch of photography. These interests lasted for years and years.

As I stated, Sendai was a city with a population of about two hundred and fifty thousand people. It had been devastated by firebombs. Our house girl said it was a terrible experience. Many of the people ran to the Kawachi River and immersed themselves in the water. She told us that the water became so hot that people could not stay in the river.

The 172nd Station Hospital was housed in a previous insurance building. This building had been spared from the fire because it was made of concrete. It accommodated itself to hospital use very well.

The Japanese people were very industrious and were busy rebuilding their city. This industry and activity was markedly missing in the Manila population.

Most of the stores had earthen floors. The stores were heated by small hibachi pots using coal. Coal was very plentiful. The damp and chilly days were very penetrating during the winter. Many War prisoners had been forced to work in the coal mines. The paved streets ended just outside of the town; then, streets turned to gravel ruts. The Japanese people were very clean. Even though soap was at a premium, many times on the way home from the hospital, several families could be seen buck naked washing in the Kawachi River. There was no litter. It seemed as though everyone was dedicated to the rebuilding of their city. The Japanese women were constantly sweeping the dirt floors of the various shops.

Most shops were "Mom and Pop" managed. Sanitation was none existent. When the rice fields were fertilized in the spring, the odor was overwhelmingly vile and penetrating. Through the hospital's activity program, we were taken on an excursion to a Leper Colony which had about five hundred patients. There were about fifty very badly affected people who were blind or had deformed fingers and toes. Most leprosy was the skin form and somewhat controllable. A person contracting leprosy in southern Japan would travel north on foot to this Leprosarium so that his/her family would not be ostracized. Leprosy is basically a filth disease.

On another excursion, we were taken to the Matsushima Bay area which was considered one of the ten most beautiful spots in the world. It had hundreds of green capped islands with picturesque bridges. It was a resort area with many hotels. While enjoying the beach, one of the Japanese hospital workers was caught in a major undertow and drowned. This put a big damper on the outing.

Mary and I tried to learn to play tennis without much success. I kept the racquets for many years long after we were back in Omaha. Learning to play bridge was another item of little interest to us. Bridge playing came and went so fast that it was almost none existent.

Chapter 11

My medical duties were varied and interesting. My mornings started out with a Troop Dispensary just a few blocks from our quarters. I would walk there at 8:00 am and handle whatever patients there were. Many of the medical problems were different types of venereal diseases. I saw more and learned more about venereal disease than I ever wanted to know. I had been very naïve in this area, but no more.

An ambulance drove me downtown to the hospital. Here, I was assigned to care for the infectious disease ward which consisted of about sixty men mostly with Viral Pneumonia, Viral Hepatitis, and Infectious Mononucleosis. These diseases had many symptoms and lab tests in common. If there were any children in the hospital, they were in my province.

If I saw a soldier in my dispensary who needed an in depth evaluation, I would refer him to the hospital for a consultation. After I arrived at the hospital, I became the consultant to do the evaluation. Ha! Ha! As the Japanese were a conquered people, we were NOT allowed to fraternize with them. This admonition was repeated ad nauseam.

There were two orphanages in Sendai, one Catholic and the other one was Baptist. When there was an orphan infant or child who was very ill, the Japanese doctor would advise the Orphanage Director to call the American Doctor. When I arrived, there usually was a need for fluids because of dehydration. This condition frequently required IV fluids. There was a severe illness named "Ekri" which occurred in infants and children. A child could be well in the morning, develop nausea, vomiting, diarrhea, convulsions, and die before evening. Dr. Dorothy

Thompson, a noted researcher from the University of Arkansas, studied this problem. She determined that the situation was probably due to a very low protein diet which creates a body state of hypoproteinemia [low proteins], and low body calcium levels (hypocalcemia). Diet changes were almost impossible to achieve for these folks.

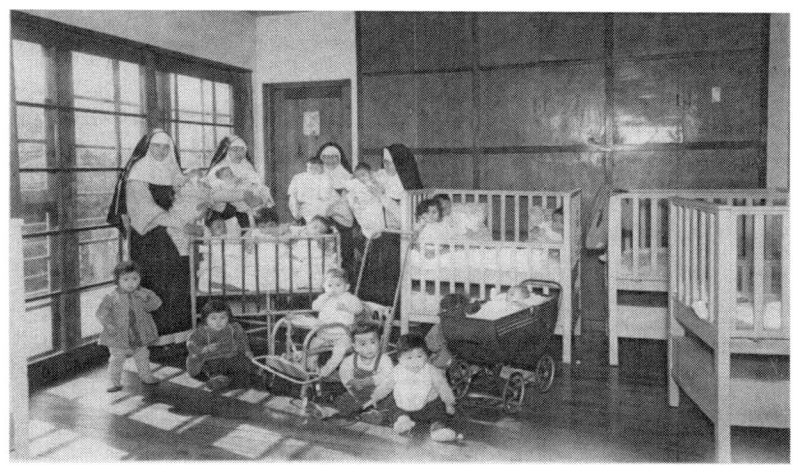

Dominican Orphanage Japan

After awhile, the Army found out about my orphanage activities and told me to stop as we were not allowed to fraternize with the occupied peoples. Instead of me going, I would send my nurse to the Orphanage. She would appraise the situation, call me, and I would tell her what to do. This system worked out fairly well for the rest of the time that I was in Japan.

There was one of the ten Imperial Medical Schools in Sendai, and it had a Pediatric ward. I would make medical rounds here every other week. This experience was a major eye opener. I saw several medical situations which were hard to believe. There was a child who suffered from seizures (convulsions) due to a calcified ascaris worm in his brain tissue. There was a child with a marked problem of Nephrosis and abdominal ascites (fluid) who needed frequent paracentesis to draw off the fluid which interfered with his breathing. The abdominal fluid would be centrifuged. All stages of the tick would be found in the acetic fluid from the larva, to the nymph, and on to the adult form of the tick. The only medication which would reduce the "Tick Count" would be antimony injections. If I had not seen it, I would not have believed it was possible. Exotic situations were rather common place due to the lack of good hygiene, poor dist, and such squalor in living conditions. It was pure, but clean, squalor in most areas.

When a child was in the hospital, the family moved in providing the nursing care, bed clothing, and food for the meals. The mother would cook on a small hibachi. It was a far cry from our immaculate and efficient State side Hospitals.

Medical Journals were very scarce and precious in this Sendai medical school. Only the head of a department was allowed to use the library facilities for specialized research problems. Everyone else had to have special permission to see and use a medical journal. The War had created havoc with the Japanese medical system as most doctors were drafted into their services. Poorly trained and, almost, but not quite physician assistants cared for most of the civilian population to their detriment. These folks were called doctors and plied their trade upon the population. The government was trying to eliminate them.

The Dean of the Medical School was a Dr. Sato, who was a famous hematologist and developer of the Hematoxyl-eosin Blood Stain which was used to differentiate the different types of white blood cells. He was a very gracious person. I had him to my hospital for a consultation several times.

Tuberculosis was a huge problem in Japan because of the poor diet, crowded living conditions, and poor sanitation. The Army started the BCG Tubercular vaccination program with great success. During the year I was in Japan, a million people were immunized. This program revolutionized the tuberculosis problem for the better.

Small pox was another major and deadly disease which was prevalent throughout the Far East. Any Army personnel had to be vaccinated for Small Pox if he or she went in or out of Japan every six months, regardless of any previous vaccinations. Malaria was another disease situation that we encountered frequently.

Many times when I was at my Dependent Clinic during the afternoon, a group of Methodist Missionaries, who had escaped out of China ahead of the Red Chinese Army, would drop by to visit. Many of these dear folks had major health problems such as rheumatic heart disease, bronchiectasis, and similar severe medical problems. While we would visit, some of them might inadvertently and on purpose receive an injection of penicillin or a needed immunization. These health measures were administered even though it was frowned upon. How could I refuse to help such wonderful people?

I had a number of interesting service personnel's children with Pediatric problems. There was a five year old child of a Medical Service Officer who developed meningococcal meningitis. She was critically ill. With a combination of sulfadiazine and penicillin, she recovered without any residual complications. For a very brief while, I was again a short lived "Hero".

When I first arrived in Japan to replace Jerry Russof, the previous Pediatrician, the Obstetrician, Jack Pritchard, informed us that he had a major rH problem on his hands. At the time of the Cesarean Section, it was apparent the infant needed an immediate exchange transfusion for the erythroblastosis fetalis problem. This exchange procedure was very new and relatively untried for both of us. Obviously, neither one of us was an expert. We were very inexperienced. We compared our few past experiences and determined a method to use. We performed a successful exchange using only twenty cc increments of blood in and out instead of the previously disastrously recommended fifty cc method. The previous method had a high mortality rate and had yielded very poor results. After the exchange was completed, the infant was evacuated to the Tokyo General Hospital for follow up care. Again, both of us were short lived "Heroes".

My worst nightmare happened when some thirteen children from one dependent area which was about fifty miles from the hospital, Camp Schimmelphening, developed polio. I had one nurse who had had any experience with an Iron Lung. This outbreak created such a concern that experts were brought over from the States. They determined that the possible cause might have been water borne. Fortunately, this situation ended without any more cases; no major paralytic residual resulted; and no need for an iron lung happened. Thank God! My exposure to polio had been nil up until this time.

I really had to grow up very fast and rely upon my incomplete training. The Island of Hokkaido was just to the north of our island of Honshu, and it had a small Army Installation. The physicians there had only nine month internships and very little exposure to pediatric problems. One doctor had a case of meningitis that was too ill to evacuate to Sendai. I would talk with this physician several times a day in the role of a consultant. This experience helped me later in my own extensive consultative practice life. The child recovered without any residual problems.

When being the "Medical Officer of the Day", everything - and I mean everything - that happened was yours to handle. I delivered many babies during my year in Japan. I am so glad for my extra time on OB during my student days and internship. I felt fairly comfortable handling most deliveries. Fortunately, I never encountered any real serious complications. There was one big, big irritation that I remember so well. It was about 2 am when a lady called and wanted to know what to do for her cat's diarrhea. Need I say more?

Rice was more than a food substance for the Japanese. It was a pillar of life. Rice was a very labor intensive crop. The rice paddies had to be hand planted with seedlings then flooded with water. Rice demanded a high source of nitrogen which necessitated the use of "Night Soil" as there was no other source of fertilizer available. This made the spring season air very pungent and odiferous. The rice farmers had city routes where they collected the human night soil using "Honey Bucket Carts".

When the rice was harvested, all sorts of methods were utilized. On a drive into the nearby countryside, you could observe people who were rolling off the rice grains by hand onto a mat. This was the same method in use 1000 years ago. Other people would be using the old flail method which had been in use for centuries. Still others used a hand held grain separator, which was about as modern as it got.

Rice was a critical material and was used in many ways besides as a foodstuff. It was used as flour for cookies and bread, and in the cooking of many dishes. Saki was a rice wine. The rice straw was made into a large hat for work in the fields, into a crude coat to shed the rain, and woven into shoe-like foot gear. The straw was fashioned into mats for the house and for bedroom for sleeping. Rice straw was mixed with adobe mud for building walls. Without rice, the Japanese would not be able to function or even to survive.

Because we were so intent on saving money while in Japan, we only bought a few mementoes and two sets of beautiful Noritaki China to take home. We had several men and women suits made as the material was cheap and the workmanship excellent. My mother sent me a kit for making a Tux. This kit included the satin for the lapels, the stiffing for the lapels, and the black silk stripe for the trousers. I can still wear this Tux today, some sixty plus years later. Frequently, I was teased about my old tux being out of date by both friends and family when I wore it at a formal occasion. Tux styles would come and go, but my tux would always come back in style if I waited long enough. I would just smile to myself and go merrily on my way. How many others could say the same thing after sixty years!

We did not travel much while in Japan but hoarded our money to buy a car when we returned to the States. We visited our classmates, the Barmores, in Yokohama by train over Thanksgiving. They came to Sendai over Christmas. We experienced several severe tropical storms and a few earthquakes. The first one was scary when we felt the house move but became used to them.

It became imperative that I make plans for completing my training before we returned to the states. I was accepted by Duke University. A Dr. Davidson, the author of the "Complete Pediatrician," was the Chairman of the Pediatric Department. Dr. Tompkins talked with Dr. Joseph A. Johnston of the Henry Ford Hospital in Detroit where he had been trained. I was accepted there and elected to go to Detroit. Dr. Johnson was world famous with his work with hormones and their influence on nitrogen (protein) and calcium metabolism. This position paid $100 per month and was much better than the previous $40 at Nebraska or the offered $50 from Duke. This decision created endless opportunities and experiences for me which was hard to comprehend at the time.

The Army did an excellent job of packing our belongings and shipped them directly to Omaha. We put them into storage. Our trip home was aboard a converted Liberty Ship, the SS Sherman. This ship was a holdover from the War. It was a far cry from the comfortable cruise ship we took to Japan. We went home via the "Great Circle Route" past the Aleutian Islands of Attu and Sitka, which were the only American territories that were under Japanese control during the War. We landed in Seattle.

It was late June when we sailed. We stayed with the Barmores prior to sailing. They were to follow us in ten days, but the Korean War interrupted their departure. There was a myth in Japan that, "If you could see Mt Fuji when leaving Japan, you would return". We were very unhappy that it was raining so hard on the day we sailed. You could not see across the street, so no Mt. Fuji was seen. We had been so very happy here that we hated to leave.

It was very cold on the ship's deck near Alaska even though it was Mid June. We put a harness on By so he wouldn't slide through the scuppers into the seas. He was a very active boy and wanted to explore everything. Sixty years later, that desire hasn't changed a bit.

Mary had to share a stateroom with six other women and children. I was bunked across the hall with three other officers. One of whom was a Ray Mellinger, who was going to Detroit and the Ford Hospital in Internal Medicine. Ultimately, he became a noted Endocrinologist. Later on, he helped me obtain Human Growth Hormone for a special growth failure problem.

Chapter 12

We arrived in port in Seattle with the band playing. I went directly to Fort Lewis Washington where I was quickly discharged from the service. We flew to Omaha. Mary and our son stayed with her Mother while I flew on to Detroit. As I had a few days before my residency started, I spent this time getting our apartment at 1215 West Bethune Street ready for Mary and By to join me. Dr. Elmer Mueller, from Fort Dix, had arranged for the apartment for us as he was already at Ford's. It was one room with a Murphy pull down bed, a small kitchenette, and an enclosed porch which we used for By's bedroom. During the winter, this room was chilly to cold. We would dress By in two warm pajama suits with the attached feet so if he became uncovered he would stay warm. Without fail and after kissing him good night, as we would be closing the door, this little voice would say, "I have to go pee pee". Grrr! We would have to undo all the clothes, attend to or not the business, and start all over. Oh! The price of parenthood is costly and/or aggravating at times. This apartment was a far cry from our Japanese quarters. Our rooms were just across the street from the beautiful Hospital lawn and flower gardens. Our parish church was down the street about four blocks.

I talked to Mary in Omaha each night. During one call she said, "By, had a terrible accident today". Naturally, being a doctor, all kinds of horrible thoughts raced through my mind, I asked, "What happened?" Mary replied, "By fell down Grandma's basement steps and broke his clavicle (Collar Bone)". With immense relief and without thinking,

I said, "Is that all"? Well! Ice quickly formed at the other end of the telephone line. Boy! Was I ever in the dog house?

Meanwhile, the Korean War broke out while we were in Omaha. The 172nd Station Hospital was the first medical unit sent into Korea and was part of the holding action in the Pusan Peninsula. I held my breath expecting to be called back to duty, but it didn't happen.

Because of the new war and a possible problem in the obtaining a car, I went immediately to the nearest Chevrolet Dealer. I ordered a car and had no stipulations as to color or other items except it was to be a two door sedan for our child's safety needs. After six weeks, we had a beautiful white two door sedan for which we paid cash. We traveled far and wide in our sweet car when I had free time. Because Detroit was so large, it took almost an hour, even on the many expressways, to get into the countryside. The traffic was fierce. Like driving in Philadelphia, if you could drive in Detroit, Chicago, New York, or Los Angeles, you could drive anywhere.

Through the help of one of my fellow residents, George Kempton, I was able to "Moonlight" one night a week from roughly 6:00 pm to 7:00 am at the St. Francis Hospital in Hamtramik, Michigan. This was a town within Detroit with its own police department, school system, other vital services, and necessities. It had over two hundred thousand Poles. At this time, the population was more than in any other place besides Warsaw, Poland. I worked in the Emergency Room and had an interpreter to aid in understanding the patient's needs. I delivered babies when the attendant couldn't or wouldn't come in, and handled any other tasks that needed to be done. This job paid $25 per night. The money made our budget and living conditions much more comfortable.

These many experiences helped when I was in practice in Omaha as there were hardly any emergencies that I hadn't encountered in all of our travels. By selling a pint of blood to the hospital blood bank for $25 every six weeks or so, this transaction gave us nice cushion for emergency situations. Mary had always hated it when I donated blood.

We frequently drove to the Orchard Lake area which was a beautiful spot and about an hour from our house. We traveled to the Gross Point region where the super rich lived, and Bell Island, which was a child park in the middle of the St. Claire River. We drove up the river to Port Huron across to Canada and down the Canadian side to Ottawa, then, back to Detroit. We frequently drove to the Cranbrook Art Museum and the surrounding countryside. The Irish Hills Country was not too far from Detroit and was a very pleasant trip. We enjoyed going to downtown Detroit and shopping at the big Hudson Department Store. It was similar to Gimbals' in Philadelphia. We enjoyed our life in Detroit, but it was too big and too congested for us to want to live there.

I reported to Dr. Johnston as a senior chief resident. Ordinarily, my duties would be to spend most of my time in the outpatient department. As I had had so much experience in this area while in the service, I asked permission to work on the hospital wards as a first year resident in addition to my other duties. I knew that I needed to hone some hospital skills that I had found lacking while in the Army. Dr. Johnston agreed and proceeded to add many fascinating duties to my itinerary. One of my minor jobs was to preview any talk that Dr. Johnston would be presenting at a medical meeting. He was a frequent guest speaker. I would do some literature research for him. He had authored books and many medical papers on calcium and nitrogen (protein) metabolism and the effect that various hormones had on these components. He made the point to me that when you were going to submit a paper for publication and when you think the paper is done; then, put the paper in a draw and leave it. After two months, read the paper. If it still says what you envisioned, then, submit it for publication. Much embarrassment is avoided by this action. Over the years, I subscribed to this philosophy with satisfying results. I published some 41 papers on various medical topics over time.

Dr. Johnston made daily rounds with the residents every morning at 9:00 AM. He was a very thin, short, kind, and friendly person who had trouble remembering some of the resident's names even though they had been around him for quite a while. We were amused by this situation. He loved to go fly fishing for trout. He tied his own flies. He persuaded some of the children to tie flies for him. Occasionally, I would see him clip a few feathers off of a mother's hat to make some flies. It was amusing to see the shock like expression on the lady's face

He was one of the shining lights in Pediatrics and had been one of the twenty-five original founders of the American Academy of Pediatrics in the early 1930's. The Academy started in Detroit. He originally came from the Boston area. Patients were brought from all over the States and South America to be seen by him.

During the morning rounds, he would use past experience stories to emphasize a point. Many of these stories I used later in teaching students in Omaha. After rounds on Wednesday Mornings and with Dr. Johnston accompanying us, we, residents as a group, drove to the Detroit Childrens' Hospital. We attended the Clinical Conference at 11:00 am with Dr. Paul Wherle leading the discussion. Again, we attended the Clinical Pathological Conference on Thursday mornings. This latter conference was conducted by Dr. Wolff Zuelzer. Dr. Johnston thought he was one of the new shining lights in Pediatrics, especially, in Pediatric Pathology. Interestingly, I was in Sendai with his cousin, who was an Orthopedist and in the regular army.

Over time, my role expanded into teaching the Henry Ford Hospital Student Nurses a full semester of Pediatrics. I had to prepare the entire curriculum for each one hour weekly class session, prepare exams, and grade the exams. What a learning experience this was. There was an adolescent ward in the hospital which housed long term patients who had positive TB skin tests. These mostly female adolescents were a part of the ongoing calcium and nitrogen (protein) balance studies relating to the effects of cortisone. This new hormone was just beginning to be available. Many medical centers were exploring the usefulness of this new wonder medication.

Dr. Rebuck, a noted Hematologist at Ford's, was studying cortisone's effect on different blood diseases. He made history in the treatment of leukemia. Up until now, a diagnosis of leukemia was a death warrant collectible within a few weeks of the diagnosis. Dr. Rebuck introduced a combination medication, including cortisone, approach to this disease. Survival rates went from a few weeks to three to six months. This was an incredible change. This occurrence opened the door for extensive new research.

I was listening to a well known Radio Talk Host the other day promoting his "Cureathon" for Leukemia and Lymphoma as a fund raiser. A man called in to pledge funds. He stated that he was a ten year survivor from leukemia. The Talk Host has been doing this fund raiser for twenty years. He noted that survival rates currently are measured by many years not just weeks. What remarkable progress this result has been in my lifetime. Cortisone is utilized in many different roles throughout medicine. It is a staple in the treatment of rheumatoid arthritis which my beloved Mary has.

My role in the current calcium and nitrogen project was to keep a record of the physical aspects of the patients for this study. Dr. Jim Sweeney, a Pediatric Pathology Resident, took care of the actual chemical calcium and nitrogen (protein) balance studies.

One of my favorite extra jobs was to check out a new Mercury sedan from the hospital garage, drive out to the suburb, Dearborn, and engage in my duties at the Greenfield Village Henry Ford Museum and School. My duties were that of a School Physician. This role included giving sex education talks to the high school students. Each Monday morning, Mary and By rode with me in the new Mercury to the Greenfield Village where they would explore and walk around the Museum building sites studying living history. Meanwhile, I was busy carrying out my duties. Later, we explored the fascinating Museum in detail seeing the original Wright Brother's Bicycle Shop, Lincoln's Springfield Court House, Stephen Foster's Home, and Tom Edison's Menlo Park Laboratory. There was a huge building filled with all types of transportation machines from a Pharaoh's Chariot to the most current automobile and, even, included an early version of the Ford Trimotor airplane.

There was a large collection of agriculture equipment from an old fashion flail which we saw used in rural Japan to large modern farm combines. With a bit of Imagination, one could almost visualize being present at some period in history. The Greenfield was a spectacular place to visit. We explored until it was time to go back to the Hospital by 1:00 PM and my ward work.

Mary frequently took By across the street to the Henry Ford Hospital Grounds which were lovely and filled with blooming flowers and a pond with gold fish.

One day, I received a call from the ER where By had had some stitches put in his scalp. He had been investigating a bike. It fell cutting his head. Mary was heard to say," I'll never be able to raise this boy in one piece". Little did she know what the future injuries would be with her boys?

Matt fell out of the neighbor's tree and broke an arm. When he was playing Prep Football on the Junior Varsity Team, I noticed one day that he could not raise either arm more than waist high. On examination, his upper arms seemed very hard to me. Dr. Bach, our Orthopedist, told Matt his football days were over because he had severe calcium deposits in both arms from blocking opponents with force with his upper arms. Matt caught Chicken Pox from Terry. The Pox lesions developed a secondary infection in each Pox site which caused Matt terrific pain if his bed was slightly jiggled. I slept on the floor beside him for three nights until he was better. Oh! The price of Fatherhood!

Terry was about six when he was playing with By, Matt, and some cousins in the basement. He was trying to hand walk a steel beam. He would get so far and, then, have to let go as the beam was too long for him to traverse. Naturally, his feet hurt when he landed on the cement floor. Undaunted, he tried again with the same results; only this time, his big brother, By, tried to help Terry down. Just as he grasped Terry's legs, By was jostled by a cousin; and, Terry fell like a pendulum hitting his head on the cement floor sustaining a ten inch linear skull fracture. He recovered OK and was doing well until one week later when I returned home about 3 am in the morning from Childrens' and heard him crying in his room. He told me that his head hurt. This stoic father of his went off like a Roman candle, and called Childrens' to tell them my son was coming in with meningitis and to get everything ready. I called Dr. Gedgoud out of bed for the same reason. After Dr. Gedgoud examined Terry, he told me with a very wry smile that Terry had a sinus infection, but no meningitis. I felt like a mitigated fool and took Terry home to bed. This story doesn't end here.

Ever after, when Terry played football, all I could see and keep my eyes on was that head running up and down the field. Even when there was a night game and I had to be at a meeting out of town by 8 AM, I watched that head until the game was over and, then, took the last plane to wherever I had to go. No old worried Dad with this fellow.

Terry was a good baseball player. When playing little league ball, he ran into the corner of the bleachers chasing a ball and sustained a bad gash in his lower groin area near the scrotum that had to be repaired. When playing football for Westside High, he was tackled out of bounds while carrying the ball and sustained a tremendous gash near the left elbow area which was filled with grass and dirt. This accident happened on a water pipe which was situated too near the sidelines. It took a long time to cleanse this wound before it could be stitched.

When By was in 8th Grade and playing football against Boy's Town, he was fielding a punt and two large opponents tackled him one from each side with a crunch. By sustained another broken clavicle [collar bone] right in front of his father from this vicious tackling by these two fellows. When sliding into third base while playing CYO Ball in his last year at Prep, he tore the cartilage in his knee. This did not bother him until he and Dale B. hid in a car trunk sneaking in an outdoor movie. He could not straighten out his leg when he tried to get out of the trunk due to the torn cartilage. Obviously, this knee had to be operated on as a major procedure in those days. Arthroscopic surgery was a long ways from this incident. When By went to Marquette for his Pre-Med studies; he played Club Football during his first year. Naturally, old worry wart Dad had to fly to Milwaukee for the games to be sure that there were no injuries.

Whenever one of the boys would get sick during the night, it was my big toe they used to pinch me awake rather than awaken their Mother. There just wasn't any justice in our house. So much for the trials and tribulations that Mary had to endure with her quiet and sedentary boys. Ha!

Mary joined a group of resident wives while at Ford's and took By with her on many occasions. One of the interns, by the name of Rupe Lovelace, had a TV set. Several of us, residents, with our families would congregate at his apartment and watch the Tuesday night prize fights. We had a pleasant social life while in Detroit.

We bought a large and thick shag rug for our combination living room and bedroom. We used a Murphy bed which was stored in a closet in the living room. By got a hold of a box of granular detergent and sprinkled it liberally over the rug. No matter how hard I tried with a hand vacuum or a broom to remove the detergent I could not I get it all out of the rug. The rug was too big to shake out. Getting up at night to answer a call to the ER was an uncomfortable experience with all the grains of detergent between my bare toes. Grrr. I wanted to crown him. When I let my mind wander, I can still feel those granules to this day some sixty years later.

As a general rule, Ford Pediatric residents spent three months at the Herman Kieffer Contagious Hospital where they were exposed to an array of diseases including polio. By design, I was not a part of this rotation. There were enough polio cases within the Pediatric Department at Ford's for me to obtain a good exposure to polio and its treatment modalities. The most dramatic case I experienced was an eighteen year old handsome and husky male who had been on a camp outing in upper Michigan. He developed bulbar polio. This type was the most serious form of polio. We tried to dehydrate the brain swelling using a hypertonic solution of fifty percent glucose as a concentrated crystalloid solution. This approach was designed to draw off the fluid from the brain tissue. This injection was followed immediately by an injection of twice concentrated human plasma. This plasma was to hold the fluids within the vascular system until it was excreted through the kidneys. This routine helped many of the polio cases, but not this big beautiful boy. He died. I brought this therapy for polio with me to Omaha along with a much better self assuredness about handling polio than I had had in Japan.

On several occasions, Dr. Johnston asked me to drive out to Henry Ford II's home on Gross Pointe where the rich mansions were located. The two Ford daughters may have needed some immunizations for a trip to Europe or to be checked for an illness. I would do so; then, I would call Dr. Johnston and report what I found. Because of the extensive security to protect the Ford family, it was like going into Fort Knox to get in and out of the home. In some ways, this security was a bit unnerving.

As I had had more but a very limited experience with rH Infant problems than anyone at Ford's, I became the major point person to handle these situations when they would occur in the Ford OB Department. I perfected the technique of using ten cc increments of blood during the exchange transfusion, instead of the twenty cc's which were recommended, with excellent success. This experience was of great importance when I returned to Omaha.

Dr. Johnston made arrangements for me to be a temporary Instructor in Pediatrics at Wayne State University, School of Nursing so that I could teach. I gave a six week course on the neonate and again, on the premature infant. I seemed to end up with many special projects during my time at Ford's in addition to the routine resident work. The different types of work seemed to flow my way just as it had at Nebraska.

There was in Detroit a special prestige, progressive, and expensive Preschool and Kindergarten school, named the Merrill Palmer School. This school specialized in studying early childhood growth and development. The school offered lectures in the evening to the parents. Dr. Johnston made arrangements for me to attend these lectures. They were interesting, but not nearly as useful as Dr. Tompkins' parent lectures, which I had previously attended as a Nebraska resident.

When I went to Ford's, I had planned on staying for two years instead of the required one that I needed in order to be eligible to take my Pediatric Board exams. I thought that I would go into an academic career. My eyes were opened wide when Dr. Jim Sweeny was trying to find an academic position at the completion of his residency time. It was almost six months before he had a job with Dr. Mitch Rubin, a noted Nephrologist, at the University of Buffalo.

Chapter 13

I had a week's vacation coming which I took in March of 1951. We drove all night from Detroit so that, hopefully, By would sleep a good share of the time. Everything went well until we arrived near Des Moines, Iowa, which was about two hundred miles east of Omaha. We ran into a miserable winter snow storm. We drove very slowly the rest of the way to Omaha and worried about the huge semitrailer trucks behind us when going downhill.

While in Omaha, I had several detailed conversations with Drs. Tompkins and Gedgoud. They offered me an easy and practical way to establish a practice with them. I would become associated with them and utilize a draw for money instead of a salary and would not have to pay any rent for office space. I readily accepted their offer and planned to begin around July 1, 1951. I had received several offers to join Pediatric Practices in Detroit and its suburbs, but we did not want to stay in Detroit. I wanted to become established soon as Mary's parents were getting along in years. I knew that her Father would not be able to work much longer. The same held true for my Mother.

When I returned to Detroit, I informed Dr. Johnston about my intentions and plans. He said he was sorry to lose me but had felt that it was inevitable. We promised our Detroit apartment to a Dr. Robert Slabaugh who was coming from Omaha to do a residency in Internal Medicine. He subsequently became a noted Omaha Internist. There were a number of "Ford Graduates" practicing in Omaha.

Because of the nature and type of training, a graduate of the Henry Ford Hospital was at least three years ahead in practice polish than someone who was trained in a State University program. This discrepancy was because you were taught how to deal and relate to patients per Se, their families, and near relatives.

As I reflected back on this year, my exposure to different medical situations was multifold and varied. I was much better prepared for starting my practice. I had achieved the added hospital exposure and treatment that I had sought upon my return from Japan. My pediatric knowledge had been greatly enhanced. My teaching skills had been honed and improved. It had been a very interesting, exciting, and worthwhile year.

Drs. Tompkins and Gedgoud owned the duplex which housed the offices. It was on an Island on forty-second and Farnam. In addition, they owned a two story house next door, which had been made into an apartment upstairs and another one on the first floor. We were very happy to have a temporary place to live on the first floor without the pain of trying to locate a house. We paid the rent.

At the office, they established a $500 monthly draw in lieu of a salary. My money put upon the books was totaled and subtracted from the draw. By October, I had worked my way out of the money draw hole and was earning my own way. This fact was amazing to me in just how fast it had occurred. My dreams were well on their way to become a reality.

Mary's Brother-in-Law, Paul Welge, was the top salesman for the Graybar Electric Company. He was able to obtain for us at wholesale prices a washing machine, clothes dryer, refrigerator, and TV set. These acquisitions were a big assist on the budget. Mary's other Brother-in-Law, Robert Arfmann, was a salesman for R.J. Reynolds Tobacco Company and an avid tennis player. When he came in off the road from western Nebraska on Friday afternoons, he tried to teach me the finer points of tennis without much success. Oh well! There was always "Tiddle Winks". It was with great anticipation that I looked forward to becoming an established pediatrician and to provide for my family. The next ten years were filled with many different challenges and opportunities.

Part III to Follow
Back to Omaha
Establishing Our Practice

Part III

Back to Omaha 1950 to 1959
Establishing Our Practice

The beginning of the pursuit of my passion for Pediatric Medicine began when I returned to Omaha. These were heady days as I could practice the way I deemed best for my patients. Early on, I had to accept and make a difficult decision which put me at conflict between my wonderful family and my pediatric practice. I could not bring home and discuss patient matters at home with my wonderful Mary. Medical care and any patient happenings are a privacy matter and an ethical one; so, from the very beginning, I lived in two totally different worlds. Sweet siren Medicine already had her clutches on me and, thus, began a lifelong struggle to maintain a proper balance between family and medicine. This mighty struggle will be apparent throughout this story. When I closed the office door and opened the family home door, I entered into a different world and circumstances.

It was wonderful having a walking textbook in Dr. Gedgoud at my fingertips. I could put in a dime asking for some information and go off with a dollars worth of data. One personal experience surprised and hurt me. When I left Omaha for the Service, I was well liked and was everyone's "Fair Haired" person. Now, I was a competitor; and some of the same physicians acted as though I was taking food off of their table.

Chapter 14

When I left Omaha, there were twenty Pediatricians and Family Physicians who saw many children. This group comprised the people responsible for setting up the necessary medical aspects for Childrens' Hospital. Dr. Donald Nilsson returned from the service in 1950 to Omaha as Pediatrician number twenty-one. When I came back to Omaha in 1951, I was number twenty-two. Dr. Nilsson was an excellent and well trained Pediatrician at the Flower and Fifth Avenue Hospital in New York City. We became good competitive friends and shared many pediatric practice ideas, especially, on practice management. We frequently met in Childrens' Coffee Shop and discussed different aspects of practice. Ultimately, he became deeply interested in and committed to Pediatric Allergy. Finally, He limited his practice to this field. He and his wife died in the MGM Hotel fire in Los Vegas. He was a real loss to the medical community.

Dr. Henske decided to retire from the State Crippled Childrens' Heart Program and as the Volunteer Chairman of the Department of Pediatrics. Dr. Gedgoud took the Heart Program over for Dr. Henske and asked me to help in this clinic, which met every Saturday Morning at the Med Center. He would see and evaluate the patients and select those with interesting heart murmurs to demonstrate to a group of Junior Medical Students. The teaching was my role.

To check on our outstate patients in the western part of Nebraska, I went, first, to Alliance, Nebraska and, later on, to North Platte, Nebraska every six months. Dr. Gedgoud traveled to McCook, Nebraska in the same manner.

Usually, I would take the overnight train to North Platte for the clinic. Occasionally, I would fly as there was a small United Airline Plane that stopped in North Platte. One of our boys would go with me to the train station about 10:00 pm. We obtained our roomette and would go to bed. The train pulled out about midnight. Each one of my sons would accompany me on this short trip in rotation. The clinic occupied the morning hours. This little excursion gave each of them an adventure in riding the train and gave me some individual quality time with each one. Before we would return on the afternoon train, we would visit a lovely gift shop in downtown North Platte and pick out a figurine for their Mother. Mary still cherished each one of these little gifts many years later.

I participated in this Crippled Childrens' Program for eight years until the Medical school hired a pediatric cardiologist; and he persuaded the State that this program should be an integral part of the University. When this was accomplished, Dr. Gedgoud and my services were no longer needed. This became a standard method by which the Med Center expanded its tentacles. I was an Instructor in Pediatrics at this time.

Chapter 15

Childrens' Hospital was having some trouble with the supervision of the University residents when they rotated through Childrens. At times, the residents were not very cooperative and were rather rude to the parents, especially, in the ER area. This attitude was having an adverse effect on the public image of Childrens'. I was asked to assume the direction of the residency program. Dr. Herman Jahr, who took Dr. Henske's place, was the first part time paid Chairman of the Medical School's Pediatric Department. I was paid $500 per month for this part time job which took about two hours each day. I handled this job for about three years until my practice could no longer spare the time.

I loved this role. I made daily rounds on all hospital patients being very careful not to tread on any attending physician's toes. I established a Clinical Pathological Conference every Thursday Morning at 8:00 am. This conference was patterned after those I had attended in Philadelphia and Detroit. We had interesting cases, discussions, and excellent guest speakers. The conferences were so well received that there was good attendance from Council Bluffs, Iowa and Lincoln, Nebraska in addition to the Childrens' Medical Staff.

After awhile, we received, from an unknown donor, funds for a Conference Recording System. Dr. Donald Nilsson, Dr. Tony Lombardo, and I acted as an editorial board. We would select an outstanding conference, edit the recording, and publish it in the monthly Childrens' Hospital Bulletin which we started. This bulletin was mailed to the Pediatric Staff and the outstate Nebraska and Iowa Physicians. This endeavor was an attempt to promote Childrens' as an important regional medical facility, and the bulletin succeeded in its mission.

The resident in charge of presenting the designated case would be required to obtain several appropriate reference articles and bring them to me by Wednesday evening. In this manner, I could study the material in order to help guide the discussion. I assimilated a tremendous amount of knowledge by this system. A facsimile of this conference is still occurring to this day although is now on Friday mornings as "Childrens' Grand Rounds".

Chapter 16

Because of my previous experiences with exchange transfusions, this attribute became a tremendous entre into newborn care in Omaha. This medical pathological entity usually left a lot of devastation in its wake. There were many serious complications resulting from the rH sensitivity factors such as cerebral palsy, stillborn, deafness, fetal hydrops with a Buddha like abdominal fluid swelling, intrauterine death, and several other major catastrophes. One of the goals of treatment was to control the level of bilirubin in the infant. This bilirubin was felt to be a major player in causing brain damage in the infant. The very low red blood counts with a decreased oxygen carrying capacity and low blood proteins were other factors to be encountered and countermanded.

By exchanging two and one half times the baby's circulating blood volume, the bilirubin would usually decrease to less than one half of the original figure. There would be an expected rebound but not high enough in most conditions to require another exchange. In my hands, the need for a repeat exchange was necessary in only about one third of the times. Never did I have to do a third procedure. Other physicians mentioned the need for three or four exchanges. I never encountered this need. The more exchanges performed the greater the possibility of having major complications arise either during or after the procedure. I lost only fifteen babies out of the five hundred infants that I treated. After an autopsy, all of these infants had impossible situations to save.

With the help of Dr. Schenken and the Childrens' Pathologist's Laboratory, I studied a number of physiological changes in the infant while it was undergoing an exchange transfusion. Some of the important changes were:

1. It was important to warm the fresh O Negative blood or hypothermia (low body temperature) could result in the infant.
2. It was important to use blood under three days old as blood any older had a very high Potassium ion content and could result in a very slow infant bradycardia heart rate or death.
3. Ten ccs of blood in and out of the infant had less adverse effect on the infant's heart rate and venous pressure than larger amounts of blood.
4. It was important to measure the Venous Pressure periodically to prevent overloading the infant's vascular system.
5. It was important to keep the infant warm during the procedure to avoid chilling and producing hypothermia [low body temperature] in the infant.
   a. After a few years, the General Electric Company developed an electric blanket which eased this concern.
6. To help avoid a major bilirubin rebound, the volume of the exchange transfusion needed to be approximately two and one half times the infant's circulating blood volume. This volume of blood frequently avoided the need for another exchange.
7. The infant's heart rate needed to be constantly monitored throughout the procedure observing to be sure that the rate did not accelerate too much or become too slow.
8. One tenth of a cc of calcium gluconate needed to be given at every one hundred cc of blood pushed into the infant to help control the heart rate and to avoid the heart stopping due to a lack of calcium and relatively high potassium levels

There were many other aspects which had to be considered but they were not quite as important as the above items.

I became a subspecialty expert in this field and had a local reputation of being a neonatologist before there were trained subspecialists in this field. By the time I had successfully performed twenty-five exchanges, my reputation was made and referrals came from all different sources. The obstetricians who handled high risk pregnancies asked for me time after time. Outstate Physicians learned through the medical grapevine about my interest and success in this condition. I began being referred one or two rH problem infants every week from around the state. Many of these infants would arrive after midnight. This procedure took about three hours to complete an exchange from start to finish. This made for a very short night and a full next day with rounds starting at 6:30 AM. Fatigue became a constant companion.

Chapter 17

I was called by a very noted and popular Obstetrician for a very critical rH problem in a major infertility problem. I was introduced to the family in very glowing and praiseworthy terms emphasizing my previous successes. About one half ways through this exchange, the infant experienced a cardiac arrest which did not respond to any measures that I tried. Now, this high powered Pediatric expert had to face the family and explain that the anxiously anticipated child had died under his hands. Never have I ever or since faced a more difficult task. The mother proceeded to adopt two children. I was honored to be their Pediatrician. We had a long and close relationship throughout her children's adolescent years.

Over time, I performed over five hundred Exchange transfusions with only fifteen deaths. My worse case that survived was that of a diabetic mother whose baby was born with a red blood count of only one half million red cells, instead of the usual four to five million RBC's, with a hemoglobin of about four grams of hemoglobin. The infant was in air hunger before we started due to the low blood count. We used about three cc of packed red blood cells in the beginning until the infant was in better shape to proceed with the regular exchange routine.

I published two papers, participated in an rH Forum, and gave presentations by invitation at three different Medical Meetings regarding the handling of this rH problem.

The local pediatricians, in self defense, began doing their own exchanges. When one would get into some problem, I would be called to help him out of his difficulty. Several generations of residents had helped me perform an exchange and were able to handle these situations on their own when they went into practice.

As a result of my successes, my practice burst into being like a gigantic mushroom cloud. I was being referred newborns from all the major hospitals in Omaha. My name was prominent across the various bridge tables and other women gatherings. I would be called to see two or three healthy newborns every day in the various Omaha Hospitals. This occurrence began to create pressure on the office schedule as these infants needed to be seen every month for their well baby checks and immunizations. I began to start hospital rounds at 6:30 am in order to arrive at the office by 11:00 am. It became necessary to alternate various hospital visits. I would go to Immanuel, Methodist, Clarkson, and Childrens' Hospitals one day, and St. Catherine, St Joseph, and, again to Childrens' Hospitals on the alternate days. Mothers and their infants stayed in the hospital longer in those days.

A major time pressure problem would result when I had an infant in trouble at Immanuel and another infant at St Joseph Hospital. These two hospitals were at the opposite ends of Omaha which required a considerable amount of driving time. No one thought about restricting themselves to selected hospitals. Sometimes I would feel like I was going to blow a gasket from the stress and strain.

Some of the older Pediatricians would use me in special situations. Dr. Clyde Moore was the Pediatrician in charge of the Nebraska Crippled Childrens' Program for cleft palates. Dr. William Shearer was the Oral Surgeon who did the repairs. This program was handled at Immanuel Hospital. Occasionally, one of the infants would need a blood transfusion. Dr. Moore would call on me to give the infant a blood transfusion using a three way stopcock, syringe and a nurse to operate the syringe and stopcock. I would insert the needle into a scalp vein if possible and hold it in place while the nurse pushed in the packed red blood cells. Sometimes it was very difficult to find a vein large enough to accommodate even the smallest gauge needle that could handle the red blood cells.

Chapter 18

Because of my success, I was able to do without a money draw from the office within six months of starting practice. I was offered an opportunity to purchase a large and desirable lot in West Omaha, reasonably, for $3,700. I took Dr. Gedgoud to see the lot for his opinion. He said it was a good investment. I needed $500 for the down payment on a land contract. This occurrence was in October which contained the Feast of Christ the King and was within the confines of the brand new Catholic Parish of Christ the King. This new parish was just being established by Father Hupp. I didn't know where I would get the money, but I said that I would buy the lot. Well! Speak of miracles. The office collections were larger the month of October than were expected or ever previously experienced. It was almost unbelievable. After my draw was settled, I had both our regular living monies and the necessary $500 for the lot. Some people would say that this happening was purely coincidental. Those of us with faith can think differently.

We did not begin to build until 1955 when the major sewer line was put in our area. This wait saved many headaches from trying to use a septic tank system due to the dense clay soil. We started with a bare dirt lot and ended with a park like setting for our home over the years. We planted every blade of grass, bush, and tree on this lot. These actions were a great labor of love. When we first bought the lot, the Omaha City limits stopped at seventy-second Street; now these limits go beyond the two hundredth Street.

Dr. Gedgoud had asthma during August and needed to get five hundred miles away in any direction from Omaha. He would go to

Colorado and the Aspen Music Festival for the month. He was a very unique and gifted person. He taught himself to play the piano and then the electric organ. He would substitute as the organist when his church needed him. He became an authority on Liturgical Music. He was a dedicated ham radio operator and played chess with several people around the country on Saturday mornings. I would cover for Dr. Gedgoud when he was out of town. The two practices kept me very busy.

A group of physicians in Australia developed a method of doing an intrauterine blood transfusion in the very severely affected rH infants. A group of physicians in Winnipeg, Canada brought this procedure to North America. With the very progressive Clarkson Hospital Administrator's, Jim Canedy, permission and financial backing, I made arrangements to fly there with a medical team including an Obstetrician, Dr. Bill Rumbolz, and a Clinical Pathologist, Dr. John Grier, to observe and learn this technique. We were on call to come whenever there was a patient available to observe performing this new technique. We flew to Winnipeg in the winter time when it was thirty-two below zero. My, it was so cold that you did not want to take a breath when outside of a building.

We brought the details back to Omaha and used it several times with good results in situations that would have resulted in a stillborn infant. This procedure was both very costly and very time consuming. When someone at the Medical School became interested and desired to assume this role, we happily let him proceed and wished him well.

When the birth control "Pill" came into existence, the number of pregnancies per family diminished markedly; and so did the affected rH babies fall dramatically. This occurrence was because the "Pill" lessened the number of pregnancies and decreased the rH sensitization of the mother. With the development of RhoGam to give to rH negative mothers, during a pregnancy with the potential for an rH problem and to neutralize the rH antibodies, this medical condition almost disappeared. Today, if I had to rely on this entity to earn an income, I would be out of luck and would starve to death.

Chapter 19

Because of the experience with this specific blood problem, my interest expanded into blood clotting disorders. There were no trained Hematologists in those days; so I became somewhat interested in other blood entities thanks to my studying blood slides in Dr. Latta's office as a freshman medical student. I had as patients, the two Christiansen brothers, with Hemophilia. In those days, there was no commercial blood clotting factors available as there is today. Fresh whole blood was the only therapy available. After many, many transfusions, the problem of hemociderosis (liver loaded with iron from the blood break down) became apparent. It was no longer possible to use blood transfusions when a bleeding situation occurred. The boys' mother was a nurse. I cared for these brothers until their teen years. Being active boys, it was almost impossible to keep them from getting bruises. These actions would result in bleeding problems for all of us to cope with.

A low blood platelet count was another blood clotting difficulty which I encountered at intervals. The main entity was called thrombocytopenic purpura (too few platelets). There was no technique to separate out or to concentrate the platelets, then, as there is today. Fresh whole blood was used with as much of the plasma siphoned off as possible in order to concentrate the platelets. On rare occasions, the overly active spleen, (which destroyed the platelets) had to be removed. If the platelet count went too low, there was a major danger of bleeding into the brain. Within a few years, Dr. Peyton Pratt joined the Omaha Medical Community as the first certified Hematologist in Omaha so this vacuum was rectified. As I was no longer needed in certain blood problems, my interests turned in other directions.

Chapter 20

The year 1952 goes down in Omaha's history as a huge nightmare time. Polio came in like the whirlwind of a tornado. The epidemic was statewide. Parents were panic stricken if their child complained of a headache, stiff neck, or similar symptoms. From mid July to the freezing frost in the fall, I was rarely home. There were over three hundred and sixty children in Childrens' Hospital with polio during this summer. We used alcoves for bed space. Most of the children had lower limb paralysis. Bulbar polio was a beast to handle. There was a constant census of at least fourteen iron lungs in operation at all times. The Omaha Fire Department stored and serviced the Iron Lungs. All the Pediatricians pooled their time and made hospital rounds at staggered times. We would see our own patients and, then, check on all of the children in the lungs.

When a child was in a lung, there was a major concern because of the potential of a respiratory acidosis developing as the iron lung ran continuously. There was no in between of regulation of the iron lung for fast or slow. The body had no way to protect itself from this condition. There was no blood pH test available-not even a crude one to aid in handling this complication. There was a wonderful resident, Bill Stanage, and a Pathology resident, John Brown, with the help of Dr. Jacobi, who was the head of the UNMC Biochemistry Laboratory, and I developed a colorimetric method to crudely test blood pH. This was a big help. It was much more than we had had previously. The next year the Beckman Photometer was developed which could easily make this determination. Our findings were reported in a paper in the Journal of Pediatrics.

I can still shut my eyes after all these years and see Holly B., Pamela H., and Connie C. with their polio difficulties. Holly died. Connie should not be alive, or she should have had some major CNS problems. She was sent in from Grand Island, Nebraska because her sister and Grandmother had just died from polio. She was sent to Omaha in desperation. She had bulbar polio with temps of 106-108 F for several days. We tried to control the temperatures with cold body packs, but to no avail. These were temperatures the like of which few people had and survived. She would turn blue, have convulsions, and be in extremis. We did all the standard treatments including the dehydration routine from Ford's Hospital without any improvement. The parents asked if there was anything they could be doing to help. I told them, "You can pray for all your worth". Two days later when I made my hospital rounds, her temp had come down spontaneously; and the road to recovery started. I had a hard time accepting this miraculous change. I never thought she would have a brain cell left in her head after those severe temperatures. After she was discharged, I saw her in one month, three months, and six months. She showed no signs of any type of residual problems including limb paralysis.

When she graduated from high school, she was the class valedictorian. She won a full scholarship to a prestigious university. This nightmare happened over the Labor Day weekend of 1952. Her father sent me information on her achievements on what he called, "My lost weekend," and it surely was. Connie is a mother and lives in Bellevue, Nebraska, which was a town south of Omaha. She had no residual from her original polio and no post polio syndrome. How fortunate for her. My son, Matt, and his wife, Nancy, met Connie on one occasion at some meeting in Bellevue and exchanged thoughts. To me, Connie is living proof of the power of prayer.

This experience taught me a major lesson in the power of faith. With this exposure, I endeavored to learn about other people's faith. It became obvious to me that if I could converse with the folks within their own understandings and beliefs; it would aid the parents' peace of mind and help in the treatment of their patient. When I encountered a family whose faith did not accept the need for blood transfusions, I would explain my position of insisting and/or court use, if necessary, to give the child the necessary blood transfusion in order to save a life. The family could either accept or reject my care. The decision was left in their hands without any rancor. Fortunately, this situation never reared its ugly head. If I encountered a family who had no faith, my heart would fall into my shoes as there was very little that could be said to comfort them.

One of the most serious problems in premature and newborn babies was the pulmonary hyaline membrane entity. This was the situation with Jackie Kennedy's premature infant who died. For a long time there was very little that we could do except support the infant. It always hurt me inside when I would lose an infant or child even though there wasn't much more that I could do for the patient. My beloved Mary was a Godsend for me when this happened. She had such a knack for helping me recover from the discouragement that would descend upon me when this situation would occur.

Many times, the nursery Nurses would ask me to baptize a baby in critical distress as there were almost no provisions in the early days for faith support. Today, it is much different. At times when a child died at Childrens' and the parents knew no priest or minister; the Nurses would ask me to talk to the family. The Nurses seemed to think that I could help people with their grief. As maudlin as it may seem to some folks, I felt that part of my role as a physician was to do God's work. This faith helped to support me many times over.

Pamela H., a beautiful four year old blond child, was in an Iron Lung for over a year. Her paralysis crept up and up until it was just below her eye balls. We used everything including the kitchen sink to aid her. Gradually, the paralysis began to recede very, very slowly. At long last, she was out of the Lung and had residual paralysis from the hips downward. Her parents proceeded to learn the "Sister Kenny Method" of hot packs and exercise. Never have I ever encountered a more dedicated set of parents. They worked and worked on their child and wouldn't let her give up trying to get better. Years later and the last time I saw Pam, she was walking with only lower leg braces, had gone to college, and had a job with the State Disability Program counseling clients. To me, this was another unforeseen miracle and the result of dedicated parents.

Chapter 21

As we lived on a very busy street in 1951-52, Mary wanted to move to a quieter area. By would enjoy having tea parties on the front porch of our house. When the ambulance would turn our corner of forty-second and Farnam Street on its way to the County Hospital ER, with the sirens blaring, poor By would be so frightened that he would dash crying into the house.

Mary found a home to move to from the apartment, we had more room, a yard, and our second son joined our family at this house. Our third son, Matt, was conceived in this house. She had to handle all of the details of the move herself for I seldom was able to leave the hospital as so many of my patients were so critically ill with polio. This house was an older home just across the street from our first apartment.

My venture into tennis with Bob Arfmann was not at all rewarding so that sport was given up. Next, I tried golf. Early Sunday mornings I would go with several of my former resident mates. Never having played before, it was not considered what I would call a truly successful venture. I put off golf for a number of years. I, finally, took some lessons so that I would know which end of the club was used to hit the golf ball.

Remember, there were only thirteen deaths out of total of the three hundred and sixty plus children, who had been hospitalized in Childrens' with polio during that horrendous epidemic. A few years after this frightening nightmare, the Salk vaccine became available with its miraculous results. As an offshoot of the effects of the vaccine, children could now go swimming in the summer, go to the movies, and play with others during these months free from the fear of polio. This vaccine literally changed the summer economic scene. The ability to go on a vacation without worry became a reality.

As this medical vista righted itself, I encountered a most unusual situation. I was called to the phone on a Saturday morning while at the office. The father related that his four year old boy was suddenly in very desperate straits. He was told that I would meet him immediately at Childrens' ER. When the child arrived, I had to heartily agree with the father. As I was starting an IV and oxygen, I noted that the child's chest muscles were not moving very well.

After the child was stabilized, I asked the Father and Grandmother about the circumstances surrounding this sudden episode in a previously healthy and active boy. The grandmother had a sheepish grin on her face and admitted to giving the boy a rectal enema consisting of a package of Bull Durham tobacco steeped in a one half cup of water to cure pin worms.

I contacted Dr. Ross McIntyre, who was the head of the med center's Pharmacology Department, about the nicotine poisoning. He was a noted authority on curare, the South American Indian arrow poisoning. He explained to me that nicotine had a curare-like action in high doses; that it would paralyze the chest muscles; that it would be rapidly metabolized; and would quickly be eliminated from the body.

By the next day, four year old David W. was back to his old rambunctious self chasing around in his crib. Whenever Grandmother brought David into the office, I would tease her about treating any more pin worms. This case was reported in the Journal of Pediatrics in 1953.

In 1954, David developed a paroxysmal tachycardia (a very rapid heart rate) and on conversion to a normal rate threw a cerebral embolis (blood clot). He recovered well but was left with poor use of his right arm. Many times on the school grounds, David would be apt to use his right arm as a club on some classmates. This action did not go over well with the parents. It created strong parental protests. This case report was published in the Journal of Pediatrics.

Chapter 22

I always taught medical students and residents that when working towards an intricate diagnosis to think of the common entities but to always look for an unusual medical condition. Often this unusual finding made the handling of difficult cases more intriguing and successful. As part of his/her training, each resident was expected to research and publish a paper on some entity or case study in pediatrics. Several papers were published in the Nebraska State Medical Journal. This exercise was mandated so a resident could appreciate the effort needed in writing a scientific paper. It, also, helped him/her to critically evaluate the data in any medical paper which they read.

In 1954, I had two bright and excellent women residents who provided me with my own claim to fame. Dr. Carol Angle was brilliant, published many papers, was a Nephologist (Kidney), and, later, became the Chairperson of the Nebraska Pediatric Department. Dr. Matilda McIntyre was very active in many public health venues, was the patron saint in establishing the national poison control centers, championed safety in toys, and published over 100 papers. Both of these ladies left a terrific impact in the Omaha medical community. They were inducted with Dr. John Thomas and me into the initial class of Childrens' Hospital "Legend in Pediatrics" Hall of fame.

As part of my own continuing medical education, I evolved a personalized approach which satisfied my needs throughout my entire practice years:

1. I would endeavor to publish a paper on some aspect of Pediatrics each year based upon some of my own practice

experiences. As a result, I ended up publishing forty-one papers in my thirty-seven years of practice, one book, co-authored two others, and was a guest contributor of a chapter in another book.

2. I had an intense desire to someday become a member of a major Medical Society's National Committee. Little did I know that I was destined to be on many different National Committees in several medical societies?

I budgeted $500 per year for my medical library for books and journals. I would read at least one hour a day at home. I no longer had the luxury of time to be able to go to the medical library. At one time, I would scan fifteen to twenty different specialty journals per month looking for interesting articles to use in the residency program and for my own edification.

3. Over time, as new learning techniques became available, I utilized them and subscribed to three different monthly audiotape services: General Pediatrics, Specific Monthly Pediatric Topics, and Pediatric Psychiatry entities. I would listen to these different tapes as I drove around while making my hospital rounds.

4. After it was established, I utilized the AMA Recognition Award on the recommended three year basis to be sure that I was staying on tract to accomplish my own Continuing Medical Education Program. I received this Award in 1969, 1973, 1976, 1979, 1983, and 1985. I retired in 1988.

I planned to attend two medical meetings each year outside of Omaha on different subjects that interested me. These meetings were planned on a rotation type of basis as there were several different areas of medicine that intrigued me. I have always been a "Fiddler and Diddler" looking into areas that seem interesting. I enjoyed poking into new aspects of medicine and the adjacent subjects.

I had fallen madly head over heels in love with medicine. Medicine was so seductive that if you were not careful her embrace would push aside any other matters. All I could think of or do was related to medicine.

I had a terrifying experience on an evening out with my beautiful, neglected, beloved Mary. I promised myself that I would not think or talk about anything if it was related to medicine. Well! I sat like a bump on a log with our dance group. I could not think of one single thing to discuss that was not medically related. What a humbling and embarrassing experience that was. Obviously, many changes were in order.

We thoroughly enjoyed dancing as a pastime going clear back to our early dating days. We learned to Samba, Rumba, Cha Cha Cha, Waltz, Boogie Woogie, Polka, and the Double Shuffle. We were very accomplished Fox Trot dancers. We were very smooth dancers and glided around the dance floor. Mary's three sisters were, all, accomplished dancers. It was enjoyable to dance with them. The music in the 1940's to 1960' had been melodic, had foot taping rhythm, and had such meaningful words. Ballads and tuneful melodies generated wonderful musical sounds. The songs were much different from today's loud noises and repetitive words and phrases. Where did the romantic ballads and melodious melodies go?

Chapter 23

I took Fridays off. In the early days, this meant that I was away from the phone from the time I completed hospital rounds in the morning and checked in with the office until I went to bed somewhat near midnight; then, the phone would be turned back on. I would hope that I would obtain a fair night's sleep. When the boys were a little older, we would spend the Friday time building an HO Railroad System during the winter, and sailing, or water skiing during the summer.

Because of my embarrassing experience with our evening out, the next day I set about reorienting my priorities. My priority list became as follows:

1. My first priority was to God
2. My next priority was to my family
3. My last priority was to my practice

This approach lasted throughout the rest of my practice life come hell and high water. It was quite a struggle at times to keep these priorities in this order. It was equally difficult to maintain the wall between siren medicine and my lovely family. Like all families we had our moments and a basket of woes.

The impact of this experience began my interest in the field of "Time Management". I became more and more intrigued with the management of a private medical practice in the early 1960's.

Drs. Tompkins and Gedgoud passed on another working philosophy for the practice which withstood the test of time. This philosophy was that any new innovation test or service which was to be introduced into the practice should meet three major criteria:

1. Is this proposal good for the patient per Se or at least neutral as to its long term effect?
2. Is this proposal good for the entire practice as a whole or at least neutral as to its effect?
3. In the long run, is this proposal good for the individual physician per Se putting forth the idea for the change or at least neutral as to its effect?

After thirty-seven years of practice, these three working tenants proved their value time after time and helped to avoid some major pitfalls. Several times during an intense discussion about a proposed change in the practice, Dr. Wax would remind us that this new idea could well have an adverse effect on our families. Well! Need I say more? Nix! No dice!

Chapter 24

As my practice grew, I had to retire from managing the residency program. This realization came with great pain as I loved the challenges which it supplied and the knowledge that I acquired from the exposure to the different medical subjects.

The consultative aspects of my early practice needed some major improvement. This fact was brought home to me by Dr. James Ramsey of Atkinson, Nebraska. We had been classmates; and, periodically, he referred patients to me. One day I received a call from him with an unpleasant voice saying, "Absence makes the heart grow fonder for somebody else". I had neglected to keep him informed about a patient he had referred. The relatives were after him for some answers. Boy! Was this ever an eye opener? Ever after, I called within two days or sooner to report findings and progress and would send a detailed report soon after the patient went home. This report contained complete instructions for the patient's care, follow-up needs, and other important data. This lesson was not lost on me and helped to build my reputation as a worthwhile consultant. So often, a consultant would tend to add the referred patient to his own practice with never a "Thank you" to the referral attending physician; so the patient was never seen again by the original referring doctor. The Med Center was notorious and still is the culprit for this type of activity.

For my part, I would ask the referring doctor if he/she wanted to handle the follow-up care on a complicated case or would he/she want me to address those needs of the patient. All other care would be kept in the hands of the referring physician. Most of the time, I was elected to handle the difficult aspects of the problem.

Chapter 25

Boy! Oh Boy! Talk about a missed opportunity. There was a young investor guru, Warren Buffet, in Omaha who asked ten young physicians, including me, to invest $10,000 from each doctor for a long term investment. My fellow former residents had the money. I did not; so I gracefully declined this opportunity. All those contemporaries now are multimillionaires. Ah, so is life. However, I was the Pediatrician for Warren's family for years.

In 1951, the year I started my practice, there were two contemporary hospital administration interns that began at this same time with me, James Canady of Bishop Clarkson Hospital and John Estabrooke of Methodist Hospital. Both of these men would have a profound effect on my medical life and practice in the future. Each of them became outstanding Hospital Administrators.

When I became the medical coordinator and director of the Nebraska Residency program, I was exposed to many different types of medical situations. At this time, I was a Faculty Clinical Instructor in the Nebraska Department of Pediatrics. Because I was supervising medical students from both Nebraska and Creighton Medical Schools, I was made an Instructor in Pediatrics at Creighton Medical School. This dual appointment was the first of its kind in 50 years. This joint position helped decrease some of the marked jealous rivalry between the two schools.

I couldn't seem to say NO to offers so I was involved in teaching at several nursing schools in addition to the med school and residency needs.

Chapter 26

Our family had increased. We now had three very active boys. Mary came from a family of four girls, none of whom played sports. What an eye opener and rude introduction into the male world this was for her. She was a very graceful and feminine lady. She had to learn all about three baseball strikes and you are out; in football ten yards means a first down; and what a "take down" in wrestling means. She cared for our new home with a passion. She turned our house into a very loving home which was well appointed. She worked with a Mrs. Kennedy of the Orchard and Wilhelm Furniture Store. Mary was a cautious buyer when came to furnishing our home. She bought good quality but not costly furniture. Most of the furniture we still use in our most recent apartment. She was a wonderful home maker. It was a pleasure to come home after a full day of seeing patients. She was always a good sight for sore eyes.

We took our first vacation to the Lake of the Ozarks when By was three years old. When Terry and Matt were big enough, we began to go to Lake Okoboji, Iowa every summer, near the Fourth of July, for two weeks. Soon, I was tired of renting boats. We bought a beautiful mahogany wood twelve foot, thirty-five hp "Yellow Jacket" runabout boat. This boat began our career in helping people learn to water ski. By was eight years old when he first got up on the skis by the old tried and true method of try and try again. None of us had the slightest inkling on how to go about water skiing. Terry was about six and Matt was four years old when they made it out of the water onto the skis. Matt had very strong legs, like oak stumps.

Their mother was the most graceful skier in the family. Because of the polio problem when she was growing up, she never learned to swim. I taught her to do the breast stroke which she did very well. When she tried to teach Mrs. Bohrer how to do the breast stroke, while at Okaboji, the boys had a belly shaking laugh.

Our next venture was to try sailing. I hadn't sailed since my Sea Scout days when I was fifteen and learned on a fifteen foot X-Boat on Carter Lake near the Omaha airport. There was a Styrofoam Sailboat with a main and a jib sail which sold for $90 in a boating magazine. I could not resist. By and I tried it out at Okaboji. I did fine going down wind, but I had forgotten how to "Come About" to return to where we started. Talk about frustrations. Ugh! We finally conquered this endeavor after many, many failures. When our sailing as a family was at its peak, we had two fifteen foot "Snipes" with main and a jib sails and two eight foot aluminum "Grumman Dinghies" which had a single sail, and a very small blue and white wooden sailboat that I bought for $10.

Plastic Flite Fish Sail Boat Mary and Terry

During the summer, we ended up water skiing almost every Friday afternoon and sailing in the races every Sunday at Lake Manawa near Council Bluffs. Matt and Terry sailed the "Grumman Dinghies" in the

Junior Boat Races. These activities were great family sports and lasted until I turned seventy-five when it seemed an appropriate time to stop water skiing. I gave up the boats and donated them to our third son, Matt.

After trying many different nearby lakes, we decided to confine ourselves to Lake Manaw just across the river in Council Bluffs. There was a nice family friendly, small country club where the snipe sailors belonged. We joined the Lakeshore Country Club and were members for about 40 years. The food was good. We could play all day; and, then, we would have a pleasant meal. We would be tired but relaxed.

Chapter 27

One day, I answered the phone at home and my Sister-in-Law was on the phone; she was hysterical. Her son had fallen out of their third floor apartment window by leaning against the screen. I met her at Childrens' ER. After a detailed and very thorough physical exam, he did not have any apparent injuries. He had fallen into a group of bushes which broke his fall. The bushes gave him a bunch of scratches. His guardian angel was with him that day. He had pushed the window screen out, lost his balance, and tumbled out the window behind his Mother's back. All's well that ends well.

Our boys were growing like weeds and each had their own areas of interests, and their own interesting attributes. Matt, the youngest, had a real knack for taking things apart and successfully putting them back together. His brothers would bring their broken items for him to fix. He could visualize in his mind the way a new item needed to be put together without reading the instructions. Today, he has sharply honed those attributes and is a marvelous computer expert and a home handy dandy man. He had great concepts of space, and its relationship with objects.

Terry seemed to live in an ethereal world all of his own. In spite of whatever incentive we utilized, Terry was always a slob when it came to his room. In the end, we would close his door, walk away, and settle for a detailed Saturday clean up. He loved to read and still does so today. He became an accomplished and published poet. He has managed a writers' workshop for the city of Lincoln amongst other civic endeavors. He played a twelve string guitar. He played football, baseball, and wrestled. He has lived in Lincoln in a small apartment for a long time and manages very well.

By has always been interested in all types of outdoor activities and sports. He played football, baseball, basketball, and track. He still is a great competitor. Every Friday was Prep football night. By was an excellent player, was a fullback, and carried the ball most of the time. He was fast, had great balance, and was very agile. We went to the games with the Harvey's whose son played tackle. Whenever Prep scored a touchdown, Mary would vigorously ring a brass bell. The players waited to hear the bell after a score. On Saturdays, it seemed as though half of the team ended up in our den watching the TV games. Mary ran a short order restaurant with sandwiches and soft drinks which it seemed like forever. She really loved these times and listening to the boys' chatter.

The years that By played football he had very good competition in Johnny Rogers, who played for Tech High and became a Heisman Winner, and Guy-"The Fly"-Engles- who played for Westside High and became an All American End. By ran in the Hawaiian Ironman Triathlon and finished about 112th out of a thousand. He is a retired anesthesiologist and spends much of his time outdoors swimming, kayaking, hiking, biking, bow and arrow hunting, and cross country skiing. He just returned from a 40 day hike through the Swiss Alps with his cousin, Mark Welge. Talk about being in condition? Ugh!

Chapter 28

When By graduated from eighth grade, we finished remodeling our basement. At long last, I had my genuine dark room for my photographic interests.

This same summer we took a trip to Los Angeles in a family compartment on the Union Pacific Train, past where the golden spike was driven, and on to see Disney Land near Los Angles. While there, we went deep sea fishing and took a boat trip to Catalina Island. We rented a car and drove up the coast on "Highway 1" towards San Francisco stopping to see the many sights along the way including the Hearst Castle. We arrived at Mountain View, California at my sister, Virginia's, home. Her backyard had a great swimming pool in which the boys lived.

We returned home via the Burlington Railroad through the Feather River Canyon. It was a marvelous trip. The boys would tease me about the historical details that I would give whenever possible. I wanted them to live in and appreciate their history. Many times, if we happen to pass a historical sign the boys would pretend to yawn and sigh over the anticipated remarks. As a family, we had many wonderful times and moments.

On another trip, we traveled to Yellowstone National Park and, then, on to Sun Valley Idaho We took the beautiful highway from Cody, Wyoming to the East Gate at Yellowstone. As the accommodations were full in the Park, we stayed at the Absaroka Lodge which was just outside the East Gate to the Park. It was a lovely place with a mountain stream bubbling and singing near our door. We drove into the Park to see Old Faithful, the many hot springs, Yellowstone Falls, and the different animals. We hired a guide to help us fish on Yellowstone Lake. The boys all caught fish. Mary pulled in the biggest trout. Guess what? I was skunked once again. No fish liked my line or bait. The lodge cooked our trout which were delicious.

After Yellowstone, we traveled on to Sun Valley. We ran into Dr. Tillie McIntyre and her husband, Dean, who was a classmate of mine from med school. Tillie would take her boy and ours on rock hikes. They fell in love with her and her knowledge. We returned through Jackson Hole and the Teton Mountains and stayed in a cabin by Jenny Lake. It was a marvelous trip.

Time was passing fast during this year. We joined a neighborhood pool where I taught the boys how to swim better. They lived at and in the pool forever it seemed. There was a proposed nine hole golf course to be built near the pool area. We joined as charter members. Both the boys and I learned to play golf here. Terry never enjoyed it, but By and Matt became avid golfers and much better than their father. Not fair!

Chapter 29

As time passed, I became aware more and more of the various multiple costs that a private practice incurred outside of salaries and malpractice insurance. It was quite a major eye opener. This knowledge stimulated my interest in private practice management. This insight into management ultimately became a lifelong area of interest which I pursued avidly. Initially, Dr. Gedgoud handled the various cost factors for the office. Once again, I was a student at his knee endeavoring to understand the intricacies of a practice.

With fond memories of "Mother Mason", I devised a system for writing medical orders on a patient's chart which covered all aspects of a patient's care. In this manner, there could be very few misunderstandings and mistakes. The format of these orders was as follows:

1. What supportive care was needed to sustain the patient until a definitive treatment program could be instituted?
2. What IV fluids were needed, if any?
3. What were, if any, specific or special dietary or nutritional needs?
4. What precise and specific therapy was needed including antibiotics, heart medications, or others?
5. What about looking for the common entities via tests that might be the cause, but do not forget to look for the unusual reasons?

6. What was the S-O-A-P Examination Format and did it address all of the indicted problems? More on this item later in this story.

If a nurse had any question about what my orders stated, she was expected to call me regardless of the time day or night and relate the surrounding circumstances and problems. The nurses were expected to call me concerning any changes in the patient's condition. If they didn't call to notify and clarify their concerns, I would get upset and grumpy.

My medical horizons were expanding. Dr. Tompkins and a Psychoanalysist, Dr. G. Alexander Young, established the Institute for Human Understanding to aid Methodist Ministers to better comprehend and to help their congregations. The two of them gave talks to the ministers and their wives at regular intervals. I attended the meetings and occasionally gave discussions to these folks on a child's physical growth and development. I was becoming very interested in this aspect of Pediatrics and was on my way to becoming an authority on a child's physical and psychological development.

After eight years of unbelievable experiences with Dr. Tompkins, he announced that he had to move to Tucson, Arizona for his wife's health. She had severe rheumatoid arthritis with many deformities and had a marked problem of bronchiectasis with one lung already removed. She had lived in Tucson for a trial of six months and could appreciate the help the drier climate gave her. It was with tears in my eyes that I bid goodbye to my Hero and mentor. However, I had had the privilege and pleasure of practicing with him for eight years.

Dr. Gedgoud and I handled the practice between ourselves. When August came, I almost floundered under the combined load of three large practices as most of Dr. Tompkins' elected to stay with me. Before this decade was over, Dr. Gedgoud lost his lovely wife, Margarite, who was ravished by diabetic complications. I loved her. He subsequently married Kathleen, who was our head nurse and a single mother. I was honored to be his "Best Man". This had been a long, winding, and amazing journey from being a junior medical student to being his partner and his best man in his wedding.

There was a bright, industrious resident, Dr. Donald Glow, at Childrens who was just completing his training. Many offices were after him to join with them. We threw in our two cents to entice him to join us. He elected to become part of the Omaha Childrens' Clinic. Thank heavens! He was a great asset for the next 18 years before I lost him back to Childrens' as their Medical Director and Vice President. I couldn't complain about Childrens' choice as I was the one who was elected to formulate the Job Description for this position.

Our office worked with many different adoptive agencies within our community, i.e. The Nebraska Childrens' Home, Lutheran Family Services, and VNA Well Baby Stations. Some of the Omaha Pediatricians and General Practitioners would help TB Skin Test the Omaha School Children each year. Drs. Tompkins and Gedgoud always preached that we should be involved in some civic endeavor of our own choice. This philosophy was carried on all the time I was in practice and for each member of the practice.

Early in my years of handling the teaching program at Childrens', there was a lady administrator who was not in favor of having any teaching within the hospital. I found a nice roller Chart Cart hidden in a corner, which Bob Blue modified for my use in making daily rounds with the residents and students. This cart worked very well. One day, I came for rounds; and the cart was gone. She had sold the cart out from under me. Well! I went to the Medical Staff Officers and gave them my side of the story. Mrs. Barber was gone within the month.

Chapter 30

Fortunately for me, I was in on the beginning of the "Golden Age of Medicine". World War II had demonstrated the value and usefulness of the Tetanus Toxoid vaccine. I had written my senior thesis on Tetanus and the Tetanus Toxoid. There were very few reported US war casualties who developed "Lock Jaw" [Tetanus] from being wounded after receiving the prophylactic Tetanus Toxoid Vaccine.

Diphtheria was a frightening disease as it was very contagious and had severe complications. A child could have a Diphtheria Membrane in the throat area which could suffocate the child unless a tracheotomy was done to provide an airway. This was accomplished by making a hole in the child's windpipe. At times, I had to do this procedure on an emergency basis. The Diphtheria bacillus produced a toxin which could attack the heart. The Diphtheria Toxoid vaccine mostly eliminated these worries.

Whooping Cough was another major disease entity which succumbed to the Pertussis Vaccine. Sometimes, Croup could be confused in differentiating it from Diphtheria and Whooping cough. Children with croup responded best to a steam croup tent.

I had another major lesson one night when I was called about a child with croup. I explained to the mother over the phone on how to make a "Croup Tent". When I arrived at the house about 30 minutes later, there was the most unique tent one could imagine. The mother said, "She couldn't understand my instructions at all; so she went next door to a public health nurse. This nurse really helped her".

There was a card table turned on its side with the top of the table against the head of the bed with the legs extended outward in a horizontal manner. A sheet blanket, not a bed sheet, was draped over the legs. The child was nestled in and quite comfortable with the steamer going full blast. I don't know how many times this same technique was explained by me to mothers in need.

Between the DPT Vaccine and the Polio Vaccine, many major pediatric problems were almost eliminated. Dr. Morgulis, head of the Biochemistry Department of the Med School, thought that Vitamins would soon have a big impact in medicine. He was so right. With Vitamin D, rickets with its rib and leg deformities no longer occurred. Scurvy was eliminated with Vitamin C. A type of large red blood cell anemia [Pernicious Anemia] was handled by some of the Vitamin B complex. Curative changes were occurring right before my eyes. It was difficult to keep up with the changes. Seductive siren Medicine was at her best or worst, depending upon your viewpoint.

Chapter 31

The next major advance in medicine came in the form of discovering one new antibiotic after another. In defense of the promiscuous use of antibiotics, they literally changed the medical landscape. The treatment of acute bacterial infectious diseases became a reality. The Meningococcus was a deadly bacterium. A child could be well in the morning and dead from wide spread Meningococcemia by bedtime. If the child had Meningococcal Meningitis, he/she would be dead within about ten days in spite of all the supportive care possible. With advent of Sulfadiazine, a German discovery, some of the cases would recover. When Penicillin became available and combined with Sulfa, recovery could almost be predicted; and very few residual aftermath complications would be left in its wake. Now, there is a vaccine to help counteract the spreading of this Meningococcus organism, which is fairly effective but not one hundred percent. Subsequently, there have been isolated cases which have been reported amongst college students and Army personnel.

The same results occurred with Chloromycetin when used in treating bacterial Influenza Meningitis. Pneumococcal Meningitis was a tough customer to conqueror because it produced such a thick gelatinous exudates on the meninges but usually responded to penicillin in very high doses. Pulmonary Pneumonia could now be treated without waiting for the old method of recovery by crisis. Lung abscesses, pleural empyema, and pleural effusion almost became complications of the past. Repeated bouts of Pneumonia, which could lead to the chronic condition of Bronchiectasis, became a rare entity. Repeated bouts of ear

Mastoiditis and deafness became unusual. Many other rather common bacterial disease entities succumbed to various antibiotics. For awhile, there seemed to be a new antibiotic every month. It was hard to keep abreast of the role of these new meds. Each antibiotic had its own spectrum of bacterial organisms which it could control.

One of the greatest changes in child health occurred with the Penicillin treatment of Strep Sore Throat with its aftermath of Rheumatic Fever, Rheumatoid Arthritis, and Rheumatic Heart disease. The heart involvement had the devastating complication of heart valvular damage and resulting heart failure. Penicillin cured the antecedent Strep Sore Throat infection which led to the Rheumatic Heart Disease state and, on an occasion, the problem of Rheumatoid Arthritis. These affected children had to be at bed rest for a year or longer, had to have homebound schooling, and seldom ever had the opportunity to be able to run and play again as other children could. Rheumatic Fever was a devastating disease in children.

Medicine was revolutionized with antibiotics in spite of the bad press they now receive. The next savior for children came in the form of Immunizations against Measles, Rubella, and Mumps. Every spring there seemed to be an epidemic of one of these so called and accepted, but not so benign Childhood Diseases.

Measles was by far the worst of these illnesses. It was frequently called the 'Ten Day Measles' or "Hard Measles". Many times, it left severe residual effects in its aftermath. Today, it is hard to comprehend that Measles Encephalitis could wipe out some of a child's brain functions and leave mental retardation, cognitive problems, or school difficulties as important complications in its wake. In some children, there would be the problem of Measles Encephalopathy with marked high blood pressure followed in about ten days with a kidney shut down with all its attendant complications. If one could support the child for about ten days, the renal (kidney) problem might reverse itself and recovery could occur.

There were no renal dialysis machines in those days so we had to improvise a methodology. A gastric tube would be placed in the duodenum [upper small bowel]. My previous training at the Henry Ford Hospital aided in performing this task of placing a tube into the duodenum. Another tube was placed in the stomach with a continuous lavage (washing) instituted with a Lactate Ringers Solution. The blood NPN and/or other renal tests could be dramatically reduced by this method. Another approach was to insert a tube in the right abdominal flank and on into the peritoneal cavity with another similar tube in the left flank. The fluid could be irrigated through these tubes in a like manner with similar results.

A group of physicians in Australia noted that there was a higher than expected rash of congenital anomalies occurring in the offspring of mothers who had experienced Rubella or" Three Day Measles" during their pregnancies. This finding triggered a whole host of investigations with the end result of the Rubella Vaccine causing a great reduction of these problems in mothers.

Mumps was another culprit that left deafness in its wake. Orchitis in the testicles of teenage boys with sterilization being the residual problem was a major worry. Again, that worrisome Encephalitis reared its head; but, in most instances it was not as severe as the Measles Encephalitis. The development of the MMR Vaccine aided in markedly reducing the many terrible aftermaths of these so called routine childhood illnesses. What is so sad in recent days is the failure for parents to immunize their children due to erroneous facts, forgetfulness, or simple laziness. Everyone's protection against these diseases depends upon the entire population being immunized – the "Herd Effect". A person not being immunized for whatever reason jeopardizes the entire group.

Chapter 32

Congenital heart defects were rapidly coming to the fore front with the development of the Blalock-Taussig and Potts surgical procedures. The correction of the Tetralogy of Fallot (Blue Baby Syndrome) initiated a new interest in the surgical addressing all types of congenital heart problems. Later on, adult heart surgery followed in its wake which was coupled with the great advances in anesthesiology.

This state of affairs created an inherit need for better diagnostic procedures. Cardiac catherization was just becoming available. We had to send our patients from the Nebraska Heart Clinic to Chicago for these and other detailed studies. Drs. Ralph Moore-Radiologist at Childrens', Don Nilsson, and I collaborated on devising a make-shift imaging approach to these diagnostic needs. With the help of Bob Blue, the Childrens' Handy Man, a wooden cradle shell was made to fit over a child's chest containing a slot to hold an X-ray cassette. A radioactive dye was injected into the child's vein. Cassettes were quickly pushed manually through the shell under the Fluoroscope giving us a very crude but useful cardiac image. Within a short period of time, machines became available which handled this problem with ease.

Dr. Cochran, a gifted surgeon, and I encountered another major situation when we had a child who needed prolonged gastric [stomach] suction. Little was known about the role of Potassium in fluid balance at that time. A Doctor Dan Darrow was currently studying Potassium in the production of the entity of Metabolic Alkalosis.

Our patient developed this problem. We turned to Dr. Jacobi, who was the Director of the Med Center's Biochemistry Laboratory. He helped us to devise an IV 6th Molar Ammonium Chloride Solution, which corrected this problem. The child recovered nicely. It was some time before a commercial preparation of this type was available on the market. For a long time, there had been a commercial preparation for the correction of Metabolic Acidosis in the form of an IV 6th Molar Sodium Lactate solution.

I was very knowledgeable concerning the fluid balance therapy of that day and gave lectures to the Nebraska Surgeons upon request. Later on, there was developed fluid balance parameters based upon per meter squared of body mass which further refined and defined fluid therapy capabilities.

As these acute medical situations seemed to lessen in number due to improved preventive measures, the field of Endocrinology began to catch my eye. It was triggered by a doctor's child who only weighted twelve pounds at one year of age. Her underlying cause was hypothyroidism – very low thyroid hormone. With the correction of this situation, Martha began to grow and develop until she was near normal on the growth charts. The Wetzel Grid was a big chart factor in following her progress as it compared the child to her own self growth instead of to a percentile of a group. I used this type of growth charting during all my years of practice. This chart told me so much more about the child until around twelve years of age when this chart was no longer valid. The only drawback in using this approach was the fact that this chart cost fifty cents apiece; whereas the free charts only compared a child against an age group. The costs could mount when several charts needed to be initiated each day. I thought the capital investment was more important than using the freebies.

Martha had several problems in the wake of her initial one. In the beginning, school was difficult and concentration was a big, big problem. Ritalin had just come onto the market. It was a Godsend for Martha as she could now concentrate. School became acceptable and doable. She showed some of the earliest symptoms of Autism that I had ever encountered. Martha was on Ritalin for many years and then tapered off. She graduated from high school and held several minor jobs until she went to work in her brother's medical office where she blossomed. She became a self supporting semi-sociable being and enjoyed a limited social life. She still lives with her parents, takes trips with a friend to see Donnie Osmond in various places, and still writes to me about every six months. Her most recent mailing to me was her 2009 Christmas card and letter. As I work on this story, I just received another letter from Martha. I was honored to be invited to attend her fortieth birthday party. She is now in her fifty's. Martha taught me many different lessons. One of which was, "Never, never give up on trying to help someone help himself or herself". Martha had done a remarkable job in preparing for and living her life.

My old friend, Ray Mellinger, Endocrinologist at the Henry Ford Hospital, helped me to obtain a supply of the very scarce and hard to acquire Human Growth Hormone. This hormone had to be produced from a cadaver's pituitary gland. It was like finding gold. This small for age boy fit all of the criteria and laboratory tests for the protocol for Human Growth Hormone deficiency (major growth failure). These designated tests were necessary in order to obtain this cadaver produced medication. He responded well until he developed antibodies to the Hormone. When this happened, it had to be discontinued. I found this field to be very interesting and useful. After a few years, a Pediatric Endocrinologist came to the Med Center; so my usefulness in this field was ended.

Chapter 33

By now, I was beginning to formulate a rounded approach and philosophy to the care and treatment of children. This knowledge was sparking my interest into the beginning field of Adolescent Medicine. My training and exposure at the Henry Ford Hospital spurred this interest, and I had treated many older adolescents in the Army.

My mind's eye envisioned the following theoretical three parallel tract approach to Well Child and Adolescent Growth and Development and provided a sound foundation for observations and advice. This framework was built upon own my designed patient care and programmed advice:

1. The central core of this philosophy was based upon normal Well Child Care and how to help keep him/her well via "Guided Growth Advice" utilizing immunizations, proper nutrition, vitamins, exercise, and similar needs.

2. The chronically physically Sick Child, for whatever reason, and using whatever measures were necessary to help him/her to return to the normal Well Child modality or as close to it as possible.

3. The mental and psychological Traumatized Child due to whatever cause and using whatever measures were necessary to help return him/her to the normal Well Child modality or as close to it as possible.

This philosophical approach spurred me to study and learn about as many different aspects of this intricate modality as were available to study. Over the subsequent years, I would gear my reading and medical meetings to some aspect of this approach on a rotating basis. In this manner, I could cover each area of interest on a three year cycle. This rotation would catch any new ideas or approaches in their early conceptual stages. It was a very satisfying approach to my own Continuing Medical Education Program and the way to practice pediatrics. When I would learn of a useful idea, I would study ways to incorporate this thought into my mosaic of development theory.

From this accumulated knowledge, I evolved a Parent, Child, and Adolescent Educational program from birth through the early adult years in a linear fashion. This approach helped to reinforce whatever was discussed in person "At the Annual Health Office Encounter".

In the later adolescent years when the patient came alone, I would send a report home to the parents as to what was done and what items were discussed with some privileged limitations. Over time, this educational program became a very sophisticated endeavor and was well worth the extra effort it entailed. It was gratifying to hear a class valedictorian urge his/her classmates, "To know thy self" in his/her address. These thoughts were from one of my "Teen Talks".

This philosophy gradually evolved into six separate longitudinal continuums which added up to the whole child or persona from birth throughout the years to include the senior citizen period of life. At any space in time, one could cut a cross section through these six areas, evaluate the situation, and know what needed to be discussed at that particular age point. These six developmental areas were the following:

1. Physical development
2. Sex education and the development of sexuality
3. Intellectual development
4. School adjustments, adaptations, and production
5. A Philosophy of discipline and the development of self-control and self-responsibility
6. Emotional and personality development

These six areas of growth and development were ongoing and comprised dynamic functions in every person throughout their entire life span. Each of these areas was touched someway within every Well Child/Adolescent Annual Health Review. Over time, this approach became the central theme of my care of patients and almost became "A pediatric way of life" for them within their "Medical Home". The verbal guidance I gave in the office was reinforced with encompassing parenting papers that I wrote. Some information was purchased as commercial material which was pertinent to a subject or an area. The concomitant useful presentation of the major ongoing weekly parent lectures were based on large discussion topics which could not be covered in detail within the time constraints of an office visit. These major topics would be such as "The Philosophy of Discipline" or "Fatherhood Is Important". There were about ten major topics which were covered in each lecture series. This series was repeated several times a year to accommodate family needs, times, and interests.

In addition, there would be included during the office visit the use of appropriate specific topic audiotapes, film strips on toilet training and similar adjacent topics, video tapes such as "Your Self Breast Exam" and "Your First Pelvic Exam". It was a well integrated and dynamic approach to Patient Education. The people, in general, thoroughly took to the program and told others about its value. I would constantly seek additional material to utilize in this format. This program was always being upgraded as new ideas or materials presented themselves to me. It was a very satisfying way to practice well child care and kept the routine, mundane, and boredom of office work at bay.

Chapter 34

It was expected that when I joined the Omaha Childrens' Clinic that I would join various medical societies. I passed the American Board of Pediatrics Exam on the first attempt in 1952. There were four examiners who spent thirty minutes apiece with you. Each one had several areas of expertise and could make a person really sweat blood. This initial passing wasn't always the case with many candidates including one of my partners. He was so nervous before the exam he had a hard time knowing his own name when asked.

I became a member of the American Academy of Pediatrics in 1954 as soon as I became eligible to join. During the 1950's, I belonged to the Northwest Pediatric Society, the Nebraska Pediatric Society where I was President in 1958, the Omaha Midwest Society where I was the Chairman of the Pediatric Section, the local country and state Medical Societies, the AMA, the Nebraska Heart Association, and the Catholic Physicians' Guild where I was president in 1957. As a general rule I was an active participating member of any association that I joined and not just a passive observer. These organizations provided many important contacts and experiences for me. In today's vernacular, it was early networking at its best.

I had other embarrassing lessons in my first year of practice. It was near the first days of August, and Dr. Gedgoud had left for Colorado. As he was gone, I used his office space instead of climbing the stairs to mine. A Mrs. C., who was the Director of the Hattie B. Monroe Home, which was now residing on the UNMC Campus having previously moved from the Omaha Benson area, brought her sick son, "Besee", in to be seen. After I examined him, I wrote out a prescription and started to go to the next examining room for another appointment. She grabbed my coattails in passing and said, "I know from my sister, who is a nurse at Childrens,' that you are supposed to be a "Hot Shot Pediatrician"; but you haven't told me one thing about how to care for my son. Why are you in such a hurry"? Boy! Did I ever feel like a fool? After this embarrassing episode, I made certain to take the time to explain to the parents all aspects of the needed treatment program in detail for their child.

I learned many other useful lessons during these first ten years of practice such as:

1. Mothers were the first line of care givers when there was an illness present in the family.

2. Mothers frequently knew that their child was coming down with an illness before any true signs or symptoms were manifested. This observation was certainly true with Mary and our three sons.

3. In my experience, I watched Grandparents step in to fill the gap when both parents were snatched away from their families; and they proceeded to do a great job of raising the orphaned children. I really liked grandparents and was glad to see them come to the office when their grandchild would come.

4. There were some young couples who were immature, and the marriage was doomed to fall apart usually within five years.

5. There were some couples who zoomed up into prominence within the community with Junior League type of civic activities and with much potential for good; but, after a short while, the marriage seemed to disintegrate and fall apart accomplishing nothing of value for their community.

6. There were some couples who zoomed up into prominence with the Junior League type of civic activities, plateau and, then, remained on this plane as good solid citizens contributing to their local community in many fruitful ways.

7. There was a much smaller group of couples who zoomed up into prominence, plateau for awhile, and then proceeded onward and upward to become true community leaders, movers, and shakers and helped to improve their entire community.

During this year, I made considerable progress in meeting my practice goals such as:

1. I authored or co-authored and published fifteen articles in various medical journals.
2. I became an officer in several medical organizations.
3. The Medical Center promoted me from an Instructor in Pediatrics to an Assistant Professor.
4. I was the Secretary of Childrens' Medical Staff and subsequently the Treasurer.
5. I was the Clinician in charge of Methodist's Nursery and was instrumental in establishing a Special Care Premature Nursery which was only the second one in Omaha. I was on this Hospital's Infection Control Committee.
6. I was a guest lecturer at many different PTA Meetings and Parochial Groups for many different faiths all over the city. This endeavor was a great way to gain new patients.
7. At their request. I presented papers at five different Medical Societies.

This time had been very successful and provided for very satisfying years on many different fronts such as:

1. I established a way to have considerable amount of quality time with my family.
2. My beloved Mary and I participated in different types of social events including our first love, dancing. Mary would go with me to most of the out of town medical meetings that I attended. I would plan to take her to some special restaurant and, if available, some major type of entertainment. She had a knack of letting me know when she disapproved of

something I did by giving me "The Look". I learned to pay attention to this sign of disapproval.

3. My practice was growing by leaps and bounds and had improved our financial foundation.
4. I had begun to define the various parameters of my envisioned and desired Well Child program and philosophies.
5. I was active in a number of medical organizations and was achieving some stature therein.
6. I had not recovered from the loss of Dr. Tompkins.
7. Dr. Glow joined our practice who was a great addition.
8. We bought a lot and began building our dream home in 1955. We moved in February 1956. It had four bedrooms, 2 ½ baths, three fireplaces, a great patio with a screened in porch, and a very large yard. As the boys grew, we had football and baseball games in the front yard. I frequently hit baseballs to most of the neighborhood boys after supper. Before I retired, the house was all paid for to our immense relief and satisfaction.
9. We developed many different interests in golf, swimming, sailing, and water skiing.
10. I was developing a glimmering interest in Practice Management.

We had completed a very fruitful, productive, and a satisfying ten year period.

**Part IV to follow
The Decade of the 1960's**

Part IV

The Decade of the 1960's Discovering Many Areas of Interest

The decade of the 50's was filled with many major decisions and accomplishments. My practice had become well established. We had built our dream home; which would shelter us for the next 40 years. Our family consisted of three very rambunctious boys. Different family interests were being explored such as water skiing, sailing, swimming, and golf.

Chapter 35

1960 opened with a note of sadness. Mary's Father passed away from the aftermath of a stroke. Her Mother had passed away about ten years earlier. She was now without either parent. She still had her three sisters. On December 27, 1960, we celebrated our twenty-fifth Wedding Anniversary where we were married at St John's Church on the Creighton University campus. Father Hupp and Father Decker concelebrated the Mass for us. I gave my beloved Mary a matching diamond ring to go with her original platinum set. The magic in the touch of her hands was stronger than ever.

Dr. Glow was well established in his practice, and his family was rapidly expanding. He ended up with five girls and three boys. I had the privilege of being the pediatrician for his flock.

1. We had our different medical problems with his family: Mary Kay's, the oldest, coat was caught in the school bus door. She was dragged. While in the hospital, she showed signs of a ruptured spleen, which had to be removed.
2. Tom developed Measles Encephalitis while his folks were out of town and needed to be hospitalized. He was left with some residual minor cognitive problems.
3. Ricky, the youngest, had an rH Problem at birth which I had to exchange and, then, re-exchange. Today, he is an Oral Surgeon on Childrens' Hospital Staff'.
4. I was Nancy's Godparent. When she went off to a small college in Missouri on a full tennis scholarship, she was

very homesick for her family and missed all of the confusion that was constantly present. She didn't want to worry her parents; so she would write me long broken hearted letters for most of her first year. After the first year, she did very well. I always called her, "My Nancy". She is happily married with four children. I still get cards on my birthday and Christmas from her.

Early on when they grew out of the small house they had, I co-signed a new mortgage so they could move into a bigger and more comfortable place. The rest of their brood joined the family while living in this spacious home.

Chapter 36

By gave us a big fat headache when he took the Creighton Prep entrance exams. He had always been an excellent math student and vied for the best math student honors in his class. For some unknown reason, he failed the math portion of the Prep Exams; so he was required to go to summer school for remedial math. This blow required us to change our previously extensive and detailed vacation plans. He did extremely well in summer school as we expected.

The first day home from Creighton Prep, he came into the house with a face dragging on the floor. He was reluctant to let us know what the matter was. Finally, we pried the reason out of him. He had been placed in the slower tract at Prep, which he called, "The dumb part of the class". Prep used a modified popular tract system at this time. We could not understand this Prep Tract system being compatible with our own intimate knowledge of By's capabilities. Finally, one of the young Jesuit Scholastics explained Prep's tract system to us. The top tract pupils were graded differently from the lower tract, and these students were able to take a foreign language in addition to the regular subjects. I, then, recalled having several boys in my office that ended up in the same boat as By and were totally turned off by Prep's lower tract system and never enjoyed high school.

I immediately began to plan my counterattack to offset this suspected transgression of justice. I learned that the summer school did not count for anything towards the tract placement, but it had produced a great big fat headache and inconvenience to us. This fact added salt to my wounds big time. I asked my dear friend, Francis Edwards, who was the head of the Psychological Testing Department at Omaha University, to test By. Sure enough, he had an IQ of 132 as I had expected. Without bragging, all of our boys had exceptionally good intelligence. Obviously, they took after their mother in this regard.

Armed with this information, I requested an appointment with Prep's Principal, a Father Laboy. I insisted that Father Decker to be present as a referee. I was as angry as I could be over this treatment and cavalier attitude towards a boy's future.

Mary and I arrived ahead of time. With fire in my eyes, I had both guns loaded for bear and was prepared for war. Father Decker knew that I was greatly irritated and upset. Mary was mortified and distressed that I was so angry and primed for war with Father Laboy. Father went through his rather pompous explanation of all the testing Prep did to accurately place the student. Immediately, I detested his pomposity. I let him know that his words were so much hogwash and presented him with the IQ Testing results from a more than qualified source. Well! Talk about red faces. Father Laboy looked like a Christmas Tree all lit up. We, all, agreed that By would move to the top tract in his class at the semester break. We would have him tutored in Spanish at my expense; so that he would be on a level playing field with his new classmates.

Mrs. Samardick, the mother of a patient of mine, was from Guatemala. She was a beautiful and gifted person. She met with By every Sunday. At the school semester break, By moved into the higher scholastic tract. When he graduated from Prep, he consistently had made first honors each semester and was on the National Honor Society. Father Laboy was long gone. Oh happy day! Father Ryan was the Principal and was cut from a different piece of clergy cloth. I had a much greater empathy for parents and school problems because of this experience. Sometimes, it is imperative that parents fight their children's battles whenever necessary when the child would not be able to fight back.

Chapter 37

The summer after By graduated from Prep, he entered a Surgical Tech Training Program that Methodist Hospital developed for the offspring of Staff Physicians. These trained Techs would work in the operating rooms during holidays and summer vacations to help with the vacation personnel shortage and when extra staffing was needed. This shortage would occur not only due to personnel vacations but at other times such as the Christmas Holiday season when a number of the workers would be on leave. By thoroughly enjoyed his time in the operating room, but he had no interest in pursuing surgery.

The summer before starting his pre-med studies, he obtained a construction job. I had visions of dollars and cents that I would not have to pay out when at college. Ha Ha! What a delusion. Just as By was to start this semi-lucrative job by our standards, he came to me and said," Dad, would you mind very much if I went back to the hospital because I miss it so much." With tears rolling down my face and visions of dollar bills flying out the window, what reply could I give except, "Not at all if that is what you really want to do"? This experience helped him to decide on medicine as a career and vocation. Later on he chose the field of Anesthesiology for his vocation.

I asked By this question, "Why is anesthesia a medical field of interest to you as a vocation"? He replied, "I've watched you handle and balance many different situations all at the same time. I can't do that juggling act. I only want to handle one task at a time. I don't care how long I have to work as long as it is only one patient at a time". Talk about one's own insight into self knowledge and capabilities!

The Prep pupils liked Father Ryan and his fairness. Years later, I learned that he had applied the "Board of Education" on more than one occasion to our different offspring. Good for Father! Had I known, they would have had more reminders at home to pay better attention to the school's rules.

We taught at least five hundred plus people to water ski in the forty plus years that we skied and enjoyed the water. When the boys became teens, it was girls, girls, and more girls that they wanted to bring skiing. I didn't mind. The more acquaintances I met, the better I understood the boys' relationships and interests. Father Ryan was one of our pupils. Turnabout is fair play, but we were very careful with him when he was on the skis.

Larson Ski Boat And Skiers

By kept pushing to be able to take friends skiing without an adult along. His mother was very adamant against this activity. She was too worried about an accident. I tried for a middle ground approach and had a brilliant "Man-to-Man" talk with By explaining his Mother's position and concerns. I proposed that I would sit on the bank and read a book, he would run the boat, and his friends could ski. Under no circumstances could anyone else drive the boat. I thought this brilliant approach cleared the air with a more than satisfactory solution. Well!

I came to the office on a Tuesday morning and began making my way through the stack of phone calls. As I was talking with Chrissie R.'s Mother, she inadvertently mentioned that Chrissie had had a great time skiing at the lake yesterday. OOPS! The horses were out of the barn. I was furious and felt betrayed. I called home on my lunch hour. When By answered the phone, all I said was, "I was just kicked in the stomach, and it really hurts". By replied, "Oh, so you know that I used the boat for skiing on Monday afternoon against your wishes"? I was so upset that I quickly hung up the phone. When I returned home at the end of the day, still steaming, By was long gone. He didn't come home for three days. He hid out at Grannie "O's" apartment, who was twisted around his little finger. She loved to spoil all the boys much to our dismay. Later, we learned that when Granny stayed at the house when we were away to a medical meeting. Forts were built in the living room and other forbidden activities were done. Well, back to By, my dear friend did not get near the boat for a long, long time.

By was experienced enough and skilled enough to sail the Snipe in the Sunday races. As I loved to sail, it was difficult to share the boat as he wanted to race with his friend, Dale B. When on the boat, By was a regular Captain Bligh and sailed the snipe with gusto. He was an excellent sailor. I purchased a barely used new snipe with Dr. Dan Miller, a general surgeon. We sailed together for many years and were fairly competitive.

Sail Boat Race Lake Manawa Council Bluffs, Iowa

An important point in sailing is that the same crew is essential for each race so that synchronization and coordination becomes the sailing way of life. Part of the enjoyment of sailing in a race was that you didn't have to come in first place to have fun winning. There were many smaller races within the main race. One boat would be striving to beat another nearby boat to the finish line. It was great fun to beat another boat across the finish line regardless of what place it was. It was quite a thrill to be on the starting line with twenty plus snipes all jockeying for a good start and with sails flapping in the wind.

The races are a timed start and the trick is to get to the starting line just as the starting gun is fired. If you get there too soon, one must make a three hundred and sixty degree turn and start over. If one gets to the line too late, tough luck old boy! One year when we sailed in the Labor Day Regatta, the winds were at twenty knots with gusts to twenty-five; we were sailing our best. We were having a wild and wooly ride and were leading the pack of boats until we rounded the windward buoy when a major gust of wind knocked us flat. We could not right the boat no matter how hard we tried. The wind was pushing the hull dead on and drove the mast six feet into the muddy bottom. It took two large motor boats, who worked for about two hours to pull the boat out of the mud and back to shore. We looked at the mast which now had a great big "S" bend where there was none before. Repairs cost about $800 and a new mast. We declined to race in winds that were over twelve knots after this experience.

Most races sailed a triangular course with one leg into the wind (windward leg), one leg off the wind (wind abeam where the wind would push against the side of the boat) and the last leg had the wind coming from behind the boat (the downwind leg). Having the wind abeam the boat was the fastest point of sailing. One needed to hike way out to balance the heeling over of the boat. This point of sailing was exhilarating. Naturally, the best start had a great initial advantage. I seldom experienced this advantage. Ha! You really needed to be aware of the winds many capricious activities and watch it closely in order to take full advantage of its power. Sailing was a great challenging sport and never grew old.

Father Ryan was a good sport and went water skiing with us several times. He joined us in many of our family activities and with the Harvey family. Tom Harvey first met By in fourth grade, was in boy scouts with him, and played offensive tackle at Prep while By played fullback. Fifty years later, the two of them are as close as brothers and spend a lot of time together. Their most recent activity was a forty day hike through the Swiss Alps. Ugh! Someone must have holes in their head. Tom is a graduate of West Point and retired as a Lt. Colonel from the army after twenty-five years. He has several businesses and owns a mountain in Virginia. Obviously, he and his family are doing very well.

Chapter 38

When we finished remodeling our basement, the large room at the south end of the house was made into a gym with weights, a chinning bar, a pegboard climbing exercise wall item, and a full size wrestling mat. The boys were into physical fitness and sports in a big way. All the boys were good at sports, and each had his own areas of interest in which to compete.

My beloved Mary was introduced to an unfamiliar world where she and her sisters were novices. She had to learn that three strikes meant that you were out in baseball. Also, she had to figure out that ten yards made a first down in football. Mary never cared for wrestling even though Terry was second in the State at his weight as senior in high school. As a family, we were into many sports "Big Time".

The boys were involved in music both with the piano and the electric guitar. It was a family dictum that piano lessons would be a part of their education until they left grade school. By was a good jazz piano player but never used it after high school began. Terry played a twelve string guitar and a harmonica. I enjoyed listening to him play. Matt became an excellent guitarist. After he was married to Nancy, he played in a four man band at wedding receptions, dances, and the "Belle of Brownsville" dinner excursion boat on the Missouri River. Because their band followers wanted a "Big Band Sound", Matt obtained a used saxophone and taught himself to play it. He already played the keyboard, besides the guitar, for the band. In a like manner, he obtained a used accordion; now, the group was able to play polkas. He played for a long time to earn money for his family. Two of his sons have played in groups.

His son, Conor, was and is a very gifted and popular Inde Rock Artist, known on the tour circuit as "Bright Eyes" or "Conor Oberst". He has played in the Hollywood Bowl in Los Angeles and in the "Radio City Music Hall" in New York City. He has toured Europe, Japan, New Zealand, and Australia, besides all over the US. He has been on the "Austin City Limits" program several times. He has produced many CD's and the large platter type vinyl albums. Some of his composed songs have been high on the Music Charts. His songs were number eight amongst the most frequently downloaded songs on the internet. A few of his songs have been used in movies. He was just honored as the musician of the decade in Nebraska.

Chapter 39

It has become time to address the decade of the 60's in a rather defined manner. From my training and based upon the first ten years of my practice, I learned five very important attributes that I possessed:

1. I was able to organize large divergent amounts of information into a single workable entity. This capability was a real asset to my future areas of interest.
2. I had an insatiable appetite to poke into new medical recesses and corners looking for new fields to conquer or to explore. At times, this attribute was difficult to manage. I would find myself to be over committed to many different projects and was apt to be overwhelmed with the concurrent responsibilities.
3. I could outwork almost anyone else young or old and not break a sweat in doing so. My capacity for work was great.
4. I had the capability to multitask a number of important ideas/activities at the same time resulting with a good and complete end product on each segment.
5. Medicine was a very potent seductress to contend with while I still had to learn how to share her with my family and to keep intact the wall between medicine and family.

This decade will be divided into the practice/professional components and the other part will be composed of family activities/areas of interest. I will describe each component separately for the simplicity of addressing each of these interests. These areas were so intertwined that at times it would be hard to separate one from another and to clearly explain the contents. Many different dynamics were in play in addition to my thirst, desire, and passion to explore the many different vistas of medicine. I was still struggling to keep from being drawn into medicine's seductive embrace and lost to the real world.

One of my unique medical enjoyments was to endeavor to untangle a difficult diagnostic problem which contained many different facets and challenging areas. Utilizing the "Problem Oriented Medical Record" approach to complex situations was of major assistance in unraveling an intriguing multifaceted diagnosis. My consultation practice grew in a programmed and mathematical progression rate.

Chapter 40

The location of the office on the Farnam Street Island limited any possible expansion or change. We badly needed more parking spaces for the convenience of our patients. Inside the building, there was a pressing need for more examining rooms. These simple facts were necessary in order to move the patient population more efficiently and to conserve expensive professional time which was wasted in waiting for a patient to be made ready to be seen. I was elected to find a solution to our dilemma.

One day, I received a phone call from a Mrs. Rubin, who owned and built many apartment buildings in this general neighborhood. She had the impression that I was looking for a location to which to move the office. She had some nearby property at fortieth and Dewey Avenue to offer. This location seemed to be ideal for us. I took one look at her offering and began the initial planning process. She wanted to create a building to my specifications and needs. We came to terms very readily.

I worked with her draftsman to draw the building plans. It was to be a long one story building with an apartment on each end and a garage beneath the building. The new location was just up the street from the new Clarkson Hospital and about four blocks from Childrens' Hospital. It was located very near the University of Nebraska Medical Center campus. This location could not have been better for our needs.

Mrs. Rubin was a fascinating person. She and her family had escaped from Latvia just ahead of the Germans in the early days of World War II. There were many members in her family with different business interests in Omaha. She had trouble handling English and writing. I made out many checks for her to sign for the builder's payments. I grew to love and admired her greatly.

Sometimes I would call her on the phone just to visit. She was a wonderful lady. I called her, "My little friend". She was not very big. She wanted me to buy the building at a very low interest rate, but I was leery as I had watched several medical groups break up over building and financial matters. In the long run, I was justified in my reluctance not to buy this property.

The office was designed with a race track type format. There was a central core for the bookkeeper, receptionist, laboratory space, and medical record shelves. This made for an easy access to these workers and/or materials. The main waiting room stretched across the front of the building and had the dual role of being both a waiting area and a place for our parent lecture hall. Our Lecture Schedule was posted in the waiting room. We could seat one hundred bodies in this area if necessary.

OCCPC Medical Bldg 40th Dewey

One end of the waiting room was divided off by an accordion wall as an adolescent waiting area. This area had posters and an adolescent magazine rack which would appeal to this age group. In the early days of adolescent medicine, this separation was deemed necessary. Later on, I determined that most adolescents didn't care one way or the other for their own waiting room. They did not mind waiting with babies and young children. Sometimes we assign too much exclusivity to adolescents. Most of them wanted to be treated like anyone else.

My adolescent practice took off like a Roman Candle and burst out in many different directions at the same time. I published four articles in medical journals and gave some seventeen talks to medical groups and societies on the adolescence years. I was in popular demand because of my pioneering and the newness of this field. Many of my patients stayed with me through the choice of their college and on into their college years. Some stayed into early adulthood because they were comfortable having this practice as their medical home.

I decided to stop seeing them at the ripe old age of thirty. I frequently told the girls as they became of marriageable age, "I expect you to bring your Fiancé to meet me so that I can determine if he is good enough for you". Surprisingly, many of the young ladies did that very thing. This age period was my most fascinating and satisfying time in my practice.

I ended up being a "Grandpa Doctor" over one hundred times with young people growing up, getting married, having babies, and desiring me for their Pediatrician. How satisfying this relationship was. Some of these relationships extended over a span of thirty plus years.

One of the most satisfying aspects of Pediatrics was that you had a front row seat for the stage of life. You became a part of the family with all of their cares, sorrows, and times of happiness for many years. It was not the most lucrative side of medicine, but it was the most satisfying medical life to have.

There were four physician suites in our building. Each suite had a main office and two additional examining rooms. This design aided in the movement of patients, especially, during the winter months when there were so many clothes to contend with. Each office area had unique decorations to fit a theme motif, such as the "Flower Room" or the "Captain's Cabin". There was plenty of working space.

Dr. James I. Wax, a former resident at Childrens', had ended his service time at the Offutt Air Force Base outside of Omaha as the Post Pediatrician. He joined us when he was discharged from the service.

Having four physicians instead of three made a huge difference in doctor coverage for the practice. When one physician was out of town at a meeting and another had the day off, there were two others left in the office. If an emergency Cesarean Section happened, there was coverage for both the Cesarean Section and the Office.

Whenever we were called for a Cesarean Section, it was our practice protocol that we would leave the office and proceed to the appropriate hospital to attend to the Cesarean Section's baby. The Obstetricians liked our availability to meet their patients' needs. Some pediatricians refused to leave their offices because of their office hours. There were no Neonatologists in those days. General pediatricians served that purpose. Because of my early work with rH Problems, I was a neonatologist long before there were such animals.

I was Pediatrician-in-Chief at Clarkson Hospital from 1965 to 1976. I deemed that this length of time was long enough. Dr. Ellison was having many newborns there and my number of infants was tapering off. I turned the duties over to Dr. Joseph Ellison, my partner.

For a while, I was involved with both, Clarkson Hospital where I was the Chief of Pediatrics, and at Bergan Mercy Hospital by a personal request of the Medical Chief of Staff, Dr. Joseph Gross. There were some major tension and diplomatic problems at the new Bergan shortly after it opened. Dissention was serious amongst the medical staff between the Family Practitioners and the Specialists. I was prevailed upon to help solve this staff dilemma. This headache and friction I endeavored to alleviate. More information about this dilemma will be explained later on in this story.

Chapter 41

My practice was beginning to have several different tracts within the encompassing whole. The fundamental foundation for my practice philosophy was my integrated and sophisticated "Guided Growth Well Child and Adolescent Program". I was constantly searching for new ideas and materials to incorporate into this mosaic of growth and development. Any new parameter that was deemed useful was added to its appropriate slot in this conglomerate feature. I looked for different medical seminars which would enhance and strengthen my own philosophies. I frequently would uncover a great idea which was worth its weight in gold. As an example, there was a pediatrician in Philadelphia who presented his ideas at a meeting. He separated infants and very young children into three personality categories:

1. The "Easy Child" who adapted to changes and new experiences within the family very readily.

2. The "Moderate Child" who followed the natural ups and downs of childhood and his/her family patterns without too much trouble.

3. The "Difficult Child" who was hard to handle almost from birth onward. As time passed, this group of children posed a major and a cardinal warning sign that the "The Attention Deficit Syndrome" may be a problem. This designation became a nodal finding when taking a medical history concerning a school failure situation.

As my interest in school failure problems grew, so did my zeal to aid these children. A defined approach to the various and multiple causes of this syndrome began to evolve. This medical entity was really a Syndrome meaning that there were multiple causes producing the same or similar presenting symptoms.

The first descriptive name for this entity came from the Blue Bird Clinic in Houston, Texas. They used the moniker, "Minimal Cerebral Dysfunction". This unlikely nomenclature was not nice, was totally unacceptable, and was very frightening to parents. Hyperkinesias, Hyperactive Child, and other similar designations were not uniformly accepted and utilized. Finally, the accepted terminology became the "The Attention Deficit Syndrome with and without Hyperactivity". I became very early pioneer and expert in this specialized field.

Most physicians and associated medical personnel did not have the slightest clue about this entity, what to do about it, and, what was worse, seemingly could care less to do anything about it. Most of these children in school were labeled "Behavior Problems" and/or the product of poor parenting situations. These children were placed in behavior modification classes for the want of something else to do with them or place to put them. Unfortunately, this unwarranted designation would follow these children through the rest of his/her school days to the detriment of their own self esteem.

As a general rule, boys were more apt to be identified early as being overly active, having trouble sitting still, having trouble concentrating, and might have some trouble socializing. These almost universal cardinal symptoms would call attention to the problem very quickly.

Girls were more apt to be "Day Dreamers" and as a result could slip past teachers, professionals, and other people for several years before their problem would be noted. At long last and finally, someone discovered that they could not read or would have other specific learning problems. The underlying difficulty for this entity was the attention span of the child. This defect made him/her unable to complete tasks or to stay focused upon a subject. The secondary effects of this entity ended with school failure, poor self image, and many other related symptoms. I should have written a book about this syndrome. I could have and should have written a detailed description concerning this medical problem because so many people still have major misconceptions about this entity. Unfortunately, the time for me to write about this syndrome has long since passed. With more than twenty years behind me, details are fuzzy, records are gone, and zest has vanished to reopen these closed doors.

The theme song, which followed these children wherever they would go in school and beyond, was, "You are not trying hard enough". This was a frequent admonition to the child or to the parents; whereas, the child was already blowing gaskets trying to keep up with his/her peers. The child knew he/she was as bright as the next one so their own anti theme song in return was, "How come he/she can get this answer and I can't. Here, I am blowing gaskets trying to do the assignment, and it just doesn't happen. They just keep on telling that I am not trying hard enough". What a heart rendering unanswered plea these unspoken words were, and what a sad travesty for the individual child.

In my opinion and working theory was that the underlying cause of this entity was trouble with the chemical neurotransmitters at the synaptic junctions (nerve endings) in the brain. This was basically an electrical connection problem within the brain. In many ways, the brain is a very sophisticated computer that can rapidly process a considerable amount of data within a short space of time. Some of these neurotransmitters were Sertonin, Acetylcholine, Norepinephrine, and several others. Also, there were neuroantagonists to these elements. Researchers were finally beginning to unravel this dilemma after years of trying and with a great deal of frustration. The medications, which became available, acted upon these various neurotransmitter elements in special and different ways. Ritalin was the first major helpful agent in the early days. Now, there is an entire armamentarium of meds available for use in specialized situations.

This condition was **NOT** due to poor parenting attributes, although, parents were frequently the scapegoats for placing blame for the child's poor school production/failure. Many a tear was shed in my office by both the parents and the child because of this labeling. How sad! There were a number of "crazy" theories as to the cause for this syndrome, such as too much sugar intake, red dyes, special exercises, or the need for mega vitamins. In my experience, none of these "far out" remedies helped one iota with this medical entity.

Associated with the attention span was frequently an accompanying specific learning problem. If it was in mathematics, it was called Dyscalculia. If reading was the problem, it was called Dyslexia. If it was hand writing, it was Dysgraphia, and so on through each of the specific academic subjects which were affected. One could follow the response to the medication program, in many instances, by observing the improvement in the child's handwriting. Sometimes the learning problem was so severe that correction was impossible, then, bypass strategies had to be employed.

There was a fifteen year old boy who had failed every grade and tried every remedial approach available under the sun to help his inability to read. Visual learning was impossible for him. His auditory pathways to learn needed to be utilized. The General Electric Company put all of his textbooks on audiotapes. He began to understand his subject materials, graduated from high school, and attended a small college in Texas, Trinity College, which specialized in working with students who had trouble learning. When he was out in the working world, his secretary would read aloud the titles of his trade magazine articles. She would read the designated articles he wanted onto a tape recorder for him to utilize. Because of these aids, he became a functioning member of society instead of a social drop out.

Many a hyperactive male would solve some of his own problem by working in an active outside job where it was not necessary to sit still for long periods as in an office at a desk. Construction work and farm jobs were ideal vocations for them. The use of marijuana was another approach they used to try and slow themselves down through self medication.

If a child had a severe spelling problem, have him/her learn to use a word processing program with a spellchecker. If there was a math problem, a calculator needed to be used. Frequently, a child's math improved because the figure columns were now aligned in straight columns due to the use of medications and the inadvertent following errors because of misalignment were omitted. Many a child handled basic math but could not handle abstract cognitive reasoning. Algebra and geometry were impossible subjects for these folks to solve. This person needed to stay with business math and related subjects in order to be self sufficient and independent. Learning to handle a checkbook and manage a budget were far more important skills to acquire than understanding algebra and geometry. Many of these children had a problem with cursory writing and found that printing was a better solution for them. If the writing was too illegible, then, a computer with a word processor was needed. As the old saying goes, "Any old port in a storm". Do what is necessary to help the individual to become a self-sufficient, independent, and functioning citizen. Not everyone needs to become an Einstein or be a college graduate.

One of the casualties within the older population with this entity was the fact that they couldn't hold a job which required sitting at a desk or handling boring and repetitive data. This person needed to have a job where he/she could keep moving such as in construction work and similar bodily movement vocations.

Many older folks would float from one job failure to another which further damaged their self worth and self esteem. Because of this constantly defeating situation, he/she might develop an irritating abrasive personality. A certain segment of this population would self medicate themselves with alcohol, marijuana, or other drugs which would slow their hyperactivity, but to their own detriment and their health.

I did a study on the young people who were placed in a juvenile detention center at Kearney, Nebraska when researching for the American Academy of Pediatrics' request that each state Chapter write a health plan for the children in their state. Many of the young people in this facility were school failure problems.

As I walked the halls, there would be a few boys in one room trying to learn to read a simple story such as, "Jack went up the hill". How heart rending this observation was for me. Our prisons have many of this same type of population.

Chapter 42

After a while, it became apparent to me that the single most important physical examination for a child to have was the "Pre-school Readiness Exam". If a child started off on the right foot, school moved along in a reasonable fashion and pace. The corollary of that observation was that a child who started to school out of step by starting too early or with attention problems; then rough waters were ahead for most of the school years both academically and socially.

I was never a big advocate for early childhood education as demonstrated by the Head Start Program. By the end of the first school semester, most advantages that had been previously accrued had been exhausted. At this point and at least by the end of first grade, all students were at the same starting level with no special advantages for anyone. I know that early childhood education advocates violently disagree with me. This readily observed happening is a fact of life as I saw it from my own extensive experiences.

This pre-school exam became a nodal spot within my well child spectrum. If a child showed trouble with fine finger motor coordination, poor hopping on one foot and then the other foot, and/or drew bizarre figures on the "Draw a Person" test, these indicators could signify there could be trouble and rough waters ahead. Many times, the picture of the "Draw a Person" would be hard to recognize as the eyes may be in odd places or some other body part distortion would be present. The child could blissfully identify the parts even though they were not connected into a complete entity.

A child with certain of these following adverse history items made me very suspicious that an underlying problem might be present. If a child had a history of prematurity, twinning, a prolong or very short labor, a breech delivery, post delivery breathing troubles, very low Apgar readings, or any type of difficulty such as chicken pox within the first three years of life, a high degree of suspicion would be raised in my mind. In addition, any major medical situation, such as meningitis, that occurred within the first three or four years of life became a major cause for concern. I published several papers on the importance of the preschool readiness exam

When a new patient would arrive for their appointment, I would introduce myself and say, "Before we address the reason that brought you to me, I want to ask many background questions to get a feel for your needs". After this information was obtained, I would, then, say to the parents, "Now, what brings you into my office today and how can I help you"? Many a parent replied, "I have never had a doctor ask me what my needs were. How nice of you to ask for my thoughts and feelings concerning my child's school problems. No one has bothered to ask me of my thoughts about my child's school problem before". What a sad commentary on my profession. With this breaking of the ice and the dampening down of hidden anxieties and fears, it was much easier to delve into all aspects of their problem in order to seek a solution for them

For all new problem cases, I allocated at least one hour for the initial evaluation. Sometimes, it ran longer so I charged accordingly. I rarely had any one complain about the costs. They were relieved to have someone finally listen to them. Many of these parents had gone from pillar to post seeking help for their child without success.

It was important to me that I should explore every apparent facet of their problem so that the parents would quit shopping and chasing rainbows because their child had been so thoroughly investigated and in great detail. Every patient had to undergo a detailed set of tests which I found helpful in ruling out the other common associated problems as causative agents.

The history helped in selecting the most useful medication to be prescribed. Each patient was evaluated by my own personal educational psychologist, who was very familiar with children with these problems.

They were, also, seen by a noted local Neurologist who had insight into these situations. He was utilized for consistency of approach. I tried to leave nothing to chance or left undone. This comprehensive approach helped to bring peace of mind to the parents and helped them to stop shopping from one doctor to another in the useless chasing of rainbows as so many of them had been doing. Obviously, this shopping had been all in vain and very costly. Too often, I saw children who had "Pills" thrown at them with no good rationale, or a snap diagnosis being made without any concrete reason, or families who had gone from pillar to post seeking help without success.

I had a strict protocol for these intricate problems which had to be followed if the family wanted me to proceed to work with them. After all tests were done and my own Educational Psychologist performed her evaluation, I would have a detailed family conference including the child, if over ten years of age, which was a knowledgeable age as to their situation. It was important for the older child to understand his/her situation as this child was the central player in this drama. This child would be coping with this school situation for a long time to come. It was imperative for the child to comprehend his/her own needs. Many patients would have to cope for a lifetime.

At this conference, I would explain the test results and all the aspects of their special problem. Many times my psychologist, when available, would be a part of this conference. When the parents exhausted their questions, I would lay out a course of action to be followed including ways to involve the child's teacher. The role of medications was discussed in depth and detail. I was very strict about follow up visits including the required progress phone calls every three months and regular six month re-evaluation office visits. If this approach was not acceptable to the parents, I would not handle their child. I held these Family Conferences at the 4:30 PM hour so the meeting could last as long as necessary without watching a clock. My supper was frequently late. I felt that my primary role in medicine was to help people and to lift some of their burdens.

I had a package of printed information for the parents to read and study and one for the child's teacher concerning different aspects of this syndrome. There were reports in the teacher's package to fill out and return monthly, so that I could get a feel as to how the classroom participation was progressing. Many times, our Office Marketing Nurse would visit, if practical, with the child's local teacher and would explain the situation and the goals we were striving for. This was a very defined, sophisticated, interactive, and dynamic program that I had developed over time and from many previous experiences.

Behind my back, I learned that I was called "Doctor Pill" or a charlatan, but these slights were not a deterrent to me. Frequently, I was blamed for doing too many tests and the like. Following my own dictates of thinking of the common cause but looking for the unusual reason, it was not too surprising to me as how many unusual causes there were. Cerebral (brain) calcifications, low thyroid states, seizure like patterns on the EEG were a few of the more common findings which reared their ugly heads and had to be addressed and corrected in addition to the primary problem. I always looked for signs and findings associated with lead poisoning; but seldom if ever found them which were contrary to some current thoughts.

As very few teachers, physicians, and parents knew much about this entity in these early days, or had limited interest in the problem, and because there were so many hurting children, I conjured up the idea for a community action educational program for these uninformed people.

With the permission and assistance of several School Districts in the Omaha area, I gathered several of their district staff education psychologists and learning specialists together for planning purposes. We outlined a program with objectives and goals. We named the program, "STAAR" meaning Learning Skills, Learning Techniques, Academic Ability, and Remediation. The program was designed to educate the public, parents, physicians, and school personnel about the needs and problems that these children and youth were enduring.

Our first public meeting was held at Burke High of the Omaha Public School System. Dr. Owen Knutson was the OPS Superintendent who approved the location for this meeting. I brought in a noted Psychologist from the State of Washington, with whom I had worked previously, as the central speaker. There were over nine hundred attendees of all types at this meeting. The program was off to a flying start.

Over time, this program brought in most of the known and outstanding people who were investigating and studying different approaches and aspects of this problem. These meetings were primarily for the Special Education Experts in the various school districts and were funded by the Special Ed Departments and ESU # 3. Funds were obtained through Dr. Don Warner, who was the head of the Special Ed Department for OPS, ESU # 3 contributed monies, and my own scrounging of donations from some of my more affluent parents who had children with these problems. The school districts recognized the importance of this program and granted educational points/credits to their personnel attendees.

The STAAR Program was a very successful venture. Ultimately, it joined with the National Organization for Learning Disabilities, which had emerged over time. For my efforts, I was given a Lifetime Membership in the National PTA. This honor was one of my most cherished.

Chapter 43

I saw children and adolescents with this problem from all over the country and world. The office would become excited when I would be expecting a scheduled medical progress call from Saudi Arabia, Italy, or England. I had seen a number of children who were dependents of Air Force Personnel at Offut Air Base, just south of Omaha, or the Peter Kiewit Construction Corporation, which did work everywhere under the sun. When the worker and the family were transferred to a new station or location, the same general follow up requirements continued. Progress med phone calls had to be made every three months without fail. Every child had to be seen for a detailed yearly "Annual Health Review". At times, this requirement worked a hardship on the parents, but it was necessary for the child or youth's benefit.

This annual evaluation was an important component of my "Well Child Program" and medical evaluation for all my patients. Depending upon the age, sufficient time was allocated in the appointment scheduling to accommodate this detailed type of review. If the child was 10 years old, we saved 30 minutes; if in early adolescence, the visit needed 45 minutes; and the older ones and young adults had 60 minutes of my time. My involvement time did not include patient preparation time. When I walked into the examining room, the entire allocated time was devoted to the patient and the family's needs. This concept was used for those who did not have a major medical condition as well as for those patients with problems. At a certain inconvenience to the parent, I did not see two children of theirs on the same day. I had learned from experience that one child would receive the majority of the visit time and emphasis. The other one would be slighted and would not be seen in great detail. I wanted to see and concentrate on each child in his/her entirety for their own betterment. This dictum was especially true for twins after they were four years or older. Most parents accepted my whimsical desires as worthwhile for their children.

Charges were made accordingly and without any major complaints by the parents. My practice revolved around this conceptual theory, "That any medical problem, whether major or minor, would and should become a mere milestone on the child's pathway to adulthood rather than the child or youth living from one series of repetitive medical crisis problems to another". I wanted each child to live from one growth period to the next one. I loved my consultative practice as it was so challenging.

Over the years, I cared for over 3000 of these special ADD patients. Usually, the outcome was very gratifying. Many of these patients became doctors, dentists, business men, and similar contributing members to society. Unfortunately, there were failures due to one reason or another. Patient compliance was always a big problem and a major headache. The older patients fought taking the medication for long periods of time. There was no cause for worrying about any addiction to these meds as the child/youth did not want to take the meds any longer than necessary.

In my experience, most of the patients would need their medications for extended periods of time. Boys took about five years and girls about four years before the medications could be slowly and gradually tapered off. About 60 % of the patients would not need any more medication thereafter; but there was a group who needed their meds resumed for awhile longer; and some who needed them indefinitely. With the younger children, progress could be documented by an improvement in handwriting which became more legible and math columns that would become straighter. With straight columns, math problems could be solved in a more timely and accurate fashion. Later on, I had access to the "Gordon Diagnostic Device", which was an investigative approach to measuring short attention spans and fine finger motor coordination. These changes were documented on special recording paper and used for progress comparisons. This device was very useful both in making the diagnosis and in following the improvement in the patient and the response to the medications.

Unfortunately, there were some failures along the way, but these were few by comparison. It was interesting to note that in the early days of the Attention Deficit Syndrome, these children were supposed to "Grow Out of the Problem by the time they entered adolescence." I did not find that this spontaneous improvement ever occurred. The symptoms merely changed and became somewhat more obscure or were masked by actions of the patient. Addressing these patients and their problems ended up being one of the most challenging and satisfying aspects of my medical life.

Another asinine thought floating around without any good rationale to substantiate it, was the idea that medications should be given during the week on school days, off on the weekends, and off during the summer. All this nutty idea did was to prolong the child's agony and the parent's disappointments. This approach did not allow for any continuity of treatment to achieve defined results; this pathway led to confusion, disappointment, and prolonged the agony of the child in my opinion.

Chapter 44

My interest in the many facets of the Attention Deficit Disorder Syndrome (ADD) stimulated my interest and need to look into many other aspects of medicine such as Neurology, Family Counseling, and Psychiatry. I began attending lectures and seminars in these fields to enhance my knowledge in order to assist me in helping my patients.

Speaking of Psychiatry, I was never able to accept the Freudian concepts of Id, Ego, Super Ego, anal phase, urethral phase, and/or sex as a basis for mental problems in children. These concepts never made sense to me in developmental pediatrics. However, it was difficult to find a psychiatrist who was not trained and dependent upon these Freudian concepts.

I was a disciple of Dr. Arnold Gessell of Yale and his movies which documented a child's growth and development patterns including some aspects of adolescence. Dr. Piaget, the Swiss Psychologist, who studied the child's learning concepts as illustrated by the glass half full or half empty with water, had very enlightening thoughts and ideas for me. His concepts as to how a child learned and processed information greatly impressed me. I was fortunate to attend and see Dr. Piaget in person at the opening of the newly constructed developmental center at the University of Miami at Miami, Florida. I studied and learned from many similar milestone investigators. I would incorporate their useful philosophies into my mosaic of "Guided Growth" concepts.

Chapter 45

One of my most memorable medical triumphs occurred when a set of premature twin girls was born at Methodist Hospital. One of the girls died immediately after birth, but not "Thumbelina" – my nickname. She was one tough little cookie that called upon all my previous skills as a pseudo-neonatologist and some ancient long ago used procedures which to needed to be utilized. This baby was a true fifth month gestation and weighed 1 pound and two ounces. She fit within the palm of my hand. Her weight dropped to fifteen ounces within days. She was so immature and her skin was so transparent that you could see her intestinal track through the abdominal wall. When I had Dr. Eagle, a wonderful Ophthalmologist, examine her eyes, the retina had not yet developed. We had to feed her with an eye dropper.

    I lived with the agonies of the dammed over this little mite. She had convulsions due to low calcium levels. We had to give her supplemental calcium. Her red blood count fell to far less than three million cells instead of the usual and badly needed four to five million cells. She was in air hunger due to lack of circulating oxygen via too few RBC's. I dug way back into my professional memory bank and armamentarium for a little used and long forgotten intra-abdominal blood transfusion technique. I used 3 cc of packed red cells. I was very sweaty and nervous about doing this procedure on such a tiny person. The red blood cells would be absorbed into the baby's circulation through the diaphragmatic lymphatic channels. She gradually improved in size and weight to where she could go home after months and months in the ICU for premature infants.

As one would expect, she presented a major set of medical problems. Early on, she had an attention span problem which responded to Ritalin. Fortunately she did not show any signs of cerebral palsy or other neurological handicaps. Her eyes developed normally and vision was merely aided by glasses.

Her mother was the Chief Surgical Nurse and Operating room Supervisor at Methodist Hospital in Omaha. This situation increased the feelings of tension and of my own impotence in caring for this wee bit of humanity. When "Thumbelina" was in fourth grade, we had a serious conversation about school, and her need to work extra hard. I told her specifically, "When you come into the office for your yearly physical exam and have all A's on your report card, your office visit will be free. There will be no cost what so ever". Well! Talk about having to eat my own words. When she graduated from eighth grade and had been off all meds for several years, her Mother told me that "Thumbelina" had a special surprise for me. Little did I realize what a wonderful surprise was in store for me? She reminded me of my words of long ago, and I acknowledged their content. She gave me her report card with the biggest grin on her face that almost split her lips. This grin went further than from ear to ear. There was the evidence in black and white, all A's without exception. There was no evidence of any cerebral palsy or other neurological deficits. I am afraid I became very teary eyed and had to hug her tightly. She was a miracle that never should have survived let alone not to have had some type of debilitating aftermath. Obviously, her parent's prayers had been answered more than tenfold. I still become choked up and teary eyed even when I read my words about this young lady. She is a true living miracle to me.

Chapter 46

Another medical tract which stimulated my interest was that of the physically handicapped child. My wife's sister had two daughters who had the problem of "Ataxia Telangiectasia", which is a hereditary degenerating central nervous system condition. Diane died at about ten years of age due to a viral myocarditis. Paula died at twenty-one due to a widespread pneumonia. These children had trouble handling infections. I experienced the many devastating burdens and denials that this family had undergone in their fruitless quest to obtain help for their children.

    I began to cultivate an interest into the mentally compromised child and their parents' problems of adjustment. This group of truly dedicated parents really does deeply hurt inside every day of their life. They simultaneously grieve for their child and bemoan the fact that there was very little that they could or can do to make their child's life better and/or more comfortable. Each and every one of these parents should receive a gold medal and a crown in heaven for their effort and persistence. I joined the American Association of Mental Deficiency, but found that this organization held very little interest for me.

    Because of this background, my reputation spread that I was a compassionate doctor who tried to help families. On one occasion, I had a mother come to the office for the first time with her "Down's Syndrome" child. The first question she asked me was, "Doctor, do you care for children with Down's Syndrome"? I was shocked at such a question. She stated that her previous physician would not care for these children. What a sad commentary on my profession. Over time,

I belonged to several different societies devoted to the handicapped child.

All I could say to her was," I am a doctor. If you have a problem, then, that is why I am here". We had a long and close relationship for many years. I noted that many parents had such a desperate hunger for someone to just listen to them and lend a helping hand and/or ear and to guide them in coping with their heart rending situation.

I evolved a special tract for these families per Se in which I tried to help each child to move as close to my "Well Child Tract" as possible. This practice format and philosophy served many different functions and kept my focus on my basic approach of the "Well Child" within the vast field of pediatrics and adolescent medicine. Harking back to Dr. Kennedy of the Mayo Clinic, I wanted to see people not just bodies with isolated problems.

Chapter 47

For several years during the month of March, there was a meeting devoted to the adolescent and his/her problems and needs. Dr. Roswell Gallagher of Boston was the initiating force behind this meeting. Dr. Gallagher was the God Father of adolescent medicine. This meeting was held in Washington DC in a fine hotel near the Dupont Circle in mid March. This hotel had a lovely restaurant with an English Pub motif. I looked forward to this annual meeting with relish and zest.

After the meeting, Mary and I would fly to Myrtle Beach, South Carolina where her sister and husband, Bob Arfmann, would join us for the week. They would drive down from near Winston-Salem, North Carolina to be with us. As time passed, Bob and I would walk the beach discussing various facets of Practice Management. By this time, he was a Regional manager for the RJ Reynolds Tobacco Company. When he retired, he was the Executive Vice President for the internal workings of the Sales Department. He handled the department details. Another Vice President ran the Sales Force per Se.

After a few years, there was a push by the usual group of attendees to this Washington meeting to establish a Society for Adolescent Medicine. I was one of the original twenty-five charter members in 1968 to start this group. This Society existed from 1968 to 1983; then, the Society merged and was absorbed into the American Academy of Pediatrics as a result of the action of the Chapter Chairmen's Forum. How this absorption came about will be discussed later in this tome. These interested members functioned as a Section on Adolescence within the AAP. Early on, I became a member of this Section for Adolescence.

My interest in this field grew by leaps and bounds. I was an active member of the Society for Adolescents' National Committee on Private Practice from 1971 to 1976. I chaired the subcommittee on Insurance and Other Third Party Payees from 1976 to 1978. Over time, I became an expert in the field of Adolescence and was asked to speak at many different medical meetings and teacher groups throughout the States of Nebraska, South Dakota, and Iowa including the Iowa's Capitol in Des Moines. For a long time, I was one of the few doctors doing private adolescent medicine. Most of the other physicians in this field were in the academic confines. I guess I was still a maverick at heart.

The "Town and Gown" attitude of looking down their nose at us peons out in the real practice money grubbing world was very especially prevalent amongst this group of academicians. Their book reviewer was not impressed with my first offering, but doctors reading and using the book sent me very complimentary comments as to its usefulness to them and their practice.

For a number of years, I gave a series of four Adolescent Lectures to the UNMC junior med students. These talks were well received. Years later, several physicians told me how these talks helped their perspective on medicine and their communities. I gave these talks during late February or early March. The pediatric department secretary would call to schedule the times for the lectures. One spring, no one called. I waited and waited but no call came. In frustration, I called the department and was told that these lectures had been discontinued without any reason or a "Thank for your past participation". I was frosted to say the least, but that was how the Med Center operated regardless of who was in charge.

My office adolescent lectures in the office were very popular. I gave a series of five talks twice a year - the Titles:

1. You and the Body God Gave You
2. You and Society - Social and Emotional Development
3. Boys Only Night
4. Girls Only Night
5. Parents Only Night

The waiting room at the office could seat a crowded 100 parents and teenagers. The first two talks were for both parents and teenagers. With the help of the Clarkson Video Department and with Administrator Jim Canedy's permission, these Teen Talks were videotaped and put to good use in my future office years.

Chapter 48

I tried on several different occasions to have the Childrens' Hospital Medical Staff establish a "Youth Village" for the adolescent population. These young folks were frequently stuck in a general hospital room usually with a very old patient – about my current age of now. Oh dear, how could this passage of time happen so soon! This treatment of the youth being with an older patient was not conducive to a quick recovery for the youth per Se.

It finally dawned on me that reason for the failure to obtain permission for this worthy cause was that the medical staff was jealous and did not want to enhance my practice and have me build an empire. "Oh jealousy where is thy sting"!

Well! There is more than one way to skin a cat. I spoke with a dynamic young General Practitioner, Dave W, who was active with various youth groups within his church settings, about this need. He agreed to spearhead a drive for the "Youth Village". His youth groups held fund raisers, dances, car washes, and many similar activities. Finally, the medical staff saw the light and thought a "Youth Village" was a great idea. The First North Floor of Childrens' was converted into a special area which became one of the most popular features of Childrens'.

I lost the many battles but won the war. Little did anyone suspect this current subterfuge of mine? I learned a very valuable lesson in not needing to receive the credit, accolades, or recognition for personal gain when pursuing a perceived need. It was more important to achieve the desired end results than to be praised. On more than one occasion in the future, I utilized this same technique and approach to achieve a good end result. At times, I could be very sneaky when there was an important goal to accomplish.

As the 1960's neared its end and the 1970's was approaching, a disturbing occurrence was beginning to appear amidst the teenage population. The problem of drug use was more common place than most adults suspected. There was very little useful scientific data available to use to combat this destructive problem. Most of us in this field knew from our intuition that these substances were very destructive to a person's mind and health. There were very few preventive measures which could be utilized. It seemed as though the accepted norm was that drugs were not a major health problem. Ha ha what a farce!

Father Hupp of Christ the King Church joined with Rabbi Brooks of the Temple Israel and the Rev. Bob Alward of the Westside Community Church to establish a program designed to combat this problem. They pooled resources and established "Operation Bridge" at Westside High School to address this problem of drugs and teenagers. This program included a paid director. I was asked to be a member of the Board of Directors and served from 1968 to 1973. This program eventually was absorbed into the Omaha Community Chest Agencies.

Chapter 49

An event occurred which I had never anticipated happening. Dr. Gedgoud was sued needlessly for an unmanageable situation. A baby had a malformed kidney which at nine months was declared inoperable by several Urologists including the Mayo Clinic. A local pediatric urologist declared that If he had seen this baby at five months instead of at nine months, he could have saved the kidney. Our Malpractice Insurance barely covered the demands. This occurred during the legal reign and philosophy of Melvin Beli, "The thing speaks for itself". This malformation could not be defended in court under this current legal climate.

After everything was settled, Dr. Gedgoud told me, he had had enough worrying about potential malpractice concerns. He was going back into teaching where he would be more sheltered from situations like this one. This time, he would be on Creighton's Faculty as a Professor in the Pediatric Department. He was with me for about twelve years. In a few short moments of time, l lost both of my beloved mentors. Now, I was the oldest member of the Omaha Childrens' Clinic. Oh dear me! What will I do? How will I manage this practice with all of its different aspects and connotations"?

Dr. Tompkins died at 65 from a cancer of the bladder though he had never smoked. Dr. Gedgoud, at 65, had some friends in for dinner on a New Years Eve. He felt nauseated, went upstairs, vomited, lay down on the bed, and promptly died from a massive heart attack. His earlier leaving of OCC necessitated that I become the President of the Omaha Childrens' Clinic PC, which title I held until my retirement in 1988.

Again, most of Dr. Gedgoud's patients stayed with me which created another major scheduling readjustment.

Chapter 50

A Doctor Salenberger, who was the President of the newly reactivated, reconstituted, and reborn Bellevue College in the nearby community just south of Omaha, called me and wanted to visit as soon as possible. He told me, "He was in a very difficult position. The College was scheduled to start classes in one week. He had hired a Psychologist from the New York area. When he came to Bellevue and took one look at the fledgling school, he promptly returned to New York".

Dr. Salenberger was left with students signed up for classes and no teacher. I explained to him, "I was not qualified for the job nor did I have a teaching degree". My beautiful and wonderful wife told me not to agree to anything. College, not having a teaching degree is no problem as long as you have a terminal degree such as in medicine. He had attended my adolescent lectures with his son. He continued, "I heard you lecture and you can do an excellent job at the college level". Mary was very reluctant for me to try this new adventure. After serious thought and some real soul searching, naturally, I could not refuse this new challenge and new field to explore. I hesitantly agreed to try the role for one semester.

My three hour course in "Introduction to Psychology" ran from 7:30 am until 9:00 pm on Tuesday and Thursday mornings. After class, I had to hurry and make hospital rounds in order to arrive at the office by 11:30 am for appointments. My lunch hour was donated to the spirit of the class operations.

I was listed as an Adjunct Professor of Psychology and taught for three years. When time no longer became an available luxury, I had to resign my affiliation with the college. In those three years, I ended up teaching General Psych, Abnormal Psych, Adolescent Psych, and Industrial Psych. I tried night school and summer school but didn't enjoy either one; so I did not repeat those experiences. My year at the Henry Ford Hospital and Wayne State Nursing School, where I had to develop the Nursing School Curriculum, taught me how to manage educational materials. The only painful exercise connected with the teaching was the giving and the grading of exams. I did not enjoy that exercise at all.

I would bring case histories from the office to illustrate different points and problems for the class in order to stimulate a vigorous discussion centered on an actual real life situation. With the last fifteen minutes of the class, I would pass a shoebox amongst the students for them to ask any question on any topic, what so ever, that they wanted to find out concerning my perspective. There were many questions relating to medicine and medical ethical situations such as abortion and euthanasia. I always gave a straight answer from the shoulder as I saw the question. Some students thought this segment of the class was the best part. I thoroughly enjoyed myself; but like so many enjoyable items, it had outlived its usefulness for me. I resigned with great reluctance.

During the time that I was teaching, there were several Air Force Officers wives from nearby Offutt Air base who enrolled in my classes for self improvement purposes. I had several Generals' wives in some of these classes. Bellevue College was beginning to find a needed niche within the surrounding educational community. The College converted several years later into a full-fledged University and now is going strong with many higher degree programs available. This University has made a good impact and developed its own place within the Omaha Educational climate. I cherish my past association with the school. I am sure that I learned more from the students than they did from me. I had several complementary notes from students over several years after I had resigned as to how the courses helped them personally.

Chapter 51

While all of these exciting adventures were transpiring in my professional life, life with my family was demanding its own personal time, just dues, and place in the sun. We took our regular vacations each summer at Lake Okaboji in northwest Iowa for almost ten years. We always stayed at Brooks Beach and stayed in the Edgewater Cabin on the East Okaboji Lake as it was a better lake for water skiing. The boys became so expert at skiing that they enjoyed putting on water show each afternoon around 4:00 PM for the resort patrons. They would get up backwards, go double, go triple, cross over and under each other, and do many other tricks on the skis or saucer. The folks staying at the resort would come out and enjoy the show. For skiing, now we had a Larson eighteen foot fiberglass runabout with a seventy-five HP Johnson Motor. It was a great boat. We enjoyed it for many years.

We would carry a "Grumman" eight foot, aluminum dingy with one sail on top of the ski boat so the boys could enjoy sailing. We followed this routine for many years. Once, we tried Minnesota for a change. It was a miserable disaster for the family because of so many mosquitoes and a rather shallow water lake for water skiing. I have yet to hear the end of "Dad's Debacle" lo these many years later. My wonderful wife still hasn't forgiven me for this mess. She so enjoyed her time at Okaboji and missed it, dreadfully.

Chapter 52

By had been a Cub Scout, and Mary was his Den Mother. When By turned 11, he wanted to join the Boy Scouts. The Christ the King Boy Scout Troop had been inactive for some time because of no adult leadership. Three dads, John Bohrer, Ray Bradley, and myself, decided to reactivate this Scout Troop. By the luck of the draw, I was elected/appointed/or coerced into becoming the Scoutmaster because of my past experiences with Scouting. I had been a Life Scout and had received a Scout Summer Camp "Black Diamond" award for being the honor camper.

We, dads, settled on some fundamentals about our view of how this Troop would function. We were not interested in being a spit and polish type of outfit or a fund raiser. A Boy Scout shirt and neckerchief was the only uniform a boy needed. We planned to show the boys the joy of the outdoors and God's world. There would be a monthly campout fall, winter, and spring regardless of the weather unless the roads were icy. We would have high adventure type outings at times but would not let them interfere or compete with summer baseball programs and/or family activities.

We began with eight boys including our own sons. There was one older boy as a holdover from being in the troop a few years before. With this nucleus, the Troop grew by leaps and bounds. We met on Thursday nights at 7:00 pm. The troop centered its actions geared on the monthly camp outs and having a big spring canoe trip on a river somewhere in Nebraska or Iowa.

The main Scout headquarters owned eight canoes and a trailer which the scouts could use. Before each canoe trip, there was a practice and training session at the Sea Scout Base on Carter Lake near Omaha where I had learned to canoe and sail. Troop 370 was one of the pioneer troops which made the monthly campouts and the canoe trips popular in the Omaha area.

The first spring canoe trip began with a trip down the Elkhorn River and onto the Platte River. We used four canoes. Twelve boys and four dads comprised this entourage. We had a great time. The boys became the envy of the school. More and more boys were attracted to our way of Scouting. We had very little to do or contact with the Scout Headquarters. We avoided huge collective regional Camp Outs, and operated as a rather maverick group of scouts.

The Christ the King spring canoe trip became the focal point of our adventures. With Father Hupp's permission and with the help of the principal of Christ the King School, the boys were to be excused from school on a Friday for the trip. No one could go if Sister did not approve of their behavior – not grades. She loved to have this stick in her hand as I had promised her the last word on who would be allowed to go. We rented a school bus. John Bohrer became a certified bus driver so our own driver and time could be flexible.

Canoes and Rack
By and Duke

Father Hupp, our Pastor, would obtain permission from the Archbishop to have a Catholic Mass in the field which was seldom approved without a major reason. Father Hupp would send one of his Assistant Priests along with his own WWII Mass Kit from his navy days aboard the USS Corregidor. This aircraft carrier had endured considerable action in the South Pacific. The Assistant Priest would ride in my car instead of the bus so he could say and read his daily priestly office in peace and quiet.

We would travel on Friday, camp out that night, enter the chosen river at the selected point early Saturday morning, and proceed downstream. Each canoe had a father; or, later on as the troop had more boys, one of our own older Explorer Scouts would handle a canoe. I would always be in the last canoe containing the first aid kit and oxygen equipment in case of need. It was much easier to go downstream rather than to try and fight the current going upstream if an emergency occurred. Fortunately, we never had any accidents on any of the many canoe trips we took. Throughout the entire trip, each boy had to wear his authorized life vest while in a canoe and on the water. I was a real grump when it came to water safety.

John Bohrer would stay ashore near where we were to land and come off of the water with the canoes. He would cook a huge batch of delicious Hunter's Stew, using sirloin steak conned for the scouts at a cheap price from a nearby small town grocery store. The stew would be cooked in a brand new large metal garbage can. When we arrived, the boys would put on dry clothes, have a great hot meal, and go to bed early very tired but pleased with their day. The next morning, we would pack up the equipment, have our Mass in the field, climb on the bus, and head home. I would have several of the Fathers act as Alter Servers for the Mass so the scouts could experience the importance of faith among adults. Many exaggerated stories really flew all around the school on the next Monday morning encouraging others to want to participate in the fun.

Over the next seven years, we canoed most of the usable rivers in Nebraska and Western Iowa. As an advancement incentive, in order for a boy to make the canoe trip, he had to move from being a second class scout to become a first class scout. Any scout who was first class or higher had to earn five merit badges of their own choice. Using this incentive package, the scouts really hustled to make the trip. As the troop grew, more and more dads joined in the fun. Before long, I had enough Dads to cover all of the required Merit Badges for the rank of Eagle Scout including having our own certified Red Cross Water Safety Director, Jim G. Each January, I would ask the physicians and dentists, who had boys in the troop, to help the scouts learn and understand the Second Class, First Class, and the First Aid Merit Badge requirements. These scouts became well trained in this area.

With the help of this group of willing fathers to assist in our scouting program, we had thirty-six boys achieve the high rank of Eagle Scout during the seven year period that I was the scoutmaster. This number of Eagle Scouts over the seven year period was remarkable. Each of my three boys was among the Eagle scouts. They made their Mother and me very proud.

Because of the large number of the boys becoming Eagle Scouts, Scout Headquarters doubted the veracity and quality of the training the boys received. Troop 370 was investigated not once but twice concerning these achievements. I became irritated with the second investigation so I called Willis S., the President of Northern Natural Gas Company, whose children were my patients, and Jerry D., the Revenue Accountant for Northwest Bell Telephone Company, for whom I used to work, and told them of my plight. Both men were pillars of the business community. They descended on the Scout Headquarters like a plague of locusts. I never had any more trouble or harassment from the scout headquarters.

As time passed, our planning eyes grew bigger and greedier; so we planned to visit the Canadian Boundary Waters out of Ely, Minnesota during a summer vacation time. We had thirty-six boys and five dads-two doctors, one Dentist, and two regular Dads-on this trip. This trip was the highlight of my scouting years. The only casualty I had was the Dentist whose son put a fish hook in his father's cheek. He received the prize for hooking the biggest fish. Our Packer, Cliff Wold, furnished excellent food, good equipment, and was very accommodating to our needs. We planned to portage in a great circle loop; but, after the first portage with so many young arms to carry the canoes, we, dads, decided to camp on an island and take day trips out from our base. This change exceeded my expectations and made the trip a real pleasure for all concerned. We saw loons, bear, geese, beaver, and many other interesting animals.

Our next high adventure was to pack in by horses into the Colorado Shadow Mountain region to the Lost Lake area. It was fun but not nearly as pleasurable as the Ely trip. Although the Packer was personally evaluated on his own location by some of my fathers, he left much to be desired both as to the food and the equipment.

I wanted about a ten mile hike through the mountains into the Lost Lake area; instead, we had to hike twenty-five miles in the mountains and at a high altitude. This feat was an excessive one for those little legs to travel. We had arranged for a Guide to help us. However, our guide had never been into this particular area before and didn't know his way. I fired him as soon as we arrived at Lost Lake. This trip had three doctors, the same Dentist, and two regular dads. Naturally, my only casualty was the dentist who fell on some rocks and broke a rib. I thought to myself, "If he goes on another adventure with me, I am going to have to wrap him in cotton wadding or bubble wrap for safe keeping".

While at Lost Lake, the water was too cold for swimming. The packer took groups of the boys down to his ranch where they went horseback riding. Other scouts built bridges over mountain streams to aid the trail system. Some of us endured a mild snow storm on the mountain while others were down at the ranch where it was warm.

Several of the boys enjoyed "Altitude Sickness" for a day or so but recovered nicely. For many reasons, I did not enjoy this adventure as much as the Ely one.

My role as Scoutmaster was to organize and delegate the necessary duties to make sure that these happenings would successful ventures. Several major Omaha companies encouraged their personnel to contribute time to local civic activities. Northern Natural Gas Company was a big contributor to civic endeavors. We had several of the Northern dads help us in numerous ways. I can remember overhearing one father say to another, "If you come around the troop and help out just a little, old doc will let you go on a canoe trip. You'll never have as much fun as on that adventure". Over time, there were at least 20 helper dads working to better the troop. I had my own built-in quality control over the required Merit Badges for the rank of Eagle Scout. When we were on a campout, one dad would have a group of scouts working on the Pioneering Merit Badge, another on outdoor cooking, and, still, another on the Nature Badge. Our scouts were very well trained in any of the Merit Badge requirements. If a boy became deeply interested in Scouting and stayed in the troop for about three years, it was unusual if he was not ready to achieve the Eagle rank.

At one time, the troop had about 90 boys which was quite a handful. I didn't have a hard heart to limit the number of interested boys; consequently, the troop was a bit unwieldy. There were a number of single moms who wanted their boys in scouting for the adult male influence. We welcomed their boys.

I needed to obtain more tents for campouts but did not want to suffer the pain and undertake a big fund raiser with all the related headaches. Some families could not afford to help pay for new tents. I explained my plight to Father Hupp and as to why I wanted small two men Pup Tents. The smaller tents were desired to avoid any headaches of the boys picking on each other as could and probably would happen in a larger tent housing several boys. Father said, "Go ahead and get the tents and send me the bill". The cooperation I received from the Nuns and Father was outstanding.

These Scout years gave me a wonderful laboratory in which to study and observe the young adolescent. Many of the older boys wanted to stay active in Scouting; so I established an Explorer Post to meet their needs. These were very happy and satisfying years for me. All outings had to be planned as though I might not be able to participate and go on the adventure. Fortunately, I missed very few outings.

When we were on the Colorado trip, the dads decided not to shave. The facial hair was unkempt and shaggy on most of the dads. When we arrived back in the school yard and departed the bus, Mary looked and looked for me in vain. Some bystander pointed me out to her, and she said, "Why he looks like a real old man no wonder I didn't recognize him". Oh! Such is love.

Years later when some of the older scout fellows would get together, their scouting adventures became a major topic of conversation. As time has passed, I was frequently told by former scouts, with whom I had the pleasure to encounter, "What a joy scouting was and what it meant to them". I recently received a silver dollar centennial coin commemorating the 100th anniversary of scouting from one of my former scouts. I have had many satisfied feelings over these memorable days.

To help keep the young scout leaders interested in their roles, to stay active in the troop, and when school was out for the summer, I would invite these young leaders to Lake Manawa for a day of water skiing and sailing plus a big meal. My boys were the hosts for the sailing activities. They helped me with the water skiers and the boat. Previously, By and I had taken a Coast Guard Auxiliary Small Boat Handling and Safety Course. I was fanatic on water safety and had it strongly ingrained into my boys because of all of the time we spent in and on the water. We expected the same caution and respect for the water from all others whom we brought as guests. I was a tough old German on these points.

Chapter 53

My beloved Mary and I made many good friends with the parents of the scouts during these scouting years. Some of the families have become very close to Mary and me, like the Bohrers and the Harveys. We continue to keep in touch even though they have moved away from Omaha.

Father Hupp was kept very busy building the first new Parish to be established in Omaha in forty years. The new parish was in a most desirable location for people to build nice homes and to move into a desirable school and neighborhood. The Parish grew by leaps and bounds. At times, Father seemed overwhelmed and exhausted from his numerous responsibilities. John Bohrer belonged to the Omaha Country Club, Hank Moran belonged to the Oak Hills Country Club, and I belonged to Lakeshore Country Club. Every three weeks, we would take Father Hupp for lunch and a round of golf. The wives would meet us for cocktails and dinner. We had a great time. Father Hupp would seem to be more relaxed and at ease after these outings.

Father Hupp Kneeling at Christmas Crib

For a number of years, our group would have Father Hupp as our guest at Lake Okaboji in July. We would drive up on a Thursday, play golf and go to dinner. On Friday morning and afternoon, and Saturday morning we played golf after which Father would drive back to Omaha in time for Confessions and Saturday evening Mass. These were such pleasurable times.

It all ended one Friday when we were on one of our Friday golf outings; Father was riding with me on the golf cart. He told me that against his desires and wishes, he was going to be named the new Director of Boys Town to replace Monsignor Wagner, who was becoming very aged. Father Hupp had taken the vow of obedience when he became a priest, and so the change was finality.

Obie at Golf

While at Boys Town, he became a national figure, was a delegate to the United Nations, and held several other important national positions. He changed the tenor of Boys Town by introducing the family home concept instead of the dormitories and by having girls become a part of Boys Town. He began the satellite program of replicating a Boys Town in other cities. He was a very remarkable man. It was a real pleasure and privilege to have known him.

As a human being, he was a most unique person. He was an expert hunter and fisherman, jazz piano player, and a wonderful person. He was so well known and liked that wherever we went with him, we would run into someone who knew him. This recognition was true whether on a golf course, at a restaurant, a social event, or even away from Omaha at Okaboji. He had a phenomenal memory and could remember names even though the particular person had not been seen for several years. He was able to give us a brief resume of that person. Amazing!

Chapter 54

We had many flower pots and hanging baskets on our patio. It looked like a "Better Homes and Gardens Home" magazine picture. During the winter, I enjoyed bird watching and at one time had fifteen bird feeders in operation. We attracted all kinds of birds such as Gold Finches, Cardinals, Snow Juncos, Chickadees, and many others. I would sit in my den and take pictures of the birds through the big picture window. I had my own special bird blind. I enjoyed the bird watching and was teased unmercifully by my family.

Besides the pleasure of the birds, there was the prolonged and deadly battle with the squirrels. They were such a pesky and painful irritant always getting into the feeders in spite whatever deterrent that I tried. Whenever they conquered my latest approach to keeping them out of my feeders, they would sit up and flick their tail as though they were giving me the finger. These squirrels were the most arrogant and unrepentant creatures that I had ever encountered. Ah Ha! At last, I found the solution to my dilemma. The bird feed store began stocking a large plastic half bowl that would hang over the feeder denying access to these miserable pirates. The plastic was so slick that the squirrel's claws could not get a purchase and, thus, could not attain access to the feeder. I would sit in my Den and gloat over my success. This battle had been going on for several years until I emerged as the glorious victor. Try as they might, those squirrels could not get into the feeders. Hurrah! I won and wore the sweet smile of satisfaction. There is an old adage from my childhood days when insurance salesmen would go door to door making solicitations and selling policies, "There is no one who has endurance like the man that sells insurance". When amended to address this situation, this saying fit me to a tee.

My photography took a big step forward when we finished the basement in our home. This completion was at the time when By started to Creighton Prep. I now had my darkroom and a place to conveniently work. I put it to good use. I added, to the pieces of equipment I brought from Japan, all of the photographic tools including copying equipment and a slide making photo stand that I could possibly need. Black and white, colored pictures, still pictures, movies, and the video camera were making my dreams come true.

The darkroom was adjacent to the big train room where we spent our winters building our large and complex HO railroad layout. It would take three years to create a new scenic railroad section:

1. Year one would see the track, bridges, streams, and switches established and functional.

2. Year two would see the wooden frames erected for the scenery to act as the foundation for the mountains, valleys, and streams. We would put plastic over the framework to avoid having plaster of Paris to fall onto the train track while we were working. Aluminum screen was placed over the plastic in order to avoid rusting which would occur with using regular screen. The screen acted as a base for the plaster of Paris which was molded to form the scenery contours.

3. Year three would see the finish of a particular area with the painting and detailed landscaping. In one section, there was a ski resort and town with a wedding party in front of the church. It had a working ski lift. The ambiance of this area was based upon the Vail Ski resort.

Some of the areas included the following scenic vistas:

1. The Western town had a bank robbery shootout, a boot hill, a hanging, and a gold mine.

2. Another section was devoted to a logging area, with campers, an actual real waterfall, and hunters.

3. The municipal town had a drive-in movie, a putt putt golf course, an outdoor ballroom like Peony Park, a school, a stockyards, a city dump, factories, and a major multiple car wreck.
4. There was Mount Rushmore with the famous faces which were lighted up by search lights.
5. There were many mountains, rivers, valleys, tunnels, and bridges.

Two people could run three trains at the same time over mountains, through the tunnels, past a real waterfall, and by ice skaters on a lake. In some areas, there were five levels of trackage going over and under other tracks via tunnels. We enjoyed creating scenery so much that we neglected to run the trains very often.

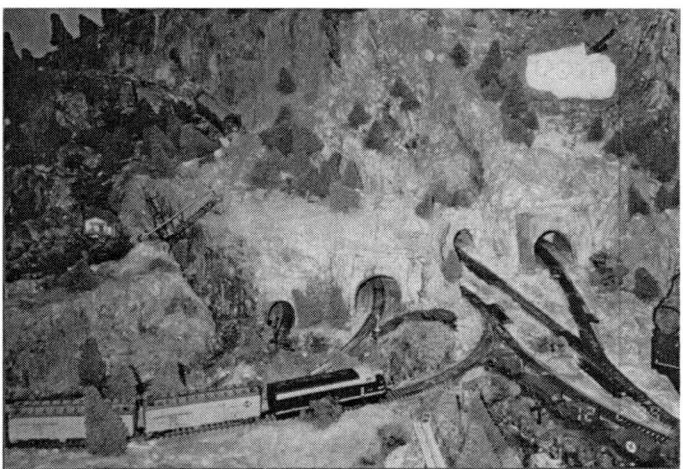

Train Room – Three Tunnels and tracks

In those days, the train track was only made of brass which oxidized readily. This impaired track made the running of the trains impossible until the tracks were cleaned. This needed cleaning took time and delayed the frequent running of the trains. Today, this problem is not a difficulty as the track is made out of nickel and does not oxidize.

The layout was spectacular when we turned out the room lights and lit the trainset lights. We used HO Gauge track and trains so we could have more scenery to build in a smaller space. The O Gauge railroad materials were too big and required too much space; so this gauge was rejected early on. This project lasted about ten years until the boys outgrew their interest and delved into sports with a big time effort.

Chapter 55

Jim Canedy, the Administrator of Clarkson hospital was very progressive and wanted an enlightened medical staff that had an appreciation for hospital management needs and policies. He brought in management experts and had the various committee chairmen undergo a three day seminar on:

1. Management by Objective
2. Management by Exception
3. Mission Statement
4. Key Objectives
5. Critical Objectives

The leader of the seminar kept making the point, "That there never were any problems but only challenges and opportunities". Some smart aleck asked this leader, "How do we handle all of our challenges and opportunities if they are not problems"?

This exposure turned on many light bulbs and my management life around. This seminar created such an intense interest for me so that it became a major component of my endeavors for the next twenty years and fostered all types of spin off areas in other directions.

About this time, Jim Canedy had a group of "System Engineers" studying all of the functions in Clarkson Hospital to improve its efficiency. For some unknown reason or another, this management approach fascinated me. I wondered how such a study could affect the Omaha Childrens' Clinic operations. Could an evaluation such as this study help our pediatric practice to become more efficient? Our collective volume of work was making us burst out at the seams. I inherently knew that our office operations were being inefficient in many ways.

With Jim Canedy' helps and with the twisting of the arms of my partners, we contracted with this group of system engineers to study our office operations for a sum of $7,000. This type of evaluation would have cost much more, but these business men were interested in accepting this challenge as they sensed another area of opportunity for their services. I was like a sponge watching them work and visiting with them about the various theories and approaches that they utilized. I quickly learned how to do "Time-Motion" Studies. This study technique I used many times over during the rest of my practice years.

As a result of the exposure to Management Theories and System studies, my mind began to segregate the various functions of a medical practice into eight different categories or Management areas:

The following four areas of management were essential for handling the business side of a successful practice

1. Administrative Management: This area is where decisions were made based upon sound research data and discussions and not whims.

2. Accounting Management: This area made the wheels go around and paid the bills.

3. Time Management: "Time" – This is a "Forgotten Resource" in most medical practices, and was a place to visit for increased revenues.

4. Marketing Management: This is the new "Buzzword" which had just come into Medicine and determined which methods could be the most successful in building the practice.

The next four areas provided a solid foundation for the handling of the medical side and patient care of a successful practice.

There were four areas of Management necessary in the medical aspects of the practice:

5. Patient Care Management: This is what Medicine basically was all about and how this care was rendered efficiently to patients.

6. Physician Management: This is the Quality Control Management of all types and facets of the practice operations including the physicians.

7. Hospital Management: This is the efficient Use of the Hospital Resources and timely Patient Care within the province of the hospital parameters.

8. Medical Information Management: This is how to cope with the volumes of new and old medical Information and how physicians should endeavor to keep current with new medical methodologies.

I came to the realization that Private Practice Management was new, exciting, and needed to be my next world to conquer. I endorsed this need with a passion. There were several questions that had to be answered to accomplish this daunting task of establishing sound practice management procedures.

It became necessary to understand several questions such as The Why? The Where? The value of a "Need Analysis" What it was? Why it was necessary? What is the approach to accomplish such an animal?

Armed with these philosophies and questions, I set out to study how other selected outstanding offices functioned and how to apply their findings to our own practice. My partners encouraged my interests and urged me to go ahead and work the game to completion. The end result was a Ten Year Long Range Plan for our practice.

Mary's Brother-in-Law

I unashamedly picked the brains of my Brother-in-Law, Bob Arfmann, who was now the Executive Vice President for the inside functioning of the RJ Reynolds Tobacco Company Sales Department. We would walk beside the ocean at Myrtle Beach, South Carolina usually in March after the Adolescent Meeting and cuss and discuss various management concepts. I unabashedly asked my Nephew-in-Law, Greg Upah, and a PhD who taught Marketing at Virginia Tech University, to assist me in the Marketing aspects of this long range plan. I learned from him the principle and use of "Focus Groups" and other techniques that were used in the Marketing World. Mary's cousin, Pat Mulvihill, was another resource that I had no shame in exploiting. He worked for IBM and ran IBM's upper Management Training endeavors at a beautiful estate on Long Island. Consciously or not, these experts gave me many thoughts, ideas, and much information to utilize in developing a sophisticated Long Range Plan. It was interesting, that when this project had been completed, my conscience did not hurt one little bit concerning the exploitation of these exceptional human resources.

Patrick Mulvihill Mary's Cousin

It took about a year to gather my data together including a trip to Tennessee to visit Dr. Billy Crook's office who had been writing about some interesting innovative practice ideas. I had taken several management seminars offered by Dr. Eddie Saltzman of Hollywood,

Florida, who was trying hard to interest the American Academy of Pediatrics into providing better concepts of practice management policies and support for the pediatricians. He claimed and exclaimed that the grass root Pediatricians needed a lot of help in this area. How right he was!

As a result of these endeavors, we revamped all aspects of the way in which the office had been functioning. We were able to increase our office volume of work 30% without any additional costs or added staff. I was a hero to my partners. We changed everything from owning our own phone system, how phone calls were handled, and to what and how which phone calls the doctors or the nurses would return. We instituted a medical team concept where each physician had a dedicated nurse and a dedicated medical assistant who served as an aid to the nurse. This change did away with the circulating nurse pool concept. The nurse became the physician's right hand person. She handled most of the phone calls and expedited any necessary schedule adjustments that needed to occur. She would handle hospital admissions, and arranged for any important follow up items that had been specified for the patient.

For my part and because of the increased number of my newborns plus the increased older patient load that was occurring within my practice and with my partners' permission, I trained Bette H., my nurse, to be a working Nurse Practitioner. This occurrence happened long before there was the concept of certified Nurse Practitioners.

She would see my newborns every other month alternating with my visits. She was a gem, and the patients loved her. This not only lightened my work load, but she handled many of the routine questions that mothers asked better than I did. She added another dimension to my practice. My partners did not adopt some of these measures but continued in their own archaic manners of the past. I learned that it was much harder and more fearful for young people to change their ways than we older duffers. In other words, we could see the light!

As I remarked before, we increased our patient volume per doctor 30% without any increase in overhead costs; had more doctor time available; avoided having a stack of 20 to 30 phone calls to return when we arrived at the office; and could go home at night not as exhausted either mentally or physically. Everyone gained-doctors, patients, and most of all the nurses as they only needed to be tuned in to one physician's whims, demands, arrogances, and idiosyncrasies. Keep in mind that all doctors were and are "Prima Donnas" – some more than others. The surgeons were the most aggressive actors of all the doctors.

Chapter 56

While I was attending a meeting in Miami, Florida I did a bit of soul searching. I knew that I was over committed by having too many interests outside of my practice per Se. I made a list of all my commitments and found to my dismay that the number was twenty. No one could do a decent job with that many irons in the fire. I culled the list to the ten most important items for me personally and resigned from the remaining ones. Unfortunately over time, the list grew long again; and the process had to be repeated. Being a Fiddler and Diddler, it was very difficult for me to turn my back on some, but nonessential, intriguing avenues to follow.

Dr. Joseph Gross, an Orthopedic Surgeon, was Chief of the Medical Staff at the new Bergan Hospital. He was an old friend from the Creighton Prep days and Boy Scouts. Bergan was the old St. Catherine's Hospital which had moved west and started over. It was going great guns and had a big OB load.

There was a great deal of friction between the General Practitioners, who had almost exclusively supported St. Catherine's in the past, and the many Specialists who, now, were extensively using the hospital. Dr. Gross pleaded with me to help him reduce the friction and antagonism.

I needed to tread slowly and to use diplomacy as many feathers had been severely ruffled. I sent letters to the GP's whenever there was to be the monthly Department of Pediatric Meeting. This letter invited them to attend, informed them of what was to be discussed, and asked them to participate. This action defused much of the intense rancor. I served in this capacity and was on the Bergan Medical Staff Board from 1965 to 1966. This problem gradually dissipated and seemed to be solved. I resigned from this post and handed over the reins to another understanding pediatrician. I was and still had continued to be Chief of the Clarkson Nursery and Pediatric Department from 1963 to 1976 during this same period. Handling both of these positions really had over extended me because of the need to attend so many and not too interesting meetings.

There was a huge omission by the architects of the new Bergan Hospital in the planning and building process. How this omission happened I'll never understand. There was no ICU Nursery for premature infants and/or distressed infants. Bergan had developed one of the biggest OB censuses in the State. When this problem was corrected, I resigned and turned over the management of the pediatric and nursery departments to others.

Over many years, I was a member of most of the major medical staff committees at Childrens', Methodist, and Clarkson Hospitals. I had been on many committees at the Med Center including the Admissions and Curriculum Committees and on the Advisory Committee to the University of Nebraska Pediatric Department Chairperson. I had been on nine major committees at Childrens' besides being a medical staff officer and president.

Chapter 57

The government began to allow Private Medical Practices to incorporate and to set up Keogh Pension Plans. This was the first major savings program available before tax deductions for physicians. Any previous savings had to be done after taxes. This latter situation limited the value of trying to save post tax dollars or to increase the work load to create more revenue; the more money you made the more taxes you paid. These actions put you in a higher tax bracket. Now, doctors' practices were being treated like any other small business.

I thought that the office had a large consultative practice; but little did I realize that we did consultation work for 120 offices outside of Omaha and plenty more within the city. The bulk of this work was done by me. What an eye opener this finding was, and what a major responsibility it was to have to help other physicians with their problems. At this time, there were about eight pediatricians in Lincoln, Nebraska; and only one resided in outstate Nebraska at Grand Island. I saw patients from the far western edges of Nebraska and well into the western aspects of Iowa almost to Des Moines. It was a huge referral territory that our office served.

The Interstate Road System was just in its infancy in being built. This condition helped to account as to why so few doctors had moved very far from the Medical Centers. Distances were too long and took too much time to travel from one place to another.

I did some mighty dumb things in my practice life and made many poor decisions in my working years in spite of my so-called management expertise. Because of my heavy office and hospital work load, I would close my practice to new patients for three months at periodic intervals except for doctor referrals. This worked well for awhile as the practice quickly rebuilt when it was re-opened; then, I was really, really stupid and dumb! I closed it for a year. This length of time was entirely the wrong decision to have made. I would only take patients who were referred by their physician. When the practice was reopened, it was hard to recover the practice momentum even though there were some parents who were willing to wait a year to see me. Why would they wait a year to see me? I don't know why, what, or how? As a side complication to this long hiatus, my newborns became a thing of the past. In the long run, this loss of newborns was a blessing in disguise.

Chapter 58

With my interest in School Learning Problems, the Attention Deficit Syndrome, The Adolescent Years, and, now, Practice Management, I had my hands full pursuing each of these enticing fields simultaneously. I was like a child in a candy shop trying to make a selection from all of the goodies.

My first area of intense desire was searching out new items and thoughts for my Guided Growth Well Child and Adolescent Program. I stumbled across Dr. Barta's, a Psychiatrist, philosophy on the "Moral Aspects of Human Behavior". His thoughts on personality development made good sense to me so that I adopted and adapted some of his tenants. For example, a child would frequently identify with the parent of the same sex and adopt a primary personality characteristic of that parent; and, then, adopt a secondary one from the opposite sex parent. By the time the child was five years old, the basic personality traits were jelled and could only be modified thereafter. The major traits consisted of Leader, Follower, Outgoing, Indwelling (shy). The psychiatrists liked the terms extrovert, introvert, dominant, submissive. I never liked these terms for children. This personality mosaic made counseling much easier when there were personality conflicts within the family constellation. For example, like versus like characteristics frequently created frictions and could result in major conflicts. A head strong child might well clash with a head strong parent time and time again to the detriment of both parties.

Fortunately, I had a great capacity for organizing large volumes of work and could handle multitasking very comfortably without too much stress. My family and, especially, my beloved Mary kept me on the straight and narrow with essential family priorities in the forefront.

Siren Medicine was still trying hard to entice me exclusively into her seductive arms. At times, it was a major struggle not to get lost in her passionate embrace. This decade was rapidly coming to a close.

Outside of my pediatric practice, I encountered a situation which stretched me to my limits. From the first shovel of dirt in the building of Childrens' Hospital, my heart and soul loved this place with all my being. During the years from 1968 through 1970, I was the Vice President and then the President of the Medical Staff. It was during this time frame period that the hospital encountered big, big problems.

Our Head Nurse retired from her post due to family needs. The Hospital Administrator left to assume a new position at St. Paul, Minnesota's Childrens' Hospital. Now, the hospital was in a very precarious position without any skilled leadership at the helm. The hospital was trying to survive by being managed temporarily by the President of the Board of Directors and me, of all people.

We searched out and hired a wonderful well qualified Chief Nurse with a PhD from Indianapolis, Indiana - the Riley Childrens' Hospital. Everyone breathed a sigh of relief until we received a negative nixing from the Chancellor of the Nebraska Med Center. Dr. C. W., by different and sometimes not all too nice means, had acquired ownership for the Med Center of the Nebraska Psychiatric Institute, the Hattie B. Munroe Nursing Home for Children, and the Meyer Rehab Center for Children. These buildings were all on the Med Center Campus, but had been free standing volunteer staff institutions until being absorbed into the University orbit. Not any more were they free standing and independent facilities, but were under the thumb and direction of the Med Center.

For a long time and by trying many different and not too subtle approaches, Dr. C.W. had tried to grab Childrens' with no avail until now. Childrens' dilemma was his great and golden opportunity to swallow up Childrens' and roll it into the University's Orbit of control.

All of these institutions, including Childrens' Hospital, had a land contract with the Med Center as these institutions were built on University property. Because of this contract, the Med Center had the last word on the hiring of a Head Nurse, the head of Radiology, and the head of Pathology at Childrens. He vetoed the hiring of the nurse under some strange and cockamamie claim. Because Childrens did not have any professional administration, he waited like a wolf for Childrens' to drop into his mouth like a ripe grape; and putting it within his grasp, and/or his orbit.

Both Methodist and Clarkson Hospitals were the premier Tertiary Care hospitals in this State and region. Clarkson was the first hospital in the state to have a heart transplant, a kidney transplant, and a corneal transplant. It, also, had the first patient bubble for the immune compromised patients. Jim Canedy, Clarkson Administrator, had the philosophy that if any bit of useful medical research was available for active use with patients, that facility should be at Clarkson. He used to teach at St. Louis' Washington School for Hospital Administrators.

He frequently called Dr. Don Nilsson and me "Rabble Rousers" for our zeal in being patient advocates wherever we worked or were involved. Remember, both Jim Canedy and John Estabrooke were hospital administrative interns when I started into practice in 1951. We had known each other for a long time.

In desperation, I went to talk with Jim Canedy of Clarkson for advice and possible help with Childrens' administration problems. The head of Childrens' Pathology Department was Dr. Rudy Schenken. He was a noted Cancer Pathologist and headed both the Pathology Department at the Med Center, at Methodist Hospital, and at Childrens'. In the same manner, Dr. Ralph Moore was the Head of the Radiology Department at Childrens', and at both Methodist, and at the Med Center. Jim Canedy suggested that I talk with John Estabrooke who was the Administrator at Methodist Hospital; because these men were already deeply involved in all three institutions. It helped in this situation that I cared for the Canedy family and knew John Esatbrooke from his early hospital intern days.

I had a wonderful meeting with John Estabrooke concerning the problem at Childrens'. All was not going to be lost according to John. He suggested that the Childrens' Medical Staff and Board of Directors enter into discussions with Methodist Hospital concerning hiring Administrative and Nursing help and support from Methodist. This major milestone was accomplished. He placed Bill P. in Childrens' as his Administrative Assistant. He designated Edna Fagin RN, his own

Chief of the Methodist School of Nursing to be the Director of Nursing of the Childrens' Nursing Department. Edna was a gigantic figure in the State of Nebraska Nursing Circles. Already, the heads of both the Radiology and Pathology Departments could not pose any entre for Dr. C.W. to create trouble for Childrens'.

Against this turn of events and being reinforced with this powerful armamentarium of involved persons, Chancellor C.W. did not have a leg to stand on any more. Childrens' has been free and independent ever since this narrow escape. Childrens' has had the ability to grow and develop to its full potential. This realization came into fruition many years later, with a new 80 million dollar hospital and now, a 50 million dollar pediatric specialty doctors' office and outpatient clinic building. This outpatient facility will be completed in the late summer of 2010. Now, Childrens' has been designated both as a Hospital and as a Childrens' Medical Center.

Meanwhile, if Dr. C. W. would run into me at a medical meeting dinner, he would not talk to me or sit at the same dinner table with me. His actions did not bother me one iota as I had the last laugh after so much blood, sweat, agony, and tears.

Chapter 59

This past ten year decade wound down with the new and exciting 1970's just ahead with all of its enticements. I was so busy, that I stopped taking new patients for periods of time unless referred by their physician. As my OB contemporaries began to close down their OB Practices and concentrate more on the GYN side of their practices, my newborn population began to rapidly dwindle in an expected manner. Though this event is the natural course of history in a pediatric practice, still, it was a blow to my ego. It was a big loss in not having the fun of playing with the children under six.

I would have an enjoyable time during a physical examination with the children from the ages of three to six. When examining their ears, I would look into their ear and say, "I see a little Brownie with a red nose, green ears, and purple shoes in your ear, and he helps you to remember what your mother says". My! How big their eyes would become. It was so heartwarming and fun to behold. I heard many years later, when a number of my old patients would get together, my Brownie stories occupied a center point of some of their conversations.

It was nice to know that their visits to the office had been a pleasant one and kind thoughts remained about me. During these years, I only published two papers; and they were on the adolescent years. I was falling behind in my writing. However, I had presented fourteen papers or lectures on variations of the general topic of adolescence at medical meetings in Nebraska, Iowa, and South Dakota.

Chapter 60

As the 1960's came to a close, my medical practice was very well established and envied by others. I had developed new areas of interest and continued on with many of the old ones. I did very little Endocrinology, Hematology, Nephrology, or Cardiac work as there were trained Subspecialists available in these fields to handle these needs. My interests had turned elsewhere. I still enjoyed the general field of pediatric medicine even though I was seeing many exotic medical cases.

Research and Progress were being made on all Pediatric Medical Fronts including Pathology and Radiology. This progress helped to unravel the many challenging consultations I was encountering. The mundane and every day medical situations were certainly gone. I enjoyed having a new consultative problem, which was much like reading a new mystery story, to solve. It was important to find a way to apprehend the guilty culprit [the medical situation] and correct the transgression.

I was well established as an authority on School Learning Problems, Adolescent Medicine, the Handicapped Child, and was cultivating a major interest in Practice Management. The core of my medical practice continued to be my "Guided Growth Program" for all ages. I related and tied all of my patients to some facet of this encompassing philosophy.

Our sons were entering into their exciting Teen Years with all of their interests in sports, and girls, girls, and more girls. We were sailors and water skiers deluxe. Mary and I had a pleasant and active social life with an endearing group of friends. My wonderful Mary had decorated our house and turned it into a real home with all of its uniqueness. I had a number of interesting and stimulating hobbies. Everything was set for our next exciting decade and what challenges it would hold.

Lady Medicine was still as seductive as ever and exerted a strong pull to forego all else and succumb to her wiles. My beloved Mary kept my feet firmly fastened to the ground which was a yeoman task for her.

**Part V to follow
The Decade of the 1970's
Our First Long Range Practice Plan**

Part V

The Decade of the 1970's
Our First Long Range
Practice Plan

Little did I know what adventures and heartaches lay ahead in the years of the 1970's decade? I found several new worlds to conquer and continued to develop the many aspects of the "Guided Growth Well Child and Adolescent Program". The 1970 Long Range Plan was accepted by my partners and was being instituted in a methodical manner:

1. The medical team concept was doing very well and office efficiency had improved remarkably.

2. The many wearing and sometimes irritating patient phone calls had been conquered. It was a long standing policy of the Clinic that no phone call would be returned unless the Patient's Chart was at hand, and specific notes about the call were recorded on the Chart. This step was vital for malpractice protection if a court case would ever evolve. The legal opinion used by the Courts was, "If it is not written down, it did not occur". The terms "Negative" and/or "Normal" were unacceptable to describe a medical situation in a patient's chart. "There had to be written descriptive notes to be acceptable" to the Courts. Our attorneys made a major emphasis of this descriptive need in writing any patient notes in the office chart.

3. Each individual patient office visit had to be recorded and completed at the conclusion of the office visit and prior to the next patient being seen. This mandate avoided the big mess at the end of the day that many medical offices encountered. It was difficult when patient data needed to be recalled in detail in order to enter the necessary information into the patient's chart. Some offices might be a week or more behind in completing the patient visit charting. How could anyone remember any specific details about an individual patient visit when jumbled together with many subsequent other patient visits? Frequently, patient information could end up being inaccurate or pieces missing by trying to rely upon a physician's memory. A physician's memory, believe it or not, is not infallible. This method of memory charting

is a big fat NO NO, and is an invitation for a poor outcome in a Malpractice suit.

3.1. Over time, I had been very traumatized by having three partners sued and losing two partners by their resignation from the practice of pediatrics. Not one of these suits was justified, nor was there a sound basis for the suit

3.2. I had been an expert witness in several malpractice cases for other physicians which further sensitized me to court room antics by attorneys.

4. The patients' Chart Files were both color coded by file cover and by the patient initials using two colors coded alphabetical initials of the last name.

5. My Nurse Practitioner was being well accepted and liked.

There were many other innovations which are not listed here.

Paul Dutton CPA's Office was selected to handle our accounting needs through Jim Canedy's recommendation. The Dutton office retooled and revamped our entire bookkeeping system and made it next to impossible for any embezzlement to successfully occur. Previously, we had lost $500 in spite of our considered foolproof procedures at the time which, surprisingly, did not detect this loss. Dutton's office improved our collection techniques and procedures. Keep in mind that money on the books is not considered money for a bank loan. The only real money for a bank loan consideration comprises the hard dollars on hand or billings less than 30 days old.

At this time, the government had begun to allowed small medical practices to incorporate and to begin an elementary pension savings utilizing the Keogh plan. This action opened a host of valuable options to be considered by each physician which had not been available before this time.

Chapter 61

The many medical committee activities and task forces that I had participated in taught me several lessons for future use such as:

1. The Chairperson should lead the committee actively and not let the meetings degenerate into gabfest sessions.
2. The Chairperson should bring a defined written agenda to each meeting with copies for each member.
3. The points of direction, including the various committee charges, should be the dominant role of the committee work and not let the discussions be sidetracked by endless conversations, speculations, and gossip.
4. The inactive committee member, who was not actively participating and making contributions to the whole, should be ignored and replaced as soon as possible. There is nothing more discouraging to a committee than to have a piece of dead wood or a person who agrees to accept a responsibility and never carries it out.
5. The agenda would be developed by me, and I would keep my own committee notes; so that I would know what was happening and what work needed to be accomplished at future meetings. When someone else keeps notes, they frequently are incomplete, inaccurate, or very slow to be made available to the members.

6. The people with assigned tasks should be held accountable for their accepted responsibilities.

As I said before, our office averaged about three thousand families per physician as compared to the accepted national norm of fifteen hundred. My own patient load was nearer to four thousand plus. We, all, were very busy in the collective practice. It was not unusual for my money placed upon the books to be double the amount of that of any two of my partners pooled together.

These listed axioms stood me in good stead throughout all of the 1970's as my many different medical society roles and other involvements ensued. These different roles led to many recognized areas for my success.

My interest in ADD and Specific Learning Problems busily continued as did my extensive consultative practice. My expertise in adolescents continued to expand. My patient and parent educational programs were enhanced by my attending specific medical meetings devoted to certain aspects of a single core topic of interest rather than a general meeting with many different subjects.

My sons, Terry and Matt, worked afternoons at the office putting my patient packets of information together. We had a room in the basement garage area where there was a copy machine and many shelves. This area was where the bulk of copied items, printed materials and purchased brochures, at my own expense, were stored.

My partners, however, had no qualms of conscience to "borrow" an occasional age based information packet for their own patient's use. I never was aware that they volunteered to reimburse me or to fund some of these purchases.

My boys would assemble the material designed for the different age periods. They would keep supplied, in age order, the various packets in the upstairs office area within a large shelved closet. This proximity to my offices was readily available and convenient for my nurse assistant to obtain the precise material which was designed for each specific office visit.

Chapter 62

There was a major recession 1970 which reared its ugly head. Jobs became so scarce in the Omaha area that the husbands of some of our nurses went to Denver, Colorado searching for work. Collections were poor. Fortunately, the large volume of work that the office processed enabled us to weather this storm.

I never wanted to be considered a "Society Pediatrician". I left this questionable achievement to others. I did care for plenty of Society children. It was almost axiomatic that many of these upper crust people were the most demanding for services and were among the slowest to pay their bills. I loved the hardworking blue collar workers. They seem to appreciate the care and paid the bill promptly. During this time, pediatric office visits and immunizations were rarely covered by insurance. The family had this financial responsibility and accepted it.

I noticed another consistent family dynamic concept i.e. if a young, rather immature girl married a solid mature man, she would quickly grow into being a responsible person; and their marriage would flourish. The corollary of that observation was the opposite. If a mature woman married an immature man, the marriage union would frequently fall apart within about five years. I saw this phenomena happen time and time again. For some reason or another, nurses as a group did the poorest job of picking a mate. The divorce rate seemed to be excessively high amongst this group of parents.

Chapter 63

I encountered the worst nightmare that could be possibly being imagined during this decade. The STAAR Program was slowly creeping along and needed new and better advertizing to become more widely known. I received a phone call one day from a Bob Maynard of the Washington Post Newspaper in Washington, D.C. He said that he had heard of the STAAR program and was interested to learn more about it. I inquired, "How did you hear about the STAAR Program in Washington, D.C. when it was barely known in Omaha." He hummed and hawed around with some garbled answer, but I was far too naïve and ignorant to catch the hedging. He wanted to come to Omaha and do a story on the STAAR Program. This seemed like an easy way to broadcast information about the STAAR Program; so I agreed.

I made arrangements for the interview to occur in Dr. Don Warner's office. He was the Director for Special Education Services for the Omaha Public Schools. We met with the reporter. He showed us his credentials, which were in order. The interview began. I explained the origin and purpose of the STAAR Program; but it was apparent from the very first that he wasn't really interested in the STAAR Program. He kept asking question after question about Ritalin, Ritalin, and more Ritalin. It didn't dawn on me that he must have an ulterior motive for all of the Ritalin questions. No matter how hard I tried to change the subject to the role of other meds in this condition, he would return to the subject of Ritalin. The interview lasted better than an hour. After he left, Don Warner's Secretary said, "There goes an evil man". Little did we know how true those remarks were to be?

I promptly forgot about the interview as soon as it was over. A few weeks later when I arrived at the office, the girls said that a radio station in Chicago had been burning up the telephone lines wanting to talk to me. "Why me"? I returned the call. The station wanted to know about the drug experiment that was going on in the Omaha Public Schools. I was dumbfounded and said, "What drug experiment in what public school system?"

The inquiring station reporter said, "You are quoted extensively throughout this AP Report that came over the wire this morning". I was floored and totally dismayed. I requested that the station send me the article so I could study it and give an intelligent response. The station was impatient for an answer and wanted to read to me the article over the phone, which they did. After a few lines, I interrupted and said,"That is not right". This remark was repeated by me several times during the first several paragraphs of the article. The station acknowledged that there seemed to be several major discrepancies in the article. When the phone call was over, I wondered where these misunderstandings had originated; then, it dawned upon me about the Maynard interview. I was furious, but there was little that I could do to offset the damage which had already been accomplished.

By now, everything really began to hit the fan. For the next two weeks, all I could do was to try to fend off all types of news media people. I was ill prepared for this overwhelming onslaught. There were reporters from "Life" magazine and many other national rags, innumerable reporters from different newspapers; and, above all, representatives from the three major TV news services. ABC and CBS did not give me the courtesy of an interview. They went to the militant activist responsible for this dilemma, interviewed him, filmed him, and put his damaging interview on the TV tube in prime time.

I talked with my lawyer and friend, Don Erickson, several times a day as to how I should handle each new situation as it would arise. Many of the reporters that interviewed me tried to ask a very startling unexpected question so that I would either look shocked, be embarrassed, or would give an incriminating answer. Ritalin and the OPS children, who supposedly were part of a nonexistent experiment, was the main focus of this national attention. Sometimes they worked in pairs using a "Good Cop Bad Cop" motif.

I lost two weeks out of my office schedule at the cost of about $10,000 of non recoverable revenue, which was not put upon the books. None of my colleagues, who knew me well, including some of those whose children I had cared for with this problem, came to my defense. I was devastated that some so called friends and competitors seemed to delight in my discomfort. Professional jealousy is a mean insidious beast. I never have felt quite the same about many of my so called colleagues after this experience. The local Omaha Medical Society investigated me and found nothing untoward. The current head of the Med Center Pediatric Department at that time, Dr. Gordon Gibbs, and one lone pediatrician were the only people to say a kind word in my defense.

This was a terrible time for me and my family. My sanity was kept intact by my wonderful wife going every day to morning Mass and praying for me. She was frightened to death because our house had been egged. A car sat up the street from our home for a number of days with a load of people in it watching the house.

However in my defense, many parents of my patients came forward and did a yeoman's job in monitoring the various local radio talk shows. They would call in to correct false information that was being portrayed over the air. To these, my parents, I was and still am forever grateful.

Ron Nessan of NBC TV was the only honest interviewer I encountered. When we sat down to go over the format of the interview, I wanted to know if there would be any surprise questions similar to those that I had encountered previously. He said, "No, we do not interview that way". He was true to his word. The interview was a positive one and was aired in prime time. I will always be grateful to him.

I made front page stories in many European papers. Some of the parents of my patients brought home German papers with big headlines and false stories. A radio station in Australia arranged for a phone line to my office without my permission for a radio talk show. I politely refused this kind offer.

It seemed as though this nightmare would never end. My oldest son, By, was in Scotland on a psychiatric clerkship from the Med Center; and when he called he asked, "Dad, what in the Hell are they doing to you"? My other two boys were teased at high school for having a "Timothy Leary" for a father. Life was terrible. This happening was like living in a huge nightmare with no end in sight.

Finally, a ray of light and hope began to glimmer. Apparently, The Boston Globe began to ask questions of various physicians around its part of the country. The paper found out there was nothing new about Ritalin being used in children for this condition. Within a few days, the news outlets pulled their reporters away from Omaha as there was no outlandish story to report.

A long time later, I learned that Bob Maynard was an acquaintance and tool of the militant activist responsible for this situation and had been to Omaha earlier for a visit with him. The activist was upset over his incompetent brother being fired from the Omaha Public School System; and he used this false drama to embarrass Dr. Owen Knutson, the Superintendent of the Omaha Public Schools.

For a long, long time, I was so sensitized by this problem that I refused to take any new children with this entity. This feeling lasted for over two years when I, finally, decided that I had lived with enough doom and gloom of self pity and self flagellation. It was time for me to pull up the shades, change socks, expunge the demons and nightmares, let the sun shine in, and walk in a different pathway. It was important to me to not just exist in medicine and go through the programmed motions of medical care; but to resume an active and dynamic role with children and adolescents. Prior to this occurrence, I would literally cringe whenever Ritalin was mentioned.

In order to finally reach closure with this feeling, I submitted a detailed protocol to the Scientific Program Committee of the AAP. This protocol detailed a presentation consisting of a three hour "Round Table" on this subject at the New Orleans Spring Meeting of the American Academy of Pediatrics in April 1977. To paraphrase the words of my hero under whom I had served in Japan, General Douglas MacArthur, and "I shall return to the fight of an active medical life helping these young people". My round table was well received. My ghosts were expunged. Thank heavens! It was almost like a laser treatment to scar tissue that restored my mind's health to a more positive attitude.

Once again, I had an intense desire to move on to new challenges. As soon as the word was out that I was taking new patients with school problems, the line started forming and kept growing longer. I was privy to the experimental use of the Gordon Diagnostic System, which measured fine finger coordination and the attention span. This instrument provided hard copy evidence both for the diagnostic aspects of the child undergoing a current evaluation, and, in documenting the response the patient had to his/her medication program. The Gordon Device was in its early testing stages. I found this instrument to be both useful and helpful in investigating and following the response to medications for these problems

Chapter 64

Our office always had medical students, various types of nursing students, and pediatric residents under foot in a training capacity in their selected clerkships. Having a student in tow added at least an hour to the working day due to all the questions that were generated and needed to be explained and answered. My son, By, elected to spend two different clerkships with me. It was a thrill to introduce my son to families as a fledgling doctor. We were able to cuss and discuss the different facets of medicine from a practical standpoint.

I had volunteer management sessions for the pediatric residents in the evening at my house about once a month. I covered subjects such as how to evaluate a practice position being offered, how to understand business contracts, and covered many other practical subjects which a resident might encounter.

One of my prize residents was a Dr. Tom Tonniges, who later established his pediatric practice in Hastings, Nebraska. He instituted several innovative services in his practice. He was cited by the Academy for some of these innovations. Later on, we became reacquainted when I was associated with Medical Computer Management, Inc. as the company's Medical Advisor. He had installed the MCMI AMOS Computer System in his office. He left his practice to become the head of the Division of Membership for the Academy. He worked there for a number of years. Now, he is the Pediatric Director for the Boys Town brand new National Research Hospital in Omaha. He is one of my claims to fame. Interesting enough, he recently came to my apartment to interview me regarding the various history making changes that I was involved with during my active days in the Academy of Pediatrics.

I noticed that several aspects of the attitude and techniques of the current crop of Medical Center teachers had not changed much from earlier days when I was deeply involved with the Med Center:

1. The Academician's attitude was still alive and more intense than ever at looking down upon the money grubbing private practitioner in spite of all the gratis teaching the volunteers gave to UNMC without any type of remuneration or added privileges.

2. Within the Hospital Ward Rounds System, the Medical Staff seemed to have forfeited their leadership role and their teaching responsibilities by having the Chief Resident teaching the other level residents. The first and second level residents taught the medical students. The Staff doctors were very prominent in their absence. When I think back to my personal rounds with Drs. Gedgoud and Johnston, how much the current students and residents really miss!

3. The General Rotating Internship had been long gone and forgotten. It was replaced by the student going directly into the selected field of his/her supposed interest. I thought the experiences gained in a general rotating internship, by participating in the different medical and surgical services, gave a neophyte physician a much better insight into the dynamics and impacts which the various fields of medicine had upon the patient. Today, I believe a student ends up with a type of tunnel vision as regards his/her chosen medical field. I suspect that there is a difficult time trying to look outside the defined parameters of his/her chosen specialty. To me, this change was a big loss in the medical training programs as it encourages junior medical students to decide upon their career path much too soon. This early choice allows for dissatisfaction with their field of selection to set in. After being thoroughly committed to a goal, it becomes much too late or too expensive to change fields.

4. Medical school has become so expensive that students frequently decide upon high income procedure producing specialties because of their huge debt that must be amortized.

5. Medical Center Staff physicians were under a constant major pressure to obtain grants, do research, and publish papers. Teaching had become a byproduct of being a faculty member instead of the primary goal and for the real reason for a medical school to exist. Sir William Osler, the patron saint of modern medicine, must be turning over in his grave.

Chapter 65

Jim Canedy was the most outstanding and enlightened administrator of a very progressive tertiary care hospital, Clarkson. He sent the heads of all the medical departments and major committees to Ann Arbor, Michigan to the Institute for Quality Assurance. This three day seminar was a foreseen need as it was one of the coming requirements by the Joint Commission for Hospital Accreditation. The coming push was to be able to demonstrate that patient care, hospital days, and hospital functions were what they were really supposed to be. Statistics of all sizes, shapes, length of stay, and many different groups of numbers were gathered and compared. These facts and figures were to become the basis and Bible for the comparison of one hospital's outcome with another as to length of stay and other parameters of care. For better and many times for worse, this bureaucracy was thrusting its nosy head into all aspects of hospital functions creating many problems, much anxiety and greatly adding to the costs of care.

In the very early days, computers were huge mainframe machines that had to be kept in a cool environment. Learning about the computer's capabilities was astounding to me. This was one of the most stimulating experiences that I had had to date. Realizing the amount of data a computer could store and compare and generate results piqued my interest beyond reality. My interest in computer applications to medicine took off like a proverbial Roman candle. Thoughts flew around my mind a mile a minute like a rapid game of ping pong.

The information we obtained was interesting and stimulating. The Clarkson group of committee heads developed a nice camaraderie while at Ann Arbor. We ate together several times at a unique restaurant, "The Gandy Dancer". The motif of this restaurant was based upon the hard working railroad spike drivers laying railroad track, and displayed other railroad memorabilia. The food was good, and the atmosphere was great.

All the time I was at Ann Arbor and on the way back home, the wheels in my brain were working at high speed and in high gear. My mind was spinning endlessly in overtime. I continually kept wondering how the computer could be harnessed to aid in running an office and storing a patient's medical record. After a bit of time and with some crude but unrelated ideas and thoughts, I went to visit my mentor in practice management. Jim Canedy listened to my thoughts and rough ideas.

After awhile he came to the conclusion that my ideas were not too farfetched or so unacceptable. We decided to use the Omaha Childrens' Clinic PC as the laboratory base. The objective was to produce a useful program of financial and medical applications for the Clarkson medical staff using Clarkson's Computer Main Frames and computer personnel. Clarkson's computer resources, at that time, were extensive.

Dr. Bill Rumbolz, an OB-GYN office, and Dr. John Kirchner, a Family Physician, were enlisted to ensure that the needs of other medical offices would be met rather than that of just Pediatrics. We gathered several times to discuss the overview of thoughts and ideas. A major Systems Manager from Clarkson's computer staff was assigned to this project. We took a trip to Greensboro, South Carolina to study a Public Health Computer Application for the recording of immunizations and, subsequently, of notifying patients for recall purposes as to when the next shot were due.

We traveled to the White Plains, New Mexico Indian Reservation to study a Public Health brief electronic medical record. This record needed to be readily available for a patient who had diabetes, alcoholism, or some other long term serious medical problem. The patient might be seen in one place today and tomorrow might check in a health facility 200 miles away. If this same patient traveled to another part of the reservation, some type of inclusive health record was essential for the local care givers to utilize in providing for ongoing care to this patient.

The basis for the accounting and business management aspects of this project were already available through the hospital's own system. This hospital program could be easily modified for office applications. We pondered how a medical diagnosis, related laboratory tests, x-ray reports, immunizations, cardinal points in a past medical history, brief essential family history concerning genetic possibilities, and similar information could be tied together for recall purposes in one inclusive bundle regarding a single patient. The old medical record with sheets and sheets of scribbled notes and scattered hidden laboratory reports had no rhyme, nor reason, or pattern to it. Most medical records were a hodge-podge of papers both large and small. To locate an important piece of medical information on a certain patient was like looking for the proverbial needle in a hay stack. With a computerized system, this patient information could be tied together for recalling all the data related to a specific identified diagnosis and/or medical problem.

After many brainstorming sessions, the solution was so simple that it made us feel foolish. All data relating to a certain diagnosis would be coded and attached within the confines of the chart by using the same medical problem number for that particular diagnosis. This would include blood tests, X-ray reports, immunizations, and similar medical information.

For Example: Problem No. 1 might be used to log and record all Preventive Care data including immunizations, preventive tests, x-rays, and body measurements. All these items would be labeled with and attached to No. 1. When the data was put into the computer under this single identifying number all of the attached data would be retrieved by recalling this single number. Any subsequent data relating to this medical entity would be tied to this same problem number facilitating an easy recall of all current available information when needed. This approach would tie all relevant data concerning a specific medical diagnosis or condition together into a neat package for recall purposes.

Each medical problem would have different number in any given chart and would be different in other patients' charts; but this was not an insurmountable problem. Each patient and his/her medical history points were unique and specific to that individual person. The problem number would be able to recall all of the data related to an individual medical problem, and this was the concept that mattered. The proof of the pudding was that this approach worked extremely well.

A Dr. Larry Weed, from the Boston area, began proposing a different medical history format called the "Problem Oriented Medical Record". It made so much practical sense to me that I quickly became a disciple of his thoughts and methods. He described an approach using a "SOAP" format. "S" stands for Subjective Findings. In the old medical terminology, "Subjective" was synonymous to the medical history. The "O" was for Objective relating to physical findings and various lab and x-ray tests. The "A" was for assessment relating to the study and evaluation of the patient's data. The "P" was for the plan related to the treatment approach and follow-up needs for the patient. Each individual medical problem the patient encountered would have its own unique problem number and a separate SOAP method of approach. I read everything I could lay my hands on describing this methodology as it made such good common sense to me. I began utilizing this concept manually with my own office medical records. I refined my record format and redesigned it so that this medical record concept could readily be adapted to the computer. One of my future Holy Grail quests was to produce an electronic medical record. My partners began utilizing this same approach to their patient records.

I had a new field to conquer relating to computer use in Healthcare and Healthcare Delivery. This adventure continued on and on throughout the rest of my medical life; like the proverbial "Energizer Bunny" that keeps going and going.

Chapter 66

Up until this point in time, medical offices such as Internal Medicine and Pediatrics had very little contact with Health Insurance Companies except for the hospitalization of a patient. Very little insurance coverage was available for office medical care, immunizations, and/or laboratory tests. The various surgical specialties had been very early users and collaborators with the Health Insurance Industry relating to different individual surgical procedures. Most of a surgeon's work was done within the hospital walls except for a brief follow-up visit after surgery. Because the surgical specialties had a procedure for all aspects of their usually encountered medical situations, this method became a procedure based reimbursement schedule. This approach to payments ensured that the surgeons would be reimbursed hard dollars very quickly without many collection problems. The surgical specialty procedure method pre-determined much in the way that insurance companies began to address the other medical specialties. A diagnosis had to have the appropriate ICD Code {International Code for Diseases}. Each disease entity had a specific descriptive and unique code assigned to it in this International Code System; which was universally accepted by most modern countries.

At times, I used to help the Medical Record Librarian at Childrens' Hospital decide what and how a Hospital Chart Diagnoses should be coded for reporting purposes. Finding the right diagnosis to code a physician's unscientific or having no specific code available for his/her diagnoses could be quite a sleuthing task. Not many physicians understood the coding systems.

Each medical procedure per Se was assigned a CPT Code {Current Procedure Terminology} and was assigned a RVS {Relative Value Scale) number. This approach grouped each medical and/or surgical procedure together with similar medical entities. Those procedures which were more difficult, more complex or less difficult and less complex had different RVS code numbers. The RVS and the CPT codes became the basis for physicians of all specialties to be financially reimbursed by Third Party Payers. The main disadvantage of this system was that most Internal Medical Specialties and Pediatrics had very few procedures except for immunizations and laboratory tests to be coded for reimbursement purposes. Medical office visits per Se needed to be "Time Used" as a basis for equitable reimbursement purposes. The insurance companies shied away from this approach for a long while. Early on, the medical oriented doctors were at a great disadvantage to the surgical procedure doctors regarding insurance reimbursements. As ugly as it seems, reimbursement is what began to pay the medical practice bills and became a real true to life defined entity and process.

Later on, the government and Medicare assumed almost complete control of this approach for reimbursement reasons. Even though this coding system was never designed for reimbursement purposes, the government decreed that it would be the basis for reimbursement, period. It became imperative for physicians and their office staffs to become very knowledgeable about these three codes and how to use them. Training seminars regarding proper coding use popped up in vast numbers like toad stools. A new industry was created. Over time, both the government and the insurance industry made these codes the Bible by which they conducted business. Sometimes the ICD and/or CPT codes worked to the detriment of the physician' income and caused inadequate reimbursement. This discrepancy was due to the use of improper coding. Claims would be submitted, refused, and resubmitted ad infinitum without recourse to a fair solution. Medical offices had to hire additional personnel to handle the increased paper work and to have them become knowledgeable concerning these codes.

I was a participant in a Round Table for the Minnesota Chapter of the American Academy of Pediatrics on understanding the "Relative Value Scale" and its applications. The use of these various codes became a subset of computer use in medical offices and became another avenue of computer applications for me to explore. The importance to understand the codes, how to apply them, and what specific codes to use grew in greater significance as time passed. With government's further intrusion into medicine, its influence progressed onward ever ever onward in a relentless manner. The horrendous mish mash of the current 2010 health insurance bill has attested to this far reaching intrusion in medicine. This intrusion will have to ultimately include rationing of care because of costs and too few practicing primary care physicians.

Because of the need for an accurate input of data into the computer, which at this time had to be done manually at Clarkson Hospital, it became apparent that a better office charge slip must be designed. With my partners, we designed and used one of the first "Super Bills" for office charges. It contained all of the various ICD and CPT Codes that were commonly utilized within our office setting. The "Charge Slip" listed all of the immunizations and laboratory tests with their corresponding CPT Codes and the more commonly encountered medical diagnoses with their ICD Codes were on the slip. This "Bill" became the data input mechanism for entering accurate information into the big main frame computers at Clarkson. This "Bill" was comprised of three copies on a pressure sensitive paper. One copy was for the patient, one for the direct computer input at Clarkson Hospital, and the other one was for use when submitting an insurance claim. This approach made an almost hopeless and insurmountable situation much easier to manage.

The secondary and an almost more important spinoff of these transactions for me was that I could gather an almost endless collection of data on the different aspects of our office practice. This action made study and analysis of the practice practical and intriguing. (These ideas reminded me of the spinoff benefits from the old Ann Arbor, Michigan meeting}. In the near future, Paul Dutton and I would carry out many useful and important analyses of our practice. The data concerning the patient's medical aspects of a medical office visit was entered into the computer. The charge slip utilized a special segment designed for the input of the physical findings such as blood pressure, height, weight, and similar related medical data.

At Jim Canedy's prompting, I joined the Society for Computer Medicine and was subsidized in attending these meetings by Clarkson Hospital for a number of years. I became a member of the Committee on

Standards of this Society from 1974 to 1982 and was the Chairman of this Committee from 1980 to 1982. I became acquainted with some of the brightest minds in the medical computing field including Dr. Larry Weed of the Problem Oriented Record approach to medical records and Dr. Marion Ball, who headed the Department of Information Technology at Temple University and the author of many books; subsequently, she moved to Jefferson Medical School in Philadelphia. Dr. Phil Manning, Dean of the University Of Southern California School Of Continuing Medical Education, ran the finest continuing medical education programs in the country. I was privileged to become well acquainted with him and to share some unique and stimulating experiences which became germane in the near future. From my viewpoint, it was a delight to observe the thinking and analytical processes portrayed by these people. I was a guest contributor of a Chapter to one of Dr. Ball's books.

Marion was a remarkable and unique woman. She visited our office during one year to observe how the office functioned. We had a number of authorities who expressed an interest in how our office handled its day to day operations.

Chapter 67

My knowledge of Practice Management was increasing in an ongoing, organized, and intense manner. I became an expert in the field of Office Medical Practice Management and was on the lecture circuit at many different types of meetings including both medical and computer sessions.

After the Clarkson Project encompassing the computer program for the Medical staff became functional, I used this data as a foundation for many other presentations starting in Miami, Florida in 1974. I gave the first detailed discussion entitled, "A Total Health Care System" at a Seminar on Health Care Delivery Systems, which was sponsored by the University of Miami. From this point onward, I gave some twenty-three presentations on various aspects of computer use in medicine and healthcare. The organization, content, and format of an electronic and encompassing Medical Record became another area of expertise for me. I presented a number of papers on this topic at a Medical Record Meeting in Boston and many other meetings over the next few years.

As time passed, these different presentations would zero in and become focused upon the various aspects of my eight divisions of Medical Management in a private medical practice. My name became an authority within the American Academy of Pediatrics concerning computers and practice management. I was a part of the faculty of the first Academy's Continuing Medical Education Course in Monterey, California in 1976 on aspects of practice management.

The Academy was in the dark ages when it came to Practice Management per Se and/or any thoughts about computers in health care were purely coincidental. It seemed to me that Pandora's Box had been opened, and I could help myself to any of the goodies contained therein as desired. One new area of extreme interest reared its head in the form of the Electronic Medical Record, itself. More on this topic of electronic medical records will be addressed later in this story.

Meanwhile, my interest in Adolescent Medicine was in full flower and requests for presentations were multiple. I gave some twenty lectures over the next few years on many different aspects of this age period. As part of my comprehensive preventive care approach, my adolescent patients received a detailed medical, psychological, emotional, social, and physical evaluation annually.

To record all the necessary information of this type of a detailed visit, I redesigned and upgraded my office medical history forms at regular intervals. An example of some of the many physical aspects examined during a teen's physical was an exercise tolerance test. This test was given to each adolescent from the age of twelve onward. The patient had to run over a metal two step exercise stairs for a defined timed interval. After this exercise, the heart rate and blood pressure were recorded at specific intervals; and a ratio was determined. It was readily obvious which patients did not engage in any exercise program and needed encouragement to do so. Advice would be given as what should be done to correct this poor test results. This test would be repeated at the next year's visit and comparisons would be made for evidence of improvement. Another item of the examination was to measure with calipers an area on the posterior [back] aspect of the upper arm to determine fat content. Generally, it took a fair amount of time by the Medical Assistant to prepare a patient to be seen by me. When I walked into an examining room, all of the necessary details had been accomplished; my time with the patient was solely devoted to the person at hand. I did not spend time doing the mundane measurements and other preparation details.

A young mother, who had been a patient of mine for a long time, brought in her new baby to be checked. After renewing old times, she asked me, "Do you still have those steps I had to run over". I answered,"Yes, it is still a part of the examination". She replied, "Oh! how I hated that damn test". We both laughed.

As time passed, the repeatedly redesigned medical office history and physical examination form began to evolve into a major ongoing. Continuous and longitudinal Health Record. I began to toy with the idea of how to collect medical history data by an automated method and how to design key questions which would trigger any potential medical problem area. The next step to be accomplished would be to how to put the data into the computer in a simple non manual manner. Manual input on the keyboard was not practical as it was too labor intensive. There many current methodologies being considered or in use.

I devised a medical history form that asked questions which could only be answered by "Yes or No". There were specific key questions in this format which if answered with a "Yes"; then, this answer indicated the possibility that there might be an underlying identifiable medical situation. This identified area could be further explored during the personal history interview time. The future mechanism for data input to utilize would most likely be a scanning device. This method of input would avoid the difficulty of the manual intensive input methods. Unfortunately, at this point in time, scanners were in the infancy of their development; so this method was not yet practical. Bar Coding was another possibility, but I did not pursue this approach.

I developed an entire menu of History and Physical Forms consisting of the comprehensive Initial Medical History and followed this by subsequent age specific Annual Health Review Forms from one year of age through to the young adult years of thirty. These different forms were used by me manually until I retired. My Medical Tech would mail out the appropriate form a month before the patient's visit. When the form would be returned, she would review it and highlight the key questions that were answered which indicated a possible problem area. When the patient came for the appointment, I could concentrate in a more detailed manner upon the key questions and utilize a cursory review of the rest of the history.

The Problem Oriented Medical Record lent itself readily to computerization. This was another area in which I was considered an expert. I gave a number of lectures on the need and contents of a potential electronic medical record. The Clarkson Medical Synopsis was a good start in this direction. I obtained, for gathering some additional teen history data, a new small computer which generated an adolescent medical questionnaire. The teen would answer the questions on the computer while waiting for his/her office visit. This print out was immediately available to me and was added to my history armamentarium before the personal patient interview. This questionnaire asked about situations and activities which, when asked face to face, were usually dodged such as drug use or sexual activity. This approach revealed many areas of importance regarding the patient's lifestyle which would identify items for discussion. Depending upon the seriousness of the answer, sometimes I might need to schedule another visit to provide time to evaluate this personal health matter whether it would be to counteract drug use, to evaluate some type of depressive problem, or to explore suicidal thoughts. Suicide was the first or second cause, next to accidents, as a reason for death in the adolescent population. Suicide was an ever present worry with some adolescents. Some authorities felt that many accidents were actual suicide attempts or calls for help.

We would receive the print out of the Clarkson medical synopsis each morning by courier. The charge slips, which had been generated during the previous day's office visits, were the vehicles that supplied the input data. This new synopsis was filed in the patient's chart. When the family came in for the next visit, I would give the parent this previous synopsis as a new one would be generated and available by the next day. The parents loved having this record. In the same vein of thought, I would give to the parent's copies of the hospital discharge summary and any copies of the reports which I sent to their referring physician. As an off chute of this detailed parent record approach, there was greater protection from malpractice suits. The family could never claim that they had not been kept fully informed as to the patient's or the family's medical situation. I learned about this aspect of protection from the lawyers at the Williamsburg Meeting on Adolescent Medical Records and Privacy.

When we moved our office west along with the new Childrens' Hospital, the Clarkson Obstetricians urged us to keep a satellite office in the vicinity of Clarkson. By having the medical synopsis readily available for every patient in our practice, this request for a second office became a practical reality. We invested roughly $10,000 into this experiment. However, the Clarkson Obstetricians did not refer to our office the number of infants they said would be forthcoming. Some of my patients resented having me spend time in this office when they lived nearer to the main location; and other patients did not like to be going to different places to see me or seeing someone else in the office when I was at the satellite office. After a two year trial, we abandoned this ill-fated venture and chalked it up to profit and loss. Dr. Wax had alternated using the satellite office with me and agreed with me to forget this venture.

The major disadvantage of this computer system was the lack of a random access by the computer to the data. String access was the only available method at this point in time. This method meant that in order to retrieve a desired piece of data, one always had to start at the very beginning of the information string and go to where the data resided or on to the end of the data. The random access technology would not be readily available for several years to come.

Over time, I published nine papers on the comprehensive medical record, gave three specific seminar presentations on this detailed medical record, authored a chapter in one of Marion Ball's Books, and authored and/or co-authored two books on computers and practice management concepts.

Chapter 68

In October 1970 my old partner and mentor, Dr. Charles Tompkins, and I gave a one half day Round Table on "Anticipatory Guidance and Well Child Care" at the fall annual meeting of the American Academy of Pediatrics in San Francisco. This presentation was well received. Shortly after the completion of the Round Table, a staff person for the Charles C. Thomas, Medical Publishers sought me. He wanted to know if I would be interested in writing a book based upon the details of this Round Table. Naturally, I was flabbergasted. Me! Write a book? He must be kidding! This book would be my first attempt on a project of this magnitude. This task of writing a book was going to be the biggest feat of my life to date. Help!

I spent the next year writing in my basement on a yellow pad in my spare time as I had never learned to type. My medical typist would have to first decipher my scribbles and then transcribe my handwriting into a readable format for editing and re-editing. This painful process seemed to be an endless chore to me. My son, Terry, who was an English Major at Brown University, edited my final endeavors. At that time, he was not very kind with his corrections to his father's masterpiece. Ha!

I eagerly awaited the publication and birth of my baby, "Practical Guidelines for General Pediatric and Adolescent Office Practice". The publishing date came, and I scoured the pediatric meeting vendor's area for the Charles C. Thomas Book Booth. I could not find the publisher's booth in any nook or cranny. At past meetings, their booth had always had a very prominent place in the exhibit hall. Later to my dismay, I learned that the company's advertising policy had changed.

The company decided to promote their cadre of books by direct mail, only. What a blow! This book needed to be browsed by the reader to determine its usefulness to him or her.

My contract stated that before I received any royalty money, one thousand copies had to be sold to cover the production costs. How sad! About seven hundred copies of my book were sold. I think that I bought three hundred of them to give away to friends and others. My anguish was soothed somewhat when several purchasers wrote to me about how this book helped them in their practice. Their kudos was ample reward for the time and effort that went into writing my masterpiece. I learned a lot about writing a book that held me in good stead in the future years. This experience was a very valuable lesson in the practicalities of the real world.

Chapter 69

My second nightmare occurred later during this decade. My beloved Mary became ill and could not remember on Wednesday that I had come to visit her at the hospital on the previous Sunday. I was devastated and totally lost. Much time went by, and no major change occurred. Finally, her several physicians told me, "They thought that she had early Alzheimer's disease". I was devastated. I had a hard time accepting this diagnosis. It was recommended that I should look at Nursing Homes for her long term care.

My son, Matt, and I looked and looked. The Monteclare Nursing Home seemed to be the nicest and best managed place at that time and place. This facility was noted for rendering excellent care. I made a tentative reservation and gave them a deposit. When faced with the nightmare of my beloved Mary spending her next ten to fifteen years in an institution, it was almost more than I could bear. The light had gone out of my life, and I felt engulfed in darkness.

Several weeks later, the miracles of miracles happened when I came for my regular biweekly visit to see her. Low and behold, she recognized me. She remembered that I had been to see her the previous Sunday. I asked an excellent Neurologist to see her for another opinion as all the other physicians had been so negative. He gave her a detailed physical examination and reviewed her multitude of tests. He told me, "She is recovering from some type of encephalitis and should be alright soon". Talk about the family prayers being answered? It was several months before I had both the nerve and the courage enough to bring myself to cancel the nursing home reservation and receive my deposit back. I breathed a great sigh of relief. The thoughts of having my beloved Mary in a nursing home for years just about did me in. She was, has been, and always will be the source of my happiness, the light of my life, and provide my zest for living.

Chapter 70

Within a short space of time and after we had moved into the new offices on 40th and Dewey, the apartment on the East end of the building next to my office suite became empty. I lobbied my partners to let me expand into this space. They gave their approval. The area was remodeled into two additional Exam Rooms which were across the hall from my original two rooms. This space gave me the ability to see my scheduled patients while my nurse practitioner was seeing some of my newborns and infants in my original work area. Her rooms had sliding doors on each side of the rooms so that I had easy access to check her work, to do a cursory check of the infant, and to personally visit with the parents with ease.

The former living room was quite large with an artificial fireplace where I installed an electric log for atmosphere. My large desk was "U" shaped with a large credenza piece occupying the far side of the desk. Now, there was plenty of room to spread out work so that I could address several projects at the same time sandwiched between patient visits and/or phone calls. When the new telephone system was installed, each physician office had a speaker phone. My speaker phone was utilized considerably as I could work at something and talk with a patient at the same time. Keep in mind that I could do multiple tasks easily and simultaneously.

The remainder of the living room space was converted into my family counseling area. The room walls were covered with a wood paneling which had a restful moss green hue to it. This wood addition removed the stark and sterile atmosphere present in so many medical settings. There were four comfortable chairs grouped around a black slate top coffee table. When tense and anxious parents would come into the room, you could almost see and feel them relax and be at ease because of the room's ambiance.

This area had many tears and anxieties dispelled in it. Just the atmosphere of this room alone became a real counseling asset for me. With this office and the four examining rooms, I was the envy of my partners. I felt as though I was in fat city! It was pure joy to go to work as I could see my patients much easier, more completely, faster, and hopefully better.

As the reputation of the practice grew, there began to be visiting physicians coming from elsewhere to study our operations. The Chairman of the Department of Pediatrics and Adolescent Medicine of the University of Helsinki, Finland was in the States and came and remained several days observing our methods. I received an invitation from him to give several presentations at his school in Finland, but could not find a way or the time to go that far away and stay away so long. I did not want to be away from my family, especially, my beloved Mary as I had not yet recovered from my intense scare about her health. I had a similar invitation to go to South America, but it was not feasible for me to do so.

In 1977, I was promoted to be a full Professor of Pediatrics at the University of Nebraska College of Medicine. I held this position from 1977 until 1988 when I retired from practice; then I became a Senior Consultant to the Pediatric Department. The old academician's looking down upon those of us in private practice was still alive and active. Surprising to their knowledge, it was my taxes that helped pay their salaries.

In April 1978, representatives of the freshman class of medical students asked me to give them a course on Medical Economics for "NO" credit hours. It would be a voluntary course with no accountability and no exams. I developed a rounded curriculum and included Dr. Roger Mason, who was the current Medical Director and Vice-President of the Nebraska Blue Cross-Blue Shield Company. I did consultative work for him when he was in practice in McCook, Nebraska. He spoke about the coming impact of insurance on the practice of medicine. Over time, I had served on several different committees in various medical organizations dealing with insurance and management in medicine.

This course was well received. Almost the entire class attended this voluntary venture. They liked the material so well that the class petitioned the Med School Curriculum Committee to make this course become a permanent part of the class load with a one hour credit. Instead of agreeing, the Committee would not allow the course to be given the next year even on a volunteer no credit basis. Great Heavens! Could Doctors possibly be talking about money, never could this disgraceful conversation be allowed to happen in this medical school! How gross an idea was this proposal!

The **real** world of medical practice and overhead factors was a big fat "No No" to most academic people. Most academicians did not have the slightest clue as to what constituted medical cost factors and could care less. Obviously, costs and cost factors comprised an unknown foreign language for them to consider. This decision ended my excursion into the world of preparing students on how to become real live doctors, who had to meet payrolls, and how to manage to control office overhead.

Unfortunately soon, these students would have to go out into the real world, earn a living, and control practice costs without any preparation. Was it any wonder that so many medical offices were run on such an inefficient basis? I am certain that this lack of preparation of physicians added to the escalating costs of medical care.

From my past experiences with the Med Center, this attitude about practice and income was not unexpected. Too Bad! This was both the Med Center's and the student's loss. Once again, the Med Center could have been a pioneer in this area and could have broken new important ground in behalf of the students. It is very difficult to change archaic and obsolete thoughts which are so ingrained in tradition and protocol and granite-like thinking heads.

Chapter 71

Dr. Glow performed an Exchange Transfusion for Dr. B. on a severe rH Problem and had to perform a re-exchange in about eight hours. The infant did well but was complicated by deafness as an aftermath problem. This was always a potential complication. Dr. Glow was sued based upon the fact that the re-exchange transfusion should have been accomplished within four hours instead of eight. This outlandish assumption was very much in error, but so was this assumption to be used as a basis for an unjustifiable malpractice suit. This case dragged in and out of the courts for seven years. It would be scheduled; and just a few days before the trial, the trial would be abruptly cancelled. Apparently, these actions were standard legal delaying tactics by prosecutors to wear out the defendant in order to force the defendant to throw in the sponge and give up.

    Dr. Glow became very upset from the time and time again of needing to be ready to face the court and, then, have it cancelled just at the last minute. After the last cancellation, he came to me and said,"I can't even write a prescription any more. I am going to quit our medical practice and do something else".

    Unfortunately at Childrens' Medical Staff's request, I, previously, had written the job description for the position of Medical Director for the Medical Staff of Childrens' Hospital. What a bummer for me was his decision to leave, and what a blessing for Childrens' Hospital as he fit this job description to a tee. He was offered this position, accepted it, and helped guide the Hospital through the ideas, the details and the trials of a move from Forty-fourth and Dewey west to Eighty-fourth and Dodge Road. Childrens' leased four floors of space in the new tower which Methodist Hospital had recently constructed. In spite of the close relationship with Methodist Hospital, Childrens' was able to keep its own identity and independence with a great deal of thanks due to the efforts and leadership of Dr. Glow.

It was obvious that with the process of Childrens' moving West and because our office was the last Pediatric Office located East of Seventy-second Street, we would have to move the office in order to stay close to most of our patients. We began the process of looking for a location for the office. Finding the new location site was aided by Jennie Ujdur, Mary's third sister. She just happened to drive past this building site and thought we might be interested in this area. This location suited us to a tee.

The move was an arduous task and an extremely important one due to its specific impact upon the practice per Se. The times were changing and along with the times, patient attitudes were changing towards doctors. The intense patient loyalty to his/her own personal physician was beginning to wane. In many instances, the pediatric office had become a mere stop between the parent's work place and the grocery store, beauty shop, and/or pharmacy.

Just before I retired, not infrequently a new patient's family would come into the office with an attitude of having a "Chip on their Shoulder". These folks seemed to feel that they were about to be exploited by the medical profession and by the doctors in particular. The people conveyed the feeling that they were at this office against their will and/or desires. This situation was a far cry from the close relationships in my earlier days in practice. I found this new attitude hard to accept and swallow.

Chapter 72

Up until this point in time, the various medical societies' meetings were a gathering of individuals with a common interest where scientific information could be exchanged and fellowship enjoyed. This was primarily true both locally and nationally. Economics and pushes by many different external forces to hold doctors more accountable for their decisions became the major change and the norm. There was a concerted national endeavor to force physicians to keep current in medical knowledge. This demand was echoed by many facets of society. I wondered how many physicians failed to keep abreast of the ongoing medical changes that were occurring around them. My going to various medical meetings would contest this false assumption by the attendance figures. This push was creating a force which was putting pressure on physicians nationally for creating a recertification process. The specter of the need for recertification in one's specialty came over the horizon like a hurricane enhanced by mandates from the American Boards of Medical Specialties. This group of examiners could smell the power and the money re-examination would produce under the guise of improving the health care of the public.

    I was totally against all of the premises that were put forth trying to justify this intrusion into my medical life. Several years before, I had opposed the Academy's thoughts and interest concerning joining this movement. I felt that one encounter with this group of examiners was more than enough for a lifetime. Nevertheless, the drum beat went on and in a few years recertification became a reality or nightmare depending upon your viewpoint. It did entail considerable costs and physician learning time, which is money out of pocket, to achieve the necessary background information for the new examinations. Unfortunately, some of this new and costly data would never be needed or used in a particular type of practice. Every medical practice was a bit different and the patient population seen was different. What one doctor needed to know could be a complete waste of time and money for another one in a similar but entirely different practice? This variation was due to types of medical entities which were encountered.

In self defense of this recertification concept, the local pediatric societies began to worry and were concerned that the American Academy was top heavy with too many Academicians. This situation was to the disadvantage of we, peons, out in the real working medical world. There began in California a movement to counteract the influence and role of being governed by the top heavy AAP Board with academicians. Various state pediatric societies joined in this effort by linking up with the newly created American Association of Pediatric Societies. In the beginning, this new society was a "Grass Roots" based endeavor and was rapidly gaining steam and interest by participants in many different states.

Meanwhile, I served on several different Committees for the Omaha Medical Society and the Nebraska Medical Society. None of these societies were in favor of this type of trend at this time.

The Nebraska Pediatric Society was a very weak and tenuous affiliate of the Academy. We went our own way and only sent a token delegate to represent Nebraska at the Academy level. Dr. Don Blim of Kansas City, who was the AAP Alternate District VI Chairman and was destined to become the future President of the Academy, came to Omaha to discuss the alternatives and choices that were available for our Society. He pressed for a more vigorous local Academy State Chapter to influence the Academy from within. Hobart Wallace and Ken Fijan of Lincoln, Warren Bosley of Grand Island, and I bought into this idea.

The four of us set about to accomplish this task of rejuvenation of the Nebraska Academy Chapter. Hobart became the first Nebraska Chapter Chairman from 1970 to 1972, and Ken Fijan was the Alternate Chairman. These two men helped to actively start this rejuvenation process. At this time, I chaired the Chapter's Committee on Youth and, simultaneously, the Committee on Medical Practice Activities.

As Chapter activities and actions began to happen, Interest by the near dormant membership began to increase and grow within the confines of the Nebraska Chapter. This interest enabled the Chapter to become an active, participating AAP member. Ultimately, the Nebraska Pediatric Society per Se was discontinued in favor of the AAP Chapter affiliation.

Ken Fijan became the Chapter Chairman from 1974 to 1976, and I was elected to be the Alternate Chapter Chairman. Every year in conjunction with the annual fall Meeting of the Academy, there was a one sided briefing by the Academy's Board of Directors, who would speak down to the level of the various State Chapter Chairmen. The Board told the Chairmen what the Academy was doing for and to the membership without any direct or indirect input from the grass root peon forces. A serious pugnacious attitude had been developing within the grass roots membership within the various AAP State Chapters. This talking down to the academy membership did not go over very well anymore and antagonism was rapidly increasing. This action really rubbed salt into some open and raw wounds

I endeavored to attend this briefing by the Board as the Alternate Chapter Chairman. I was bluntly told that I was not invited and not welcome. Needless to say, this cavalier attitude really irritated me and stuck in my craw like a huge lump of coal. This feeling lasted for a long, long time. My day in court was yet to come.

From 1976 to 1979, I was the Nebraska Chapter Chairman. By now our Chapter was up, running, and firing on all cylinders. The Academy charged each Chapter to develop a Health Plan for the children and youth of their respective states. Meanwhile, with the push and influence of Don Blim, I had been appointed to the Academy's National Committee on Child Health Standards. This Committee set the parameters and tests concerning what should be accomplished at each Well Child visit. Up until this point, the Academy only considered, within its province, the infant and child up to the age of twelve and not any years beyond this age.

Along with another pediatrician, Birt Harvey, from Palo Alto, California, we lobbied long and hard within our Committee to extend the age bracket up to the age of college. This age was a lost group who received very little medical care except through student health services if in college. This place of care left a lot to be desired. Finally, we succeeded in convincing the Committee members of the value and need for this recommendation. The Committee began to develop Standards (Guidelines) for each Well Adolescent Visit from the age of 13 through 19. The Committee recommended the preventive health items which should be covered at each adolescent office visit.

About this time, many "Eagle Beagle" Lawyers began to sue the Academy for setting "The Standards of Child Health Care". These actions caused many related headaches for the Academy. The Academy went into a panic mode and changed the name of the Committee to the Committee on Child Health Guidelines. Prior to this point, Pediatricians had rarely been sued; now, it was becoming more commonplace and seemingly more in vogue in legal circles. Three of my partners had been sued for no just cause.

The Nebraska Chapter did a yeoman's job of collecting all types of data on the various aspects of the health of this States' children and youth. This data included immunization percentages, the plight of the migrant workers encompassing those who worked the sugar beet fields, and the transient workers with the traveling harvest combines.

A family of mine ran a harvesting crew that started in Texas in the spring, worked their way north, and ended in Canada. This owner did harvesting of crops twice a year to handle both the winter and the fall wheat crops. He gave me an insight into all types of almost impossible to obtain information on the problems, and situations which were encountered by the harvesting crews. Provisions for the workers' children's school availability while traveling north had to be pre-planned ahead of the harvesting progress as well as for emergency medical care for the workers. These needs had to arranged for along the various stops as the crews worked their way north.

Dr. Matilda McIntyre and I were appointed to the local "Health Planning Council of the Midlands" for Douglas County of Nebraska. This group was charged with making recommendations regarding different aspects of health care for the regional population. We met once per month and talked a lot. As expected, not many results appeared from this Council but words and more words. I cannot recall any concrete and positive results from this Planning Council.

Dr. McIntyre and I were on this Council to protect the needs and interests of children and youth. The data generated from this Council was of great usefulness in my coming project of developing the AAP State Health Plan for Infants, Children, and Adolescents. It was not of much realistic value for any other use. Not unexpectedly, there was way too much talk and very few accomplishments.

With all kinds of data from all types of sources, I set forth to organize and write the Nebraska Child and Youth Health Plan myself in order to complete this task within a reasonable time frame. The Nebraska Chapter approved the end results. This Plan was such a success that the Academy used it as a prototype for twenty-five other states. I was asked to come to Florida by Dr. Robert Grayson, the Florida Chapter Chairman, as a consultant for the Florida Plan.

Because of the success of the Nebraska Plan, the Nebraska Chapter won the "Best Small Chapter Award" given yearly by the Academy. This honor set into motion a series of events that changed the governance of the Academy forever.

The Academy has three functioning divisions:

1. The Division of Membership - The membership was divided into nine Districts with several State Chapters in each District and a total about twenty-five hundred pediatricians in each District.

2. The Division of Committees - there was twenty-one National Committees at this time which addressed different facets of children health needs such as immunization recommendations and the like..

3. The Division of Sections - Sections were groups of pediatricians with a common bond in a specific area of medical interest. At this time, there were twenty Sections dealing with different areas of pediatric specialties i.e. neonatology, allergy, and others.

The winners of the current Small Chapter and the Large Chapter Awards along with the winner of last year's large Chapter Award were charged with developing the format and agenda for the very dull annual Chapter Chairmen's Meeting where the Chapter Chairmen were briefed by the Board. This meeting always occurred in association with the

Academy's Fall Meeting. This agenda charge provided an opportunity for me to try and make some grass roots changes in the format of this one sided meeting.

This opportunity was especially germane at this time with the unrest within many of the State Chapters and the increasing interest in the American Association of Pediatric Societies. Chapter Chairmen and Alternate Chapter Chairman served a term of three years. I had not forgotten nor forgiven my rebuff to try and attend this meeting when I was the Alternate Chairman.

Having learned the importance of being well prepared and to be able to put forth a good offense and not just try to fight a rear guard action, I spent a considerable amount of time and thought on how to construct an aggressive strategy to make changes within the Academy decision making process. These changes needed to include grass roots input into this decision process. To me, the Chapter Chairmen's Meeting should be a participating Senate type of forum. This Senate would be able to give to the AAP Board of Directors input from the grass roots in order to aid in the Board's decision making. Dr. Bill Montgomery of Michigan, Dr. Bill Conklin of Texas, and I met with AAP President Saul Robinson of California and Vice President Ed Kendig of Virginia in Chicago at the Airport Hilton for a weekend in March. After the preliminary meaningless talk and nonsense was over, I explained my proposal regarding the needed changes in the Meeting format. A number of reasons were given by us as to why these changes were imperative with the current state of membership unrest. Drs. Montgomery and Conklin had accepted my proposal with enthusiasm. Well! Drs Robinson and Kendig looked upon this suggestion with great disfavor, distain, and as though we had grown two heads. To have the audacity to change the Academy's way of doing business was a big No No!

The three of us explained the coming hazards and danger to the Academy by the rapidly evolving American Association of Pediatric Societies. After awhile and with many heated remarks on both sides of this proposal, the AAP Officers began to see the light and reluctantly agreed to have a separate gathering away from the annual meeting. The Chapter Chairman and Alternate Chairman would comprise the active members of the Meeting/Forum. The Board members were to be invited to be guests along with some selected AAP staff personnel but would

"NOT" have an active role or any input unless specifically asked for some data. We would operate under Robert's Rules of Order with Dr. Warren Bosley of Grand Island, Nebraska as the Parliamentarian. He was very familiar with these rules from his close work with the Nebraska State Legislature. He would make any necessary parliamentary rulings. The Meeting would act as a Senate, not as a population based House of Representatives. This Senate approach avoided having the very large Chapters over whelm and dominate the smaller Chapters.

We left Chicago feeling good over our accomplishments. About three weeks later, it was leaked to me from an unknown source that there would be NO Meeting. I immediately got in touch with my fellow conspirators. We divided the many state Chapters into three groups. We called each Chapter Chairman personally and explained our proposed Meeting, the acceptance by the President and Vice President, and, now, a behind the scenes a secret unannounced reneging and cancellation of the meeting. We urged the Chairmen along with as many of their own members as possible to storm and flood the Academy Office in protest. The Chapters agreed with enthusiasm and set to work. As a result, the Academy office was swamped; and the Meeting went on as we had previously planned.

This Chapters' Meeting occurred a few weeks before the Annual Meeting outside of Chicago in a suburb and the expenses were paid by the Academy. By default, I was the Chairman of this first Chapter Chairmen's Forum in 1978 and, again, the following year, 1979. In 1980, I was asked to be a consultant to the Meeting's Planning Committee for the purpose of continuity of thought and purpose. The Planning Committee always gathered about six months prior to the actual Meeting to ensure a well planned operation.

A Resolution proposed by a specific State Chapter had to have detailed supportive information available to explain the resolution and why this action was needed. Off the cuff and strange whims were to be discouraged and would not be considered at the Forum. Each resolution was to be discussed in detail, and would be voted upon either yes or no. The enthusiasm and participation of the Chapter representatives was very apparent. Many finer details of the meeting's protocol, rules, and activities were negotiated with the various Chapters as items of importance were raised and solutions offered.

The evening before the Meeting was to begin; another critical snag and crisis reared its ugly head. Our nemesis said that there would be no voting on any subjects and/or proposals. Well! Everything really hit the fan this time! The three of us backed the two of them into a quiet corner and read them the riot act. If there was no vote, blood would be spilt upon the floor. Their negative decision would be told to the entire group with the recommendation from us that all the AAP Chapters join the American Association of Pediatric Societies forth with.

We held their feet to the fire and settled on making a nonbinding vote to indicate Chapter preferences. We felt the vote was necessary to aid the Board in making decisions based upon grass roots input. We realized that we should not try to tie the Board's decision making capabilities as that occurrence would be counterproductive. The Chapter Chairmen's Forum was a huge success and changed many aspects of the governance of the Academy forever more. The meeting has continued through to this past year with very few changes in the Forum format.

The various resolutions proposed and passed by the Forum were published in the Monthly AAP News along with the Board of Directors' ultimate decisions to ensure transparency of the actions taken. Dr. Montgomery passed away. Dr. Conklin and I were invited to be guest speakers as the twenty-fifth anniversary of the Forum. We were charged to review the manner and history in which the Forum had come into existence. The current members of the Forum were pleased and enlightened with our remarks. I have to admit that as an old war horse that there was a great sense of satisfaction talking to the Forum once more in fond memory of my distant rebuff. So there too! By nature, I am not vindictive! Ha!

As a member of the Committee of Child Health Guidelines and with the Committee's permission, I introduced to the Forum in 1978 the need to extend the recommended AAP Guidelines through the High School Years to include College. It was discussed in great detail but was not passed as a recommendation until the next year's 1979 Meeting. At last, the adolescents would receive their needed attention within the Academy and have their own medical home.

This Forum launched me into a very active role within the Academy. I was elected to be the Alternate Chairman for District VI for a three year period. In this role, I represented twenty-five hundred members in six states in the Midwest.

From 1979 through 1983, Drs. Wallace, Bosley, Fijan, and I were frequently called the "Nebraska Mafia" because of the many different aspects of the Academy in which we were involved. When it was time to be re-elected to the Alternate post, I was defeated by 25 votes. A person from a much larger state with many more pediatricians ran against me. This defeat was a blessing in disguise. The next step in the AAP ladder upward would almost make certain a position on the Academy's Board of Directors. This position would pose an impossible situation for me in private practice. This role would take about six weeks of working days each year for Academy business. There was no way that I could afford to be away from the office or my family for that much time. After awhile, my intense interest in the Academy began to wane. It seemed as though there were greener pastures and fields waiting to be explored and plowed. During these past years regarding Academy business, I had done my damnedest, vented my spleen on many occasions, and accomplished more than I ever thought possible.

Chapter 73

Home front activities were moving right along. My beloved Mary was back in good health. Our oldest son, By, graduated from UNMC, married, and served a general rotating internship in Kalamazoo, Michigan. He finished an Anesthesia Residency at the University of Washington with an extra year's training in pediatric anesthesia at the Hospital for Sick Children in Toronto, Canada and at the Seattle Childrens' Hospital. He joined a group of anesthesiologists in Eugene, Oregon at the tertiary care St Joseph Hospital. This hospital served as the referring hospital for Southwest Oregon area.

Terry looked at many different schools for a strong English Creative Writing Department. These schools included the Fels Institute, Northwestern University, Amherst, Williams College, Harvard, and Yale. At last, he decided upon Brown University in Providence, Rhode Island. After all this looking, his choice was a disaster for him as it was a completely unstructured learning environment. This environment left too many decisions to the discretion of the novice and inexperienced student. I missed the boat badly as Terry required a certain amount of organization and structure within which to operate and to become successful. After his third semester at Brown, I brought him home. He floundered around from one local college to another for several years earning many miscellaneous credit hours. For having a supposedly knowledgeable father with much experience in advising others, I had goofed very badly with Terry.

Finally, he graduated with a BA Degree in English and, subsequently, a Masters Degree in Creative Writing from the University of Nebraska at

Lincoln. He settled in Lincoln, published a number of books of poetry, managed a Writers Workshop every other week, and was engaged in several civic art endeavors within the city. He was doing very well at long last and after a very circuitous route to success. We were and are so proud of how he has developed himself.

Matt looked into engineering at the Drexel Institute, Leigh, Ball State, Notre Dame, and, at last, settled on Vanderbilt in Nashville, Tennessee. However, Nancy, his first and only love, was too far away. He returned home at the end of the first semester. Matt and Nancy had met at their very first school dance as freshmen and never dated another person. They were married when Matt turned 20 years old. They helped each other complete school by alternating one person going to school full time and working part time. The reversal would occur with other one going to school full time while working part time. Nancy earned an Elementary Teaching Degree with a secondary major in Special Education. Subsequently, Nancy acquired a Master's Degree in School Administration. Nancy was hired by the Omaha Public School System and worked with children having hearing difficulties and visually handicapped young people. Nancy was certified in the Braille Method of reading.

Ultimately, Matt received a degree with a major in Math and a minor in Sociology. He taught both subjects at Papillion High School and assisted in the school's wrestling program. Matt belonged to a four person music group which played for receptions, dances, and the Belle of Brownsville Missouri River Dinner Excursion Boat. Initially, he played the keyboard, which he carried over from his piano lesson days, and the guitar. To satisfy requests for a "Big Band Sound", Matt bought a used saxophone and taught himself to play this instrument. In a like manner, the need for Polka Music encouraged him to obtain a used accordion. Matt was a very gifted and versatile musician. He still enjoys jamming with friends; though he has long since retired from the band.

Matt and Nancy's first child was a sweet little boy. My beloved Mary lobbied for a starter house for them. I never could refuse any of my Mary's requests. We found one near Elmwod Park and not too far from the University of Nebraska at Omaha. Matt handled the mortgage details and house closing details like a veteran. All I did was to stay quiet and co-sign the papers as he was still just twenty. They lived in this home for several years before moving to a bigger place.

As frequently happens in many families, Grandma Mary helped raise young Matty as both parents needed to work. She helped out for three years until Nancy's many brothers and sisters took over the job. Mary and Matty have had a very special relationship all these years even though he now is in his thirties and has two children of his own.

Mary and I had several different groups of special friends:

1. Our "Deer Club" friends, who were described in the 1960 decade, were still active.

2. We had a social group of people with whom we attended the Omaha Community Playhouse, the Pops Symphony Orchestra, and the Soiree Dance Club. We would go to dinner as a group before each activity. Mary and I loved to dance and were very graceful on the floor. Dancing was our favorite past time.

3. We continued to do many different activities with our dear friends, the Harvey Family.

4. We began to go on cruises with Mary's sister, Josephine, and her husband, Bob Arfmann, Leon Arfmann, Bob's brother and his wife Vonda, and Mary's Cousin, Pat Mulvihill and his wife Marg.

    4.1. Our first cruise was "The Song of Norway" which carried about 800 passengers. From sailing on different vessels, we concluded that we enjoyed the smaller vessels not those with two thousand or more passengers. Over the years, we visited most of the Caribbean Islands. My favorite was Antigua with English Harbor where Captain Horatio Nelson was stationed during the Revolutionary War. He was my sailing hero. He was the architect of the British victory over the French Napoleon Naval Fleet at the battle of Trafalgar which was critical for sea control during the Napoleonic Wars. He died during this engagement.

    We went through this vessel when we toured southern England later on in our travels.

4.2. St. Marteen and Barbados were our other favorite islands.

4.3. The Island of Guadalupe was the least friendly from our stand point. This Island was not a very desirable place for us to want to revisit.

Naturally, I signed up for some obvious tourist traps. This discomfort occurred during several different travels to result in everyone's amusement but mine. Will I never learn? These advertised trips did not have the outcomes that were portrayed to be seen or encountered.

When we were at Puerto Rico, I took a trip to the Rain Forest. No one wanted to join me. Well, the tour bus wandered around and around for a long, long time. The bus came to a spot in the forest which had a lookout tower that looked over some more trees; there was nearby, a very small waterfall. Those two gems were the extent of the rain forest excursion. The tour headed back to town. What a rip off. I still get teased about this excursion.

Mary and I flew to St. Croix for another vacation. I was anxious to visit the Underwater National Park near Buck's Island which had been written up glowingly in the National Geographic Magazine. Bah! This trip was another bust! The trouble with this adventure was that the advertised underwater trail was less than a block long; and the tropical fish near the reef were few and far between. What a big disappointment this looked for event turned out to be. Over time, Mary and I enjoyed eight different cruises alone or with our group. We thoroughly enjoyed the ease and convenience of a cruise.

The group decided to try the newly refurbished "El de France" which was renamed the "SS Norway". It stopped at St. Thomas and at a company owned island for a big beach party. These were only two stops. It was a large vessel with two thousand plus passengers.

Bob Arfmann and I took snorkeling lessons aboard ship. When we landed on the island, Bob could not enjoy snorkeling as his nose was rather prominent and would not accommodate to his issued face mask. Oh, how we laughed. I still tease him about that occasion. On factious occasions, I called him "Eagle Beak" as he reminded me of having the great eagle bird of prey's beak, which was used for tearing food.

I was and am an avid reader of many different types of books as a side hobby. Many of the subjects I enjoyed were western novels, historical books, sailing stories, medieval novels, a few mysteries, romance, and action/intrigue stories. As a result, these cruises were filled with many interesting attractions for me to visit due to the settings in my extensive readings. Still today, I enjoy reading very much. In the year 2009 by the Library List count, I read two hundred and sixty books and am on schedule for one hundred and ninety in 2010. The overwhelming volume of reading that medical schools required made speed reading a virtual necessity. I usually read afternoons and early evenings.

Chapter 74

It is about time to include in this story a few meaningful patient anecdotes that come to mind after all these years. Mrs. K. was a lovely mother. I was privileged to be their family pediatrician. Her young son fell down an open freight elevator shaft at a local furniture store. He died from a massive skull fracture and brain trauma. We were sitting in the doctor's lounge in the first Childrens' Hospital talking. She turned to me and said, "Dr. Oberst, I am just an uneducated person; you are going to have to tell me what I should do". Never have I felt so inadequate or at a loss for words.

The L. family had three brilliant children-two girls and a boy. They had attended the Teen Talks. One of the daughters was the Class Valedictorian. Sometime later, I heard that she had included in her address to the class; "Students, it is important that above all, you should Know Thyself". I almost cried as that concept was one of the central themes of my Teen Talks. Somewhere, somehow a message penetrated and registered with someone.

On another occasion, I received a phone call from a male student at Northwestern University in Chicago. He said, "Doctor Oberst, I think that I am going to die. I went to Student Health, and they didn't help me". Well, he had an acute gastroenteritis with vomiting and diarrhea. With a few simple suggestions, he recovered without any complications. Once again, I was a short term hero to him.

My Nancy Glow's home sickness comes to mind every so often. She so missed the noise, confusion, and activities of her seven siblings. There was always something going on or someone dropping in her home. Don

Glow bought his meat by the side of beef and had it processed. Most of it went into hamburger meat as Joanne was a creative wife and had at least a "thousand recipes" for hamburger based dinners. They never knew when one of their children would invite a friend to stay for supper. With a hamburger dish and another mouth to feed, it never created a problem in making the food stretch as far as needed.

There was a seventeen year old girl referred from a nearby town in Iowa with Meningococcus Meningitis. She recovered nicely, went home, and returned in about two weeks with convulsions. She had a small brain abscess which was the cause of the seizures. Subsequently, she needed to be on a continuous anticonvulsive regime. She returned for follow up visits regularly. She started to a local practical nursing school, became pregnant, got married, and continued to see me. Her husband and child would come in the office with her during the visits. We had a great relationship. At the age of 30, it was time for her to be followed by a neurologist and arrangements were made. We had some tears when parting because of so many pitfalls and special moments that we had shared. My medical life was filled with many such tender moments.

As a front line pediatrician, who had dealt with many grave medical situations, and, sometimes, unexplainable recoveries, I am convinced beyond a shadow of a doubt that there is no place in medicine for atheists. There must be a Higher Power than we mere mortals. I always felt that I was just an instrument to help people cope with their medical problems.

Chapter 75

My photography interests took a turn. I realized that I would never become a Master Photographer. I had joined the Omaha Camera Club to increase my skills, especially, on picture composition. My many different lectures and seminars dictated from a cost standpoint that I make my own slides for these lectures. I had a copy lens, and I bought a copy stand. There was a great medical artist at Clarkson Hospital who could take any of my ideas and convert them into eye appealing cartoons illustrating the points that I wished to convey. I imposed upon her many times. She helped to make my medical talks imaginative and amusing for my various Practice Management Lectures. Over time, I had about 50 prepared slide talks ensconced in projector carousels from which I could pull together a lecture on almost any medical subject that was needed to be given by me.

I had purchased upon our different cruises to the Virgin Islands most of my camera equipment because it was so inexpensive in St Thomas and St Croix. After the advent of the discount stores in the States, there was no longer any major savings in the islands. I had two Nikon Bodies. One Nikon had a regular lens; the other body had a zoom lens. I acquired a copy lens, a wide angle lens, and a 400 mm long distance lens. I had a full complement of filters plus large and small tripods. When we were traveling, my family enjoyed making fun of me. I would have one camera loaded with a regular lens, one with the zoom lens, plus my video camera. I looked like the typical tourist; and I was.

I made a video studio in the basement where the boys' gym had been previously housed. This area had a neutral paper backdrop for the pictures' background. I made several teaching videos on School Learning Problems and related subject material for use by teachers and in my office. This creative activity required that a script had to be developed; and, at times, background music had to be selected and added. This was an interesting but short lived endeavor. The process took too much time for me as I had too many other fish to fry and irons to heat in the fire.

When my family traveled, both my cameras and my video camera would let me document our sights and sounds very well. I accumulated hundreds of slides over the years starting with Japan. Just a few years ago, I put together on four CD's about nineteen hundred slides with captions relating to our ongoing family life for my immediate family. There were many activities recorded with our three sons and three grandsons. These CD's were complete with the associated romantic mood music that Mary and I had enjoyed and loved over the years. I had a set made for each son and grandchild.

At By's request concerning the Oberst family tree, I wrote the story of the Oberst Family which covered about the first seventy years of our life. The story was entitled "The Oberst Saga". It was professionally bound and given to each member of the family and a few selected friends.

Chapter 76

I was still very active in the Society for Computer Medicine and was a member of the Board of Directors from 1976 to 1977 and as Chairman of the Committee on Standards from 1980 to 1982. I presented a paper on "Methods of a Health Care Audit in Private Practice" for the Society of Computer Medicine at the New Orleans, Louisiana Meeting in 1974. There was a workshop on Medical Records and Related Data at the Annual Meeting in Boston in 1976 where I presented several papers on different aspects of a longitudinal lifetime medical record.

There were many wonderful bright minds in this Society. One of the brightest lights was a Dr. Don Lindberg, who had just been made the Director of the National Library of Medicine. He opened the doors and let in fresh air, and guided the Library into a useful, functioning entity for the physician in the field as well as for the researcher. He was responsible for the Library to "Go online" and become readily available for anyone who wished to use it without any fees or costs. This free use of both medical textbooks and medical articles was a magnificent feat and greatly aided all aspects of the population and researchers, in particular, in many ways.

As an offshoot from my involvement in the Society for Computer Medicine, I was asked to join the Medical Board of Advisors to PHYCOM {Physicians Communication Company). There were eight of us including my friends, Marion Ball PhD and Phil Manning M.D. Except for me; the other members were noted experts in their various fields. I was there as a representative of the system to be used by private practitioners, and for ways to utilize office statistics in practice management. This endeavor was to provide to the practicing physicians a means of communication with other doctors via the rudimentary E-mail System, have access to the National Library of Medicine, and have available a drug-drug interaction/reaction resource. It was free to the physicians and was funded through advertising. The parent company was the "Readers Digest" Division of the Fisher-Stevens Company. Subsequently, this computer endeavor experienced several different changes in ownership. The various owners moved this endeavor from PHYCOM to Physicians-on-Line to WebMD. Finally, the original PHYCOM was purchased, inactivated, and placed upon a shelf and never was seen again.

This group of PHYCOM advisors had meetings about every six months. We met at Lake Tahoe, Hilton Head Island, and Tucson, Arizona. Our expenses were paid by the company. Our spouses were invited to come as guests of the company. This new innovation was sold into oblivion to a competitor just as it was becoming popular and useful to the practicing physician. From my standpoint, this was a new language and modus operandi to learn and absorb. It provided me with a major insight into big business operations.

Chapter 77

Going back to the American Academy of Pediatrics activities, I was elected to the position of Alternate District VI Chairman, from 1979 to 1983. There were nine Alternate District Chairmen in the Academy. Each of us related to one of the nine Academy Districts. We, collectively, lobbied for an increased role within the Academy's various thrusts and influences, rather than just being an onlooker without a portfolio.

The past role of this office was very similar to the few duties of the US Vice President had to handle. As a result with this new role we acquired, it made me a participant in many different Academy activities and interests such as being:

1. A member of the National Committee on Practice and Ambulatory Medicine 1979 to 1980, which the Academy finally saw the light and established to address the members management needs.

2. A member of the National Committee on Legislative Issues 1979 to 1980 where we would meet in Washington D.C. every six months with appointments to visit with the staff of selected Congressional and Senate Offices to lobby for the needs of children.

    2.1. The Academy's position was that whatever benefited children would be good for the pediatrician. It did not push for benefits for the pediatrician per Se. It was astounding to me how young the various Congressional staffers were. These young people did the research and interviews to acquire information for the Congressional member. These folks had a great deal of influence upon the particular Congress person's legislative thoughts and actions.

2.2. We seldom visited directly with the Senator or Congress person, but talked with the staff person in charge of pending health legislation.

2.3. This role was a major lesson in civics on how our government works. Obviously, the congressional person was subject to the bias of his/her staff's input.

3. There was a Panel on the little desired possibility, but the inevitability, of the ugly presence of the mandatory Recertification process. My voice was raised in strong opposition against this very intrusive animal into my medical practice confines. I neither desired nor wanted this recertification beast to become a reality. I had my own well rounded Continuing Medical Education Program which met my needs and then some. However, over time I lost both many battles and this War.

4. The Committee on Child and Adolescent Health Guidelines had a Workshop on Patient Education at the annual Meeting in Chicago 1976.

5. There was a Continuing Medical Education Course at Monterey, California at which I was asked to give presentations on the following practice management subjects:

    5.1. Office Management- The effective Use of Time

    5.2. Management Planning and Techniques for Quality Control

    5.3. Cost Accounting, Budgets, and Overhead Components

    5.4. A General Workshop on Office Management

6. When I was on the Committee for Medical Education, the objective was to evaluate the various meeting host cities and convention facilities where a Meeting might be held. In another role of this Committee, a member would

monitor a Continuing Medical Education Course as to the content and competency of the speakers. We would report back our impressions to the entire Committee about these presentations. I had a really very difficult assignment from this Committee when there was a trip to Puerto Rico for me to monitor a course. What a penance this trip imposed on me, ha?

7. When I was a member of the Committee for Scientific Meetings, the objective of this Committee was to evaluate the contents and competence of the speakers who presented half day "Round Tables" to the Academy members. The Committee would meet for breakfast each morning at 7:00 AM and receive assignments for the day as to who and what we would be monitoring and evaluating. The work of both of these Committees was very revealing and important. We would meet the next morning and report our impressions to the group as a whole. We would give our opinion as to whether or not the speaker should be invited back for a future meeting. If any Academy member was going to spend his/her money to attend a "Round Table", it was an important responsibility of the Academy to be sure that the member would receive his/her money's worth for the time, money, and effort spent.

8. Dr. Warren Bosley from Grand Island, Nebraska and I had a fascinating week at Williamsburg, Virginia, We were part of an AAP Task Force to study and make recommendations on "The Privacy of the Adolescent Medical Record". This Task Force was an interesting mixture of individuals and professions. There were lawyers, social workers, nurses, ethicists, and we, two, pediatricians. We were assembled for this important task as it related to the Academy's fledgling interests in this age period.

    8.1 We were divided into different discussion groups to review the ramifications of a particular topic or subject of need; then, we gathered together to report on the results of the discussions to the other groups as a whole. There was a different mixture of people in each group in both the morning and afternoon sessions. There were essential selected topics pertaining to the subject matter to be addressed. It was a fascinating week of discussions with many different venues to explore. I learned that the lawyers thought and came to conclusions in a manner far far different from the rest of us poor mortals. The lawyers always looked for the exceptions to the norm while the rest of us would strive for a consensus of thought. This inherent difference was both very revealing and eye opening. The many different discussions were edited, collated, and published as a report under the auspices of the Academy. This report became the norm and standard for the Academy on this subject.

We had fairly long lunch hours during this week so Dr. Bosley and I would take the bus to the Village Museum. We wandered around through the various historic buildings and exhibits enjoying the history that was portrayed by the museum. The week went by much too fast. The many aspects and results of the task Force were both revealing and enlightening.

Dr. Kenneth Fijan of Lincoln and his wife, Mary, attended many of the same Academy Meetings that my Mary and I did. We became well acquainted and very good friends. We would frequently dine together. There were several social and entertainment meeting functions that we attended together. When in New York City, we attended several Broad Way Musicals. The two Mary's would take different AAP Family Tours which were offered in the different meetings' cities. Occasionally, Ken and I could break away from our assignment, play hooky, and join them. I made it a meeting custom to take my beloved Mary to a fancy posh type restaurant at least once during the time when we traveled to the meetings. She was so patient at finding and doing something else to be occupied with while I was busy attending to Academy business.

I endeavored to broaden the horizons of my boys by taking each one to an Academy meeting. I took By to the Academy Meeting in New York City. He was well received by my colleagues. For insight into fancy places to eat and how to act, I would take each son out for special meals in noted restaurants. In this manner, they would know how to handle themselves when in social company. I took By to lunch at the "Four Seasons" and to dinner at the "Forum of the Twelve Caesars".

Terry went to the spring meeting in Denver where he helped me with my Round Table on "Guided Growth". We ate in an old fashioned bank made out of red bricks which had been converted into a fancy restaurant, which was near the Brown Palace Hotel. Having one of the boys with me alone was most enjoyable.

Terry was always a big tease and had a great sense of humor. When in Chicago and passing a toupee shop, he slyly suggested that I go in and price a "Tailor Topper". What a lack of respect! What nerve! Later on, I carefully planned my revenge, and it came to pass.

Chapter 78

One day, I received a fascinating phone call from Dr. Phil R. Manning, the Dean of the University Of Southern California School Of Continuing Medical Education. It was one of the outstanding schools for this purpose in the country. He invited me to spend a weekend at the five stars "Del Coronado" Resort Hotel in San Diego, California with a group of folks from his school's library staff personnel, and a group from the Rand Think Tank Organization.

I was flabbergasted to say the least and quickly arranged to go to this meeting. This weekend was one of the most exciting and stimulating encounters that I ever had. I felt like a fish out of water as the other people were very bright and technically very knowledgeable concerning continuing education and computer use in medicine. My role, as I later learned, was to keep the conversations in a practical manner for utilization of this generated material in a doctor's practice. Because I had so many different types of office statistics, a major part of the thrust of this meeting was to determine, " How could a physician utilize his office patient data to design his/her own personalized Continuing Educational Program (Textbook) based upon what cases were seen in his/her office".

For example, a doctor might think that he/she had a big group of diabetic patients and would spend a considerable amount of time at different meetings attending diabetic sessions. When, instead of seeing many diabetics, he/she was really seeing a few diabetics many, many times. The time in attending an excessive number of diabetic sessions would be better spent learning some new ideas on other medical entities which he might encounter in the office.

For awhile, I felt like an idiot because the group kept talking about Boolean Searches and Concepts. I had never heard this term before and had no idea what kind of an animal it was. Finally, in desperation, I asked what they were talking about and please speak in the King's English so I could understand what was being said. At last, I learned that it was a fancy method to do internet database research in a broad or narrow manner by the construction of the "Either/ Or Commands" and similar type of logic commands to extract data from different reservoirs of information. Woe is me! Now, I know what Boolean concepts are and how they are applied. When the weekend was over, there were so many ideas spinning around in my head that it was hard for my mind to settle down and to concentrate on one idea at a time. The possibilities of applications generated from this meeting really boggled my mind. More information will be forthcoming on this weekend later on in this story.

Chapter 79

Meanwhile back at the Omaha office, I managed to publish 17 articles in the 1970's on various computer applications to office management, and Preventive Care of Children subjects. My first book, "Practical Guidelines for General Pediatric and Adolescent Office Practice", was published in 1973.

The practice had survived the nightmare of a vicious misrepresentation and was busier than ever. Dr. Glow left our practice. Dr. Phil Itkin joined us. He had graduated from the Nebraska Med School with my son, By, and had taken a pediatric clerkship with me. He trained at Los Angeles Childrens' Hospital with a secondary fellowship in Adolescent Medicine.

As usual, the Med Center could never bypass an opportunity to cause headaches for Childrens' Hospital. For a long time, the residents from the Med Center came to Childrens' for part of their training. The mischief began subtlety when the residents decided they didn't want to take a rotation at Childrens' so they would not show up for duty. The University refused to take any action to correct this travesty.

The Medical Staff at Childrens' decided to establish their own Residency program. We did all the paper work, and it was approved. I was delegated to contact Dr. Ted Pfundt, who had been Chairman of the Department at Creighton Medical School. He was well liked and had performed well at Creighton as Chairman of the Department. He was in Houston at this time working in a medical school clinic. He agreed to come to Childrens' and manage the new residency program.

Childrens' residency program went along well for a number of years. After a period of many years, the American Board of Pediatric Examiners demanded and stated that all residencies needed to be connected to a Medical School, had to have so many available beds for patients, and could no longer be a free standing program; thus, ended Childrens' residency program.

Deep in my Memory and Heart dwelled both Joy and Sadness:

> Dr. Charles A. Tompkins died during March 1970 from cancer of the bladder at the age of 65.
>
> Dr. John L. Gedgoud died on New Year's Eve 1979 from a massive heart attack at the age of 65.

I lost both of my dear mentors in the same year. I was devastated for a while until I recalled how much they had invested in me. I, always, felt that my professional attributes were an amalgamation of Drs. Tompkins, Gedgoud, and Johnston. My successes were due to their skill and guidance. It was noteworthy how they helped me to learn about the field of Pediatrics.

**Part VI to follow
The New Office
And
The 1980 Long Range Practice Plan**

Part VI

Our New Office and the New
Long Range Plan
The 1980's

Chapter 80

With Childrens' moving west, we began searching for a new location as most of our patients had moved and now lived much further west in Omaha. We found an ideal location on one hundred and twenty-eighth on Augusta Avenue near the Millard Suburb area where the population expansion had exploded. Mary's sister, Jennie, helped me to find the location. Once again, I was delegated to be the lead person for the office layout. In anticipation of the move, I put together another ten year long range plan.

New Office 12808
Augusta Avenue

Just as the building was completed and we moved in, the devastating "Carter Recession" began with many major problems ensuing for us before we were prepared to cope with the already many added expense headaches. Interest rates were in the eighteen percent range. Medical supply costs kept going up and up with each renewal order. Our collections went down into the basement. The bank did not want to advance us any additional funds for operating expenses. This added loan would have been in addition to the financial load we had relating to the moving costs. The old time doctors had always kept six months income in their safes during the depression years. We could have use some of that hoarded cash at this point in time.

We, doctors, paid all the bills; but went without any take home money for over three months. The times were very tight to say the least. To save money, we bought our own washer and dryer rather than using and paying for a laundry service. The office personnel took turns washing and folding the examining table sheets. All salaries were frozen. Times were very tight and tough for almost a year.

We continued to use a clean cloth sheet on the examining table after each patient rather than a paper cover. Nothing is messier than a wet paper sheet after an infant's voiding. Ugh!

Because we had an X-ray machine and extensive laboratory equipment, the government, both State and Federal, demanded tons and tons of paper work and forms to fill out. Fortunately, Dr. Ellison's sister, Joann, who was a knowledgeable certified X-ray Technician, was very versed in these regulatory areas. Dr. Ellison was delegated to work with the office decorator as his contribution to the change with our blessings. I felt the office design and construction was my contribution to the group.

This anticipated move required a new "Ten Year Long Range Plan" for the office containing new ideas and concepts; so, I put on my thinking cap and got to work researching and exploring thoughts and needs.

Paul Dutton had taught me about many budget items and advanced accounting practices. Previously, he had introduced me to Fixed Costs, Variable Costs, Overhead factors, and Cash Flow which helped me considerably to obtain a better understanding of the workings of our office. I was aware of some of these facets to a limited extent before but not to the extent of these new dimensions. We were able to control our overhead costs and keep them in the fifty-five percent range.

Now, it was time to do true cost accounting on the different aspects of the various office functions. Paul Dutton and I worked out a methodology where we could compare one type of office function to another. For example: It cost the office $6.50 to give an injection even if there was only water in the syringe. This amount needed to be added to the basic cost of the vaccine material, which in the early days the cost for a multiple dose DPT vial of ten cc was $10. Now in 1980 that same ten cc vial of DPT was $125. The government added another $5 to each shot for catastrophic insurance coverage. We used to give this same injection for $5 in 1951. Now, the DPT was a $6.50 basic cost + $12.50 for the vaccine + $5 Insurance = $24; and, still, we have not made any profit. There was no allowance for any spilled, spoiled, or inadvertently discarded vaccine. Any of these situations would result in total lost revenue. When we charged $40 for this injection, some people thought we were gouging them. This was not a good PR situation as most immunizations were not covered by insurance at this time. If there was any waste so that ten injections did not come out equal from a ten cc vial, this wasted vaccine was a loss of income out of our pockets.

Using this methodology, we learned that it cost $11.00 for a patient to walk through the door even if only to leave a urine specimen. We were able to control and limit our overhead to fifty-five percent which by comparison to other offices was remarkable. Some practices had a seventy percent overhead. How gross! As I said before, my Internist, who works for a major hospital combine, had a sixty-nine percent overhead factor even with all the fancy financial personnel employed by the hospital. Why so much in overhead costs? This fact of such a percentage did not make any sense to me.

I did some time motion flow studies on the amount of time that was consumed looking for patients' charts. We would not speak to or examine a patient without his/her specific chart being available. This type of current chart documentation is critical in defending against any malpractice situation. We had been through that headache and heartache before with Drs. Gedgoud and Glow and their malpractice suits. I discovered that there were at least eight places where a Chart could go and hide, never to see the light of day. Needless to say, big changes were in order. We had previously color coded the file covers and had the first two initials of the last name attached to the file. This method was rather than using the older system of consecutive numbering of charts with a name index being utilized. This method was a much needed improvement over other systems that we had tried without much success.

During epidemic situations, the constant ringing of the phone was a real pain. When a time study was done, many days could average seven hundred calls. We needed to change the system completely and as soon as possible. We added lines so that each doctor had two lines so he/she could be talking to a patient on one line while the nurse dialed the next patient. This patient would be waiting for me to start listening to what their problem was. This change saved at least twenty-five minutes per day which was enough time to see two additional patients and increase office the revenue.

During the mornings, we had two nurses answering the phones and handling many of the routine details. This change relieved the receptionist of this task while she was trying to oversee and accomplish her myriad of other duties. The nurses could expedite the calls very easily whether advice was needed to be given to the caller or the patient was needed to be seen. These phone call changes made a nightmare situation livable. We tried to have the phone answered before it rang more than five times. We avoided using the hold button as much as possible.

Our Accountant established each doctor as a Cost Center for the handling of the financial aspects of generating income and disbursing payments. I needed to generate $150 per hour for counseling and consultative sessions; whereas, $100 per hour was satisfactory for regular office visits as there were other revenue items associated with the office visit. The patient load that our office had was still exceptional as compared with the standards of national pediatric offices. Once again, the usual population base for families was about fifteen hundred per physician. My colleagues carried three thousand families each, and I still had well over four thousand families. We saw and cared for a large segment of the Omaha and regional pediatric and adolescent population.

I did Time-Motion studies and determined that from the time a patient checked into the receptionist, moved to an examining room, and waited for the doctor to come in the room was twenty minutes of total time waiting and for twiddling of thumbs. Not too bad a wait by comparison with many other offices. Time is just as valuable to the patient/parent as it is to the physician and should be respected. To help my colleagues remember this, we had a practice rule that if a patient had to wait for more than thirty minutes without a good reason such as an emergency suture job, the professional part of the office visit was free. This simple axiom kept everyone on their toes and limited the endless visiting in the halls which disrupted the appointment schedules.

With my partners' permission, I visited with my old friend from fourth grade onward at Saratoga Grade School, Bill Shook, who was a very talented commercial artist. We discussed designing an Office Logo. He designed a wonderful Logo that depicted our patient population consisting of Infant, Children, Adolescent, and Young Adult Faces. We used this logo on all letter heads, blank prescriptions, and other office items. Bill had a large bronze copy of the logo made and mounted it on the front of the building. Our logo was well received and created many positive comments. We proceeded to have the design patented for protection purposes. In a like manner, we obtained "Copy Rights" on my office "Guided Growth Patient Education Program". We did not want to leave anything to chance as the legal climate had drastically changed and was not in a too favorable stance towards physicians. At least, based upon our past partners' legal experiences, this is the way we thought about lawyers.

As the Clarkson Computer System which we had been using until now had become inadequate and obsolete for our needs, once again my colleagues delegated me to research and locate an "In house" type of self contained (standalone) computer system for use in the office. This was an arduous task to endeavor to accomplish, required considerable thought, and included many detailed investigations of the available systems on the market. The availability of a useful system for our specific medical needs was found to be rather limited. However, such systems were slowly becoming more available and practical. Electronic medical records were still an intense desire of mine but were not close to becoming a reality. The real headache was where we can find such an animal that suited our need? The search began with the interviewing of the different vendors at the various medical and computer meetings I attended.

There was a system, which I saw at a Chicago meeting that had lots of bells and whistles and looked great at the initial demonstration. The developers were located in Boston and were very accommodating to us. We cussed and discussed the many attributes that this system possessed. It sounded worthwhile to me even though the company was a young one and did not have many systems in medical offices. Due to my hard headed negotiating, we agreed to a three month trial in our office with the company's help in training our personnel at no cost to us. As I implied, this was a rather fledgling company and did not have many systems to visualize in situ. We would be an "Alpha Site", meaning a semi-research location, with no commitments to keep the system unless we were satisfied. In turn, our office would help them design and modify the electronic medical record they were endeavoring to develop. Dr. Wax and I helped with this facet of the development of their electronic medical record. Initially, we were very enthusiastic about the system's potential possibilities.

The trainers and equipment came in with a glorious bang and filled with much enthusiasm. One of the Trainers must have been a true "Boston Blue Blood" as she could not find much about Omaha that she liked. We just tolerated her poor attitude and manners. It gradually became apparent to me that this system would not meet our total needs. The vendors kept pushing us to switch over the management books and accounting items completely onto their system. They wanted us to stop keeping duplicate records with saving time being the main reason why they pushed so hard. However, this action would lock in our office to their system with no retreat position available. We resisted this pressure to convert our system to their system entirely. Later I learned that vendors called this maneuver in the computer business relationships a "Puppy Dog" arrangement. I insisted that double books would be kept. Thank heavens we didn't buy their not so subtle system approach.

The inadequacy of this system became readily apparent to everyone when we tried to install and use the Appointment Scheduling feature. Well! Our receptionist could handle and make three appointments using our manual "Veri-Visible Scheduling System" in the same amount of time this system could manage to make one appointment. Intolerable! Back to Boston it went with no cost to us, and good riddance. The search went on and on.

Chapter 81

The basic room components of the new building were similar to our current building on 40th and Dewey Street. This time, we planned enough office space to accommodate five pediatricians and again used the race track layout. We wanted to develop a "Full Service Bank" concept of services for our patients for their convenience as well as for the generation of additional revenue. The location of the new office was near the Omaha suburb of Millard which was a very rapidly growing community.

The North side of the new building overlooked several fairways on a par three golf course. Having put the most effort into this project so far and claiming to have seniority, I declared the prerogative of picking my office first. My pick had a wonderful view of the green fairways during the summer and a most pleasant tranquil scene with the winter snows when looking across these same fairways. I could sit at my desk and muse and daydream looking out of a very large picture window. It was a great office, very comfortable, and almost like a home away from home. It made going to work a real pleasure. These digs were even more exquisite than our Dewey Avenue office.

We kept the individual room theme for all the examining rooms. Our patients gave us many, many compliments upon both the location and the décor. As I had learned from the adolescents, they didn't really desire their own waiting area; so it wasn't needed or planned. The usefulness for the large waiting room had changed to that needing a smaller size area. This fact was a foregone conclusion. The appeal of our lectures, which had been limited solely to our own practice population, was waning due to so much competition from the various hospital community teaching programs, Monday night football, and the intense competition for parents' time by other forces. These items and other reasons caused us to move the lecture location and enhance our lecture offerings to the general public at large.

The local hospitals had become our biggest competitors as they began to hire their own pediatricians and other specialists to work within the confines of their specific hospital's orbit. In self defense, we changed to community wide lecture offerings instead of limiting the lectures to our practice parents. We made arrangements to use the nearby public library as a lecture site and began to target the nearby local area population.

My practice had changed considerably. Newborns were a rarity. My fingers were not as supple as before; so my young colleagues did any suturing for me. Hospital patients were few and far between. There were no procedures to perform on hospital inpatients any more so income generation from hospital visits was almost a non entity except for a daily visit fee. Intensive Care Physicians and other hospital subspecialists assumed control of their areas in the hospital often to the dismay of those of us in private practice. Consequently, our office was the place where we generated most of our income. There were no other useful external sources of revenue available. It took a lot of dollar coated peanuts to fill up the income snack bowl.

If one of my patients needed hospitalization, one of my partners would assume the responsibilities, while in the hospital, for this case. I was responsible for the admission work and initial medical orders. All of these factors had to be accomplished prior to the patient's admission. My practice became totally office based which was far more convenient for me. This change was not much of an inconvenience to my patients, and generated very little loss in revenue.

As I neared sixty-five, I began to "toy" with the thoughts of retiring. This action was considered by me to be very unlikely to happen. This old seasoned war horse still wanted to continue to answer the fire bell. It was very apparent and discouraging to me that there was a decided greater change in new patients' attitude when they came into the practice. The parents almost seemed to have a chip on their shoulder and gave forth the impression that they felt that they were going to be taken advantage of by the doctors. Some of the pleasures of practicing medicine were going out the window.

There was another apparent attitudinal change, when we would interview young prospective doctors to join our group; they were more interested in how much money they would receive, how much time off would be available, and how few hours they would have to work. What a contrast from the earlier days in medicine? Where had patient loyalty and medical dedication gone? What happened to the Hippocratic Oath?

When I started practice there were twenty-one physicians before me practicing pediatric medicine in Omaha, now, in 2010 twenty-two years after my retirement, there are more than one hundred employed pediatricians among the various hospitals and medical conglomerates in Omaha. All of these pediatricians are owned and managed by someone or someplace. My old office and a single pediatrician in Bellevue, which is just south of Omaha, were not owned and did not owe allegiance to anyone but to themselves and to their patients. My! How times have changed. It shocked me the other day on a visit to my Internist. Why? I don't recall, but we began conversing, again, about office overhead and related matters. He told me that the institution he is affiliated still had a sixty-nine percent medical office overhead. I almost fell off my chair. "How could that be with all the fancy financial experts they have running their business", I asked? From his remarks, this type of overhead is common amongst most of these several big institutions in Omaha. Gross! "Something is not right in Denmark". There should have been a big improvement in controlling overhead after all these years.

We had our own designated and equipped Emergency room which doubled as a location for performing pelvic exams. We had a major laboratory with the capacity to do the usual and frequently needed tests; plus many additional chemistry tests that we were increasingly utilizing like aminophylline levels for asthma patients. The lab was managed by a certified level 1 Tech. There was a modern $50,000 X-ray setup with an excellent certified Technician, who was Dr. Ellison's sister. This equipment saved the patient time from chasing to other facilities for these tests and procedures. We had desired to make our office as convenient as possible for our patients.

We had a part time nutritionist and my educational psychologist on the staff; and, later, we added a Physician's Assistant.

We learned at our fortieth and Dewey Street location of the importance of having enough examining rooms. The new building called for three exam rooms plus an office for each physician. It was a necessity for good patient flow to have one exam room available for a patient to be undressing in one room, one room in which the physician was seeing the patient, and the third room in which the patient was getting dressed, receiving the "Guided Growth Educational Material", being given any necessary procedures for tests, immunizations, and the obtaining any other items that had been ordered. This arrangement helped to keep the patients flowing without any loss of time by the physician who might otherwise have to wait and twiddle his thumbs for a room to become available. Once again, there was the age old headache of valuable time being lost by physicians standing around in the halls visiting. Time is money. It needs to be used wisely and not squandered. It was a mighty ongoing and difficult task to instill this axiom amidst my younger colleagues.

There was in each area a bathroom and a hall sink. The sink was imperative so that the physician would wash his/her hands and the stethoscope between each patient being seen. Public perception required that the physician was conscious of the importance of cleanliness. We dressed in a professional way with shirt and tie, and wore a short uniform jacket that was changed each day to cover our clothing. We used blue jackets instead of long white coats so that children would be less apt to be frightened. This fact was critical for good public relations.

My three rooms had the following themes:

1. The Summer Room
2. The Winter Room
3. The Captain's Cabin which had a Sailing Motif

The parents liked to be directed to the rooms by the room name, and the patients enjoyed the different motifs. For some unknown reason, my favorite room was the Captain's Cabin. Pictures of my Snipe graced the walls.

Chapter 82

I received an investigative grant of $5,000 from the Academy to study Parent and Patient Education in the office. When the building was near completion, there was installed a TV Monitor in each of my examining rooms and a colored one in my main office. These TV sets were connected to a command video center which had the ability to play a videotape and to direct this program to the appropriate exam room or out to the waiting room if desired.

These TV's were extensively used and in many different situations, for example:

1. For the young Teen Girl who recently began having her periods, there was a demonstration film on the proper way to do a self breast exam.

2. For the older 17 or 18 Teen Girl or one who was promiscuously sexually active, there was a film on how the first pelvic exam was accomplished. This videotape was usually shown around the age of seventeen to all of the girls. When I did her first pelvic exam at the next scheduled office visit after viewing this film, there was a mirror mounted behind me on the wall so she could watch the exam in detail while it was being performed. Patient education and a patients' understanding of what was being done and why, created a feeling of security in their minds. These observations helped in developing patient comfort, compliance, and assuming the responsibility for their own health.

Here are some additional teen office protocols:

1. When a Teen was about 13 or 14, I would see him/her alone from this time onward while the parent was in my office viewing one of my Teen Talk Video Films which had been filmed by the Clarkson Video Department back in the old building.

2. When the young person came in alone for his/her annual health visit, a detailed letter was sent home the next day regarding all the appropriate details of the visit except that of privileged information. The parents were made aware of the parameters of this visit and had approved this personalized arrangement.

Over time, this entire Patient Educational Program evolved into a very sophisticated approach to detailed preventive health care and was a major adjunct to the "Guided Growth Well Health Care Program".

3. We wanted the public to know that the office had excellent quality control measures in place on many aspects of this pediatric practice. We subscribed to the American College of Clinical Pathologists for their Laboratory Quality Control Program. Their office would send to our lab tech unknown materials on each test she performed without having any knowledge of the results. We would receive a grade with the results on each test the Tech performed. Dr. Itkin supervised the lab and reviewed these results with the lab tech.

4. A certified Radiologist would re-read our own office X-ray interpretations. This over reading was critical from a malpractice prevention standpoint so that no important medical finding would be missed.

5. We had the City of Omaha Weights and Measurements Department check each of our office scales yearly and certify them as to their accuracy.

We let our parents know about these measures so that they could feel comfortable about what we were doing, why, what they were paying for, and how these measures were accomplished. The practical intent of these actions was to help the public understand the measures we took to ensure quality care without exploitation of the patient. To demonstrate the quality of services the family received in exchange for their medical dollars was a critical imperative in this increasing "Doubting Thomas" attitude of the public.

Parents were kept well informed regarding their Teen's visit by a prompt letter being sent to the family concerning the important details of the visit. What we specifically covered in the personal conversational part of the evaluation was kept between the teen and me unless it was of a life threatening or self destructive nature. If the parents needed to be informed, the Teen and I would determine, together, how it should be accomplished. The parents knew this fact and trusted me to deal with their Teen as they themselves would do so or desire to be handled.

From my past experience of having a fireplace in my counseling area which previously had been such a big assist and was very crucial in the counseling arena, I made certain that there was a similar arrangement of a fabricated fireplace in the corner of my main office with a real gas log that I lighted frequently. When my partners heard about my having a fireplace, they wanted one of their own. Ha! it came pass that we ended up with five fireplaces. This corner area was a real treat and asset in which to interview and counsel families.

Another area of annoyance was the frequency, persistence, and time consumption by the various "Sales Representatives" from the Pharmaceutical Companies who came and did not seem to have any regard for the amount of time they consumed. As Dr. Ellison was a registered Pharmacist, he was delegated to see most of these salespeople and to keep us informed as to any new medicines which were being introduced into pediatric realms.

I limited the representatives I wanted to see to a few favorite sales people. The Mead Johnson sales person was one of the honored few. I wondered why? These particular people made an appointment with the receptionist for an appointment time which was theirs to use and not to squander. I did not give out many samples, and the word spread concerning this fact, so I was not given many samples.

As the word spread that there no packages of sample medications in the office, this became a good reason why thieves would not try and break into the office looking for narcotics. We had an advanced security system in place to help to avoid this worrisome concern.

We kept all prescription pads out of sight and not displayed openly upon the room desks. I had had someone try to falsify a prescription with one of my pads. Fortunately, the sharp pharmacist had the presence of mind to call and check with me.

We moved in early 1980. Our psychologist held several focus groups with willing parents about what were their perceived needs. One of the most glaring desires was better sick time availability. Because of this important desire, we arranged to have a drop in sick call every morning from 8:00 AM to 9:30 AM. Each of the physicians rotated through these time frames in turn. We had a similar sick call hour at the end of the day from 4:30 to 6:00 PM. No appointment was necessary at either time. The parents would just drop in as needed with their sick child. This convenience for our patients was the greatest thing in their minds since sliced bread. Our patients loved this time availability. If a child became ill during the night, the parent could bring the child to the office at the available times, be seen, a prescription phoned in, the child dropped off at the sitter's place, and, then, go on to work without losing an entire day from their job. The parents would not have to wait until the office opened to call in for an appointment, which was usually assigned for later in the day, and have to wait and wait at home with a sick child on their hands. The child benefited from this new arrangement, and so did the practice.

Similarly, if their child became ill at the sitters or Grandma's place during the day, the parents could pick up the child, come right to the office, be checked, and go on home with the necessary instructions and medications. These simple available hours cut down on the evening phone calls to a fraction of those we had previously and almost eliminated the need for the parents to go to the very costly emergency room to be seen. This accomplishment was a win win situation for everyone. This convenience was a great addition to our Marketing Management program.

Chapter 83

One of the most innovative additions to our practice was to establish a Marketing Nurse. We subscribed to the professional company, the "Welcome Wagon", for their ability to provide significant data to our nurse. This affiliation would give to our nurse the names and addresses of the people who recently had moved into the nearby zip code areas within our designated office parameters. She learned from experience that it was necessary to contact the potentially new family within three days of their moving into the area, or this family would have already made other arrangements for their health care from information gleaned through friends or other sources.

The Nurse would explain our office modus operandi, sick call hours, parent and teen lectures, our quality controls, drop in hours, and a host of our other outstanding features. She would leave with them our professionally developed beautiful office brochure explaining many facets of our office practices. She seldom failed to sell our expertise to the prospective family.

In addition, we trained her in how to make house calls relating to seeing newborns on their second or third day at home from the hospital. In my opinion, babies were discharged from the hospital much too soon and before sufficient medical observation had been accomplished.

She checked the bilirubin levels in the infant and assessed how everything was proceeding. From past experiences, I worried that bilirubin levels over ten might be the cause of some ADD problems. Granted, this was an arbitrary figure; but it came from my own vast experience. If necessary, the nurse would suggest, after contacting one of us, sunlight on the skin or help the family to set up a Bilirubin Light under our direction. This step was to control the level of bilirubin. She would follow this case until the bilirubin was no longer a threat to the baby.

She served the practice in another dimension as a Visiting Home Nurse. I had a child with an inoperable congenital heart defect that was handled by a pediatric cardiologist. She needed to be hospitalized several times a year because of her heart failure problems. In desperation, the mother asked me if something/anything could be done to lessen the number of hospitalizations which were terrifying this child.

We checked with the family's Hospitalization Insurance Company, received permission to have our nurse make weekly house calls, and to keep oxygen available for use at home. The company agreed to try this approach to save money by paying for the house calls made by the Nurse instead of the frequently used expensive hospitalization stays.

I went to the house with our Home Nurse where we explained our proposed approach of weekly visits, having oxygen available, checking the child's blood pressure, and explaining other important parameters to the family. Lo and behold, with these few simple measures, this child stayed out of the hospital for well over a year. The child and parents were extremely happy with this outcome. In addition, we were as pleased as punch as to our results. The insurance company was delighted over the saving of money. This result only served to illustrate the old saying, "That where there is a will, there is a way".

Chapter 84

I was asked to participate in a computer seminar at the Denver Childrens' Hospital discussing networking and computer applications to office practice. During the question and answer period, I asked how many had the new portable computers which had just appeared on the market. I was floored with the large audience response. At least, one third of the group had a portable computer. Up until now, my experiences only had been with main frame computers. The portable computers began to change both the computer landscape and the healthcare landscape because of its usefulness and portability.

When I returned home, I immediately went shopping. I settled on an Osbourne Computer which had an excellent bundled software package consisting of "Word Perfect", "Super Calc", and "D-Base". Later on, there was available an inexpensive graphic program which could be utilized for Pie-Charts and other graphics to depict office costs in chart forms. I really had fun with this graphics package and brought this data to our monthly corporation meetings.

Although this computer unit was supposed to be portable, it weighed twenty-five pounds. One would not be dragging it around too many airports or places. It served my purpose very well in addition to the improved smaller computers which were becoming available. I used this machine for many years even after the more modern laptop machines were available and put to use at home.

I had an embarrassing experience after signing up for an introductory class to the "Word Perfect" word processing program. We were given a simple paragraph to transcribe into the computer. Boy! I went at this task with gusto. The room suddenly seemed to become very quiet while I was hard at work finishing the assignment. In looking around, everyone else was done, but little ole me. My hunt and peck finger method was very slow on the keyboard. In self defense, I never had to learn how to type. In my day, mostly girls took typing in high school with an occasional boy testing the waters. Still today, this hunt and peck is my preferred method of computer input. Ha! I had tried a computer typing program but became disenchanted and quit. I insisted that our three boys learn to type early on.

Chapter 85

Coming back to the thoughts and ideas generated by my weekend with the Rand Think Tank people, many, many disjointed thoughts began to jell into an organized pattern on how to apply this new knowledge. With my many thoughts rattling around in my head and with my notes in hand, I consulted my mentor, Jim Canedy at Clarkson regarding the building of one's own medical textbook based upon my own office cases. He was receptive to this idea and suggested that I write up a grant proposal. This request would be submitted to several local foundations. This plan would describe the interrelation between office medical histories, medical articles, and statistics. He would have his grant staff polish the contents of this proposal and would provide help in submitting it to the various local foundations and, ultimately, the National Library of Medicine if necessary.

After much thought and contemplation, the proposal was clearly defined and was ready to be presented to the selected parties. Just before Christmas, Jim Canedy invited me to come to his office for a visit, which I did. I was floored and astounded during this visit. He told me that there were some hospital funds which could be used to develop my ideas, concerning, "A Personalized Medical Textbook Utilizing the Computer", for the Clarkson Medical Staff. My tongue was tied in knots. If someone had asked me my name, there would have been just a big fat "Duh". The idea was to connect the statistics from the office with downloaded information from the internet and the National Library of Medicine at home; then, to connect these articles with the appropriate patient histories from the office files. The National Library of Medicine and the AMA Disease Database were readily available now for almost anyone to use.

Clarkson provided me with an IBM XT Computer, a modem, and a Laser Printer in my office's secretary and typist area and a similar setup at my home. The two systems were interconnected and could access each other in either direction of home to office and office to home. The various pieces of the equipment and software totaled $50,000 back in the days when computers were very expensive. This was real top of the line equipment and software. A computer expert from Clarkson was assigned to expedite and trouble shoot any of my illiterate computer knowledge problems.

Each software package, in those days, was a separate entity; nothing was integrated. Word processing, database, spread sheets, modem management, and similar packages of software were some of problems that I encountered while trying to utilize these various packages. I had to learn to use the different commands of each program separately and try to remember them. This was no mean feat for an old dog to try and learn so many new tricks.

After awhile, there became available on the academic and industrial research market a special software package called, "SCI-Mate", which was designed for all types of research work. This software could download, sort, and store key medical articles, facts, and figures These articles could then be attached to medical subjects or individual cases from my pediatric practice. It was possible to attach office cases to these articles, index, and file them for future retrieval. This approach was a very useful one and made the practice of medicine once again more enticing than ever, more knowledge enhancing, and more enjoyable. My seductress was back at enticing me once again to come and get lost in her arms. It was a real problem trying not to get caught up in her seductive wiles and not to lose my home versus practice balance. It was a monumental task to keep the wall between the medical practice and home intact. My seductress kept trying to breech this wall and steal me from my family. This beckoning was difficult to resist at times.

In addition to having access to the National Library of Medicine with its unlimited reference material of books, articles, and Journals now made available via Dr. Donald Lindberg's successes; the AMA decided to devote considerable funds and resources to the development of an up to date information data base on the current aspects of many medical diseases. A drug-drug interaction data base became a part of this service. Physicians could subscribe to this service for a small fee. The AMA sustained this very useful service for a number of years; but, it did not become as monetarily self sustaining as expected; so it ultimately was dropped. Web MD seems to have taken its place in today's world.

Much of my planning and development of ideas would occur while I was traveling to and from various meeting and while doing AAP Business. I belonged to the United Airlines' "Red Carpet Room" and the Eastern Airlines' "Inosphere Lounge". My yellow pad writing was done while waiting in these quiet areas between planes. Having membership in both of these lounges enabled me to find a quiet spot in almost any city where I would spend some time working while waiting for my plane connection.

Part of my equipment from Clarkson Hospital for this project was a "RadioShack" portable computer with the vast amount of memory of a whole 32 Megs. Ha! This computer cost $1,000 in those days. It was the earliest of the new generation of laptop computers. This compact machine would fit into my traveling desk briefcase. I had a briefcase which was modified by my brother-in-law", Howard Sorensen, into being a real traveling desk. This desk did a yeoman's job. I kept meeting notes and other data on the computer which were germane to my various projects. I would go to my hotel room at lunch time and again at the end of the day and input any pertinent data from the current meeting. When I used this computer on the plane, I was the object of both the envy and the curiosity of the fellow travelers.

The AAP Annual Meetings were very enjoyable from a social standpoint. There were several major special events for all the members in which to partake during the week of the meeting. Depending upon which city we were in, Alex Fielder of the Boston Pops fame would conduct the New York Symphony Orchestra in Carnegie Hall, the Chicago Music Hall with the Chicago Symphony, or at the San Francisco Opera House with the San Francisco Symphony. This entertainment was always a delightful evening.

There would be the new President of the AAP's Reception where I could visit with many pediatricians from around the country. Some of my colleagues would tease me about politicking. Early on, I had learned the value of "networking" and had no qualms of conscious about exploiting these opportunities and keeping these contacts.

After considerable amount of time, agony, blood, sweat, and tears, "A Personalized Medical Textbook Utilizing the Computer" became a reality. I gave presentations on this program at the 1985 Spring Meeting of the Academy at Atlanta, Georgia and to the 1985 American Association Medical System and Informatics Meeting in Washington DC. The cost of this program was justified as a service for the Clarkson Medical Staff. This was one of the most satisfying projects that I was ever involved with during my medical lifetime.

Chapter 86

The American Academy of Pediatrics was woefully ignorant of the interest individual members had in and around the use of computers in their practices. In fact the Academy lived in the ancient ages and in a deep dark cave without seeing the light of day regarding computers. However, the public interest in portable computers was sweeping the country by the early 1980's. It wasn't until about 1983 that the Academy began to wake up and become aware of the interest in and the need of its members in the use of computers in medical practice. The Academy conducted a half day task force discussion of which I was a part along with Dr. O.J. Sahler, a very bright lady from Syracuse, New York. We met in San Francisco; but, as so often happens in instances like this, there was a lot of talk but very little action. Nothing concrete came of this meeting.

    The Academy finally woke up to the importance of understanding the CPT #4 Coding applications. CPT # 1, 2, and 3 were already past history. I was appointed by the Academy as the Representative to the AMA Advisory Council for CPT #4 from 1983 to 1986. Each of the different Medical Associations and Organizations sent a representative to this Coding Council in addition to the representatives from the Blue Cross/Blue Shield National Company; one member was for the rest of the major Health Insurance Companies; one for the American Hospital Association; and "THE" almighty Director of the government Medicare Institution. I was amidst some high powered people and was trying to learn the ropes and procedures of this group.

I was charged by the Academy to obtain a new CPT Code [Current Procedural Terminology] for Newborn Intensive Care instead of trying to adapt the Adult Code, which was totally inadequate for pediatric needs. I experienced a rude eye opening situation at my first meeting. When my new CPT Code for newborns was proposed, I was summarily shot down in Toto and completely in the wink of an eye without so much as any discussion of by your leave.

However, when the Pathologists wanted a new CPT Code for some laboratory testing procedure, this code was approved so fast that it made my head spin. In a similar manner, the Urologists had a great success in their request.

This group of medical societies' and government was not supposed to have anything to do with fee settings. Ha Ha Ha. The Medicare Representative told the Urologists' representative that a routine Cystoscope would be reimbursed at the same rate whether the procedure was done in the office, hospital, or underneath the spreading chestnut tree in the great outdoors. In the past, there was so much bologna stated by the government in pretending not to be an agent relating to fee controls and reimbursements. Naturally, all the insurance companies were in total agreement with the government's position. There was no available recourse to this decision. This occurrence lent disbelief to the portrayal of no fee setting by the government. Government dictates will be even more common in the coming future with the new monstrosity of Health Legislation.

Chapter 87

It became imperative to me that the Academy needed to have some group within its own institution to gain a better insight regarding the role of computers and the use of computers for its own membership. The most logical approach to this need would be to establish a Section on Computers within the Council on Sections. What a stone wall I ran into when the formation of this new Computer Section was proposed. There was a Neonatologist, Dr. Joseph B., of the Denver Childrens' Hospital who was very strongly opposed to this suggestion. He was of the archaic belief that all Sections should be of a "Hands On" entity. How old fashioned were these thoughts at this advanced time and current day and age.

However, as I have said before,"there is more than one way to skin a cat" or "where is a will, there is a way" to attain the desired goal. I pulled up my socks and began to plan my campaign. The first step was to do adequate research on to how to proceed to develop a new Section. I obtained a sample copy of the "By-Laws" for any new AAP Section from the Academy's Education Office This protocol paper outlined the procedure which needed to be followed in order to establish any new Section. After a thorough study, a plausible route became apparent to me. There needed to be five members from several different states within each of the nine AAP Districts, who requested that a Section be formed. This new proposed Section's operational "By-Laws" had to be organized and developed.

Obtaining these needed signatures was duck soup because of my wide spread past networking activities. After the necessary number of names was obtained by and for me, the next stage was addressed in detail. I handpicked several pediatricians whom I knew were very interested and knowledgeable for establishing this project of a Section on Computers. We wrote a preliminary and tentative set of "By-Laws". The roster of names and the set of "By-Laws" were submitted to the twenty–one Sections which made up of -the Council on Sections.

As an invited guest to plead the case for the new Section, my detailed oral input of the importance and need for this Section to be in the Academy was permitted. During and following my presentation, the discussion became rather spirited and, at times, rather heated. The Neonatologist, Dr. Joseph B., from his high throne through being the Chairman of the Council, won this skirmish once again; so the application was denied.

Well as that other old saying goes, "When in Rome do as the Romans do"; my next approach was in utilizing the "networking" approach by lobbying the AAP Board of Directors directly about this need. Most of the Directors I knew personally, and they knew me. I had been associated with many of them as State Chairmen in the battle to establish the Chapter Chairmen's Forum. I explained the need for this Section to each Board Member personally. Well! Lo and behold, The Board of Directors held a short gathering at this AAP Annual Meeting site and summarily overturned the Council's decision. The Section on Computers and Other Technology came into existence in 1984. We had added to the name of the Section so as not to lock ourselves out from future technological developments.

By general agreement, I became the first Chairman of this new Section and held this position for three years until the Section's By-Laws were ensconced and operational. Now, the Section was really well established and functioning with defined goals and objectives. This Section was up and running in the world of reality. Interest quickly manifested itself within the AAP membership by rapidly growing to over several hundred members. The By-Laws kicked in and became the foundation for future growth and activity. The Section was a functioning entity and ready to take on any tasks sent its way by the AAP or to hew its own trail.

Within a few years, this Section put on its own annual scientific meeting within the October AAP gatherings. I presented several papers at the Section Meetings. The Section rapidly grew to a membership of well over five hundred members in a timely manner. Many of these new and younger members were well versed in computer usage. This rapid growth proved the interest and need for this particular venture. This occurrence was the twenty-second Section within the Academy, and its birth opened the door for many other areas of special interests to establish their own home of need. Today, there are some forty Sections. "So There Too" to those antiquated ideas of that archaic Neonatologist. I had the last laugh.

In 1989 after I had retired from practice, the Computer Section petitioned the AAP Board for permission to establish an annual award to be given to an outstanding physician using computers in pediatrics. The Section and the AAP Board named this award, "The Byron Oberst Award". What an honor! I was overwhelmed. This was the first award named for a pediatrician in private practice. The other twenty some AAP Awards, at that time and date, were named after someone in Academia or prominent in Research. Now, by 2009, there are some 40 different annual Awards presented by the AAP. "The "Oberst Award" is still being presented according to the AAP News which yearly lists all of the recipients of the different Awards. Most recently, this award was given to someone at the 2009 Annual AAP Meeting.

Byron Oberst Award

Here was an interesting fact of life that a simple pediatrician in a small state like Nebraska could end up having such major effects upon the functions of the American Academy of Pediatrics. The Chapter Chairmen's Forum changed the method of governance within the Academy. The Section on Computers changed the method and purpose for which the Educational Sections were designed to accomplish. The enhancement of the Committee on Child Health Guidelines projected the role of the Academy into the field of Adolescent Medicine. The push by the nine Alternate District Chairmen to enhance their role within the Academy from passive existence to one of active participation in Academy business bore excellent rewards and better insight into the many functions of the Academy. The need for the Academy to help the pediatrician with practice management measures was another major milestone. It seemed as though the Academy, like Rip Van Winkle, finally woke up from a long winter's nap and joined the modern world.

By the end of this decade, I had been a member of four National AAP Committees and a Task Force on New Technologies, an AAP Task Force on Privacy in the Adolescent Medical Record in Williamsburg, Virginia, and participated in several of the AAP Long Range Planning Sessions. My goal of being a member of one National Committee was more than satisfied. I published eleven articles in various medical journals, and organized and coordinated the first AAP Continuing Medical Education Course on Computers in Pediatric Medicine in New York City in 1985. For me, it had been a very self satisfying decade.

Chapter 88

Being a fiddler and a Diddler, there were several other medical organizations that seemed interesting enough for me to join such as:

1. The Great Plains Organization for Perinatal Health Care
2. Being a Charter Member of the Sports Safety and Health Care Society
3. American Association of Mental Deficiency
4. Pan American Medical Society
5. American Association of Medical System and Informatics

My medical life had been full of intriguing and challenging experiences. It had supplied many opportunities to me which were exciting to evaluate and tempting to conquer. My medical seductress was still striving and trying to entice me fully into her embrace to the exclusion of my family. However, my retirement thoughts were precipitated by an unusual airplane experience on our way to Maui, Hawaii to attend a medical meeting with my Anesthesiologist son, By.

Chapter 89

As we approached the time to land on Maui, the Captain came on the intercom and said, "I have some good news and some bad news for you. The good news, we are about twenty minutes from touchdown. Now for the bad news, we have trouble with our landing flaps functioning properly. We will need to divert to Honolulu where there is a very long runway which we will need in order to stop this plane with only the brakes. Please pay close attention to the cabin attendants as they review crash landing techniques and protocol". Shortly thereafter, a lady cabin attendant asked a big, strong appearing young man sitting near us to come and learn how to open the rear escape door in case anything should happen to her. Oh me, Oh my!!!! We were ill prepared for this type of news. Mary and I clutched our rosaries and each other's hand very tightly while the plane came in for its landing.

As we came in to land, the runway had been foamed; and the fire trucks were standing by. The plane landed "hot", and the brakes were applied as they were the only means to stop this huge aircraft. At last, we came to a halt near the far end of the extra long runway. The plane sat on the runway with a fire truck on each side of the plane in case a fire started in the hot brakes. We sat in the plane for about 30 minutes, after which time, we proceeded to the terminal.

Meanwhile, back on Maui, our son, By, was waiting, waiting, and waiting some more. He was not able to find out why our plane was so late. We were flown to Maui after much time had elapsed. When we were back in our condo and recapping this experience, By suggested, "Dad, You are going to be 65 soon. Why don't you think about retiring and spending more time with Mom"? This idea had never been foremost on my mind for consideration until this experience. Retirement was not something I had been interested in thinking about as my love of medicine was so strong. I originally thought that I would practice until I turned up my toes. Earlier, I had toyed with retirement thoughts very briefly and dismissed them as being irrelevant for me. Now, these additional thoughts added an entire new dimension to my thinking equation and deserved some very serious contemplation and preparation.

For the rest of our time in Hawaii, I contemplated at length the idea of retiring soon and discussed it back and forth with my beloved Mary and By. When I returned home, I sat down with my accountant and studied my financial options. We could live comfortably, but not in fat city. I decided that now was time to hang up my stethoscope and ride off into the horizons. I notified my partners and retired on December 31, 1988 at the ripe old age of 65. The appeal of spending many years with my beloved Mary was overwhelming and a "No Brainer". There was no looking back for me once the decision had been made.

During 1985, my beloved Mary and I reached our 40th wedding anniversary. Father Hupp celebrated a private Mass in our home for a number of our very close friends and relatives. This Mass was a very special favor to us. A Mass in a private home was not usually done except under special circumstances.

Later, many of our close friends and family attended a dinner and dancing to CD records at the Lakeshore Country Club on Lake Manawa. It was a memorable day for Mary and me. As I had not heard from the club by February as to the cost of the party, I sought out the manager. He informed me that our son, By, had paid the $800 bill and told him not to tell us. What a lovely unexpected gift.

My son, Matt, and I went through my record collection and pulled together a musical journey for Mary and me. We started with "Ave Maria" from our marriage, added "My Happiness" from San Antonio, Texas, songs from Japan, Detroit, back in Omaha, and many other meaningful musical memories, which had evolved over the past 40 years. This labor of love occupied four audio tapes which were later converted to four "CD's". We have played this special music at memory times. Being an old romantic at heart, I have played these records in times of intense nostalgia.

Chapter 90

Back to my search for a "Standalone" – meaning, a self contained-computer system - for the office. During my extensive search, the company name,"Medical Computer Management Inc." kept appearing again and again from several different sources. The "AMOS" System developed by this Omaha based company was endorsed and recommended by the Iowa State Medical Association. "AMOS" means Automated Medical Office Systems. Without a doubt in my mind, it was the System that we needed.

    The MCMI office was not too far from our new office location. Rob Mitchell was the Sales Manager for this company. He was very nice and accommodating to work with. I looked at the System back and forth, upside down, and downside up in their office; and, then, all over again, with their chief training people. After the System looked especially good to me, Dr. Wax was reluctantly dragged over to the MCMI office by the scruff of his neck to perform the same type of evaluation. Dr. Wax and I had worked with the Boston System to aid in developing their electronic medical record. The Boston System was not developed nearly enough to accommodate an Electronic Medical Record. If fact, that Boston company had gone belly up and failed not too long before. Having had a near disastrous escape experience, we did not want to repeat that traumatic event. MCMI had been in business for over five years and had several hundred clients throughout the Midwest.

    My partners invested in the AMOS" System which provided a great deal of satisfaction over the next many years. It gave excellent control over all aspects of the practice, especially, the administrative and accounting needs and provided me with my desired statistics. As with my Clarkson project, this System was just what the doctor ordered. However, there was no electronic medical record available on the market as yet. Electronic medical records still were light years away. With this System acquisition, a major component of the new ten years Long Range Plan had been accomplished at long last. Hurrah!

While compiling data for this next ten year plan, it was noted that there were many pediatricians residing in outstate Nebraska as contrasted to the previous ten years. There were pediatricians in Columbus, Grand Island, Kearney, North Platte, and Scottsbluff which was near the Colorado border. As expected, this outward migration of pediatricians lessened the volume of referrals from these regions. We still had referrals from 60 offices outside of the Omaha area which remained a very sizeable consultative practice.

In order to pacify several of our major referring physicians, they desired to have a pediatric consultant come to their town as a convenience to their patients. Because of the many follow up evaluations that were needed in towns such as Denison and Harlan, Iowa, I decided to give this transient consultative junket a try.

As a result, I would travel on the third Tuesday of the month to Denison, Iowa in the morning and stop at Harlan, Iowa in the afternoon on the way home. This was a very satisfactory arrangement for these communities and for the local doctors. I saw the patients in the hospital outpatient departments. These follow up visits saved the parents an inconvenient 100 mile trip to Omaha and back home, and made it easy to handle new consultations on site. This arrangement proceeded for several years. I was beginning to entice my younger partner, Dr. Gary Lerner to handle some of these trips.

The physicians in Red Oak, Iowa became interested in a similar situation for their community. We were starting to plan to accommodate them. However, the St Paul Medical Insurance Company, which supplied our Malpractice Insurance coverage, had different ideas. This company stepped in with a mighty nasty crushing demand. It seemed as though the State of Nebraska had a financial cap on possible litigation settlements in malpractice situations; whereas, the State of Iowa did not. St Paul wrote to me that for me to continue to go to Iowa to practice medicine one day a month, my insurance premium would be increased by $10,000 per year. No way Jose! Well! The income lost from being out of the office for that one day, alone, was about $1,000 of revenue by charges not being added to the books. The income generated from the trip to the two communities was about $700-800. This was a no win situation; so I had to stop going and, in addition, discontinued talks with Red Oak medical community. How sad and inconvenient for the people of those communities. Such is life. Now, the insurance companies were to able dictate how and where doctors could practice their profession because of fear of being sued and the high cost of the insurance. This was a sad commentary on the direction that medicine was headed.

Chapter 91

Our office was visited by a major medical catastrophe of the first order when Dr. Gary Lerner's wife became pregnant again and shortly, thereafter, was diagnosed with a major breast cancer. Because of the pregnancy, she could not receive any cancer arresting treatments, especially, chemotherapy and radiation. She passed away shortly after the delivery of her baby. As a result, Gary decided he needed to have a different medical life. He joined Childrens' Medical Staff as an employee and managed the "Child with Special Needs Clinic". It was a good change for him and a big loss for us. He was a very competent and compassionate young pediatrician. I really liked him.

I made a huge error in management judgment even though I had been forewarned by my mentor, Jim Canedy. He advised against having several physicians near the same age in the practice at the same time. Well, I knew better. Ha! There were three young doctors, two men and a woman, less than three years apart in age whom we had asked to join us. Jealousy soon reared its ugly head over who obtained the most newborns and similar childish items. This nasty situation became intolerable. Within a short time, they left OCCPC to the intense relief of the rest of us. I had the mistaken idea that the situation could be easily overcome and rectified. The little bit I knew about the young modern pediatrician would fill a bushel basket and still have plenty of room for me to get into this receptacle.

Chapter 92

Mary and I took many different cruises and had several trips to Hawaii with and without our special traveling friends. We fell in love with Maui in the Hawaiian Islands. On our first trip to Maui, we stayed at the Intercontinental Hotel, which was located in the drier southern part of Maui. It was a grand five star hotel. We woke up during one night and saw the moon, like a huge lamp, hanging just over the sea. It was like a romantic postcard. We stayed here several days and then moved on to Honolulu where I presented several lectures. I proceeded to talk on Practice Management to the Straub Clinic Pediatric Staff and to the Honolulu Childrens' Hospital residents and Medical staff.

On another trip to Maui, we stayed at a condo, "No Ho Nani", near the fishing village of Lahani. It was a great location and close to many excellent restaurants. Just a short distance from the village and our Condo was the Sheraton Resort Hotel. Adjacent to the hotel's beach was an underwater reef named "Black Rock". I loved snorkeling near this reef. There were more colorful tropical fish than I had ever encountered anywhere else. It spoiled me for other snorkeling adventures. I rented a camera and tried my hand at underwater photography. The fish were tricky little creatures as they would not stop to pose for a picture. How inconsiderate of them. It was important to be below the fish and to point the camera upward towards the surface. The lighting worked better, and the pictures were clearer. After a number of trials and errors, some reasonable pictures resulted but none of the showroom variety. I decided that underwater photography was not my cup of tea.

Naturally, I fell into another tourist trap. Woe is me, would I never learn. The vendors must sense that I am a big over ripe sucker. There was a snorkeling trip that advertised seeing the giant green sea turtles while out on the ocean venture. We set sail and were not too far out from shore when the boat skipper came on the speakerphone and said, "Unfortunately, the sea turtles have been absent from this particular area for some time". What a rook and a what a bummer because this snorkeling trip was nothing like that at the Black Rock Reef. We did view an underwater volcanic crater containing a sting ray fish. This magnificent experience was more than enough excitement for this old body to handle. Ha!

We would go to Sunday Mass at a small Mission Chapel north of our Condo near the area of Kanapali. It was a sweet little building. When the choir sang "Madonna of the Islands", it was beautiful and breathtaking. This song brought tears to your eyes. Not that I am sentimental or anything.

Chapter 93

Our immediate family had left our warm feathered nest and each son was making his own waves. Terry lived in Lincoln, Nebraska and had obtained a Masters Degree in Creative Writing. He, now, directed a writers' workshop twice a month. He had published a number of books of his poetry and had been involved in a number of city art type activities on the radio and television at other people's request. He was on the road to make a name for himself in Lincoln.

Matt had left teaching in the Papillion High School and started at a level one computer position at Mutual of Omaha. He climbed the corporate ladder to become a middle manager with a team ranging from twenty to twenty-five people working with and for him. This group worked with computer servers.

He and Nancy had three boys. They had moved into a new home in western part of Omaha. The commuting time to both of their jobs took about 40 minutes or more each way every day. They decided to move back into the middle of the city closer to their respective jobs. They found a lovely home which Matt had enjoyed refurbishing. He was a very "Handy Andy" with home jobs. This home was near Nancy's brothers and sisters and was facetiously called the "Mullen Compound".

Matthew's youngest son, Conor, became an Inde Rock Star who toured the States, Europe, Japan, New Zealand, and Australia. He owned two recording studios. One studio was in Omaha near his home. The other studio was in a cluster of buildings that he owned in Los Angeles. He had some type of "pad" in New York City. He has been very successful. Many of his songs have climbed high on the music charts. Some songs have been used in movies. Recently, his songs rank number eight in the top ten of downloaded songs from the internet. One of his latest movie song renditions will be coming out the spring of 2011. He was just named the musician of the decade for the State of Nebraska. He has become my main claim to fame.

Conor needed a trusted business manger to handle his many revenue streams, properties, and a myriad of other assets that he had accumulated. Matt decided that he would enjoy this role so he left Mutual after almost 30 years to conquer new fields for Conor. He is applying his computer expertise in a host of different ways to Conor's businesses. He has been happy as a lark being Conor's general manager. He has acted as my computer support person for many years as most computer advances have passed me by like an express train.

Nancy was the Director of the Visually Handicapped Child program for the Omaha Public Schools for a number of years. She was certified in Brail and worked with the hard of hearing children. After a while, she became the principal of the J.P. Lord OPS School for handicapped children. About ten years at this school was enough, she became "burned out" and wanted to change to a regular school, which she was allowed to do.

When at this new school for a few years, she was "volunteered" by the OPS Administration and was commissioned to develop a new educational concept, the"Jackson Academy". She had to hire the staff, supervise the renovation of an older school building, and devise the curriculum. After three years into this role, she did a similar job at the old, regular Jackson school which she handled very well.

There was a need for a new school in the downtown Omaha area. Nancy was tapped to work with the architects, obtain the teachers, and to work on developing parent involvement amidst the large indigent and foreign population that this school area encompassed. This school became a show piece for OPS. A few years ago, she was made the Director and Coordinator of the 61 OPS Elementary School Principals in Omaha. She was made the "Marian High Alumni of the Years", recently. She was doing very well and enjoyed the challenges that arose. In my opinion, she was and is quite a gal. On their recent move to Washington DC, to be near their new grandson, she will be working for the Gallup Organization in a consulting capacity in the new educational division.

Matt and Nancy's son, Justin, went to the University of Nebraska at Lincoln, Law School on a full scholarship. He moved to Washington DC and has been practicing environmental law. He and his wife, Mackenzie, recently had a 10 pound boy in January 2010. They are doing very well.

Young Matthew, Matt's oldest son, lives near Raleigh, North Carolina and teaches the 7th and 8th Grade History and English in a Montessori School. He has his Master's Degree in English and wants to become a budding author. He has been looking for a publisher for his first novel. He had a son, John, ten and a daughter, Annabelle, seven.

Chapter 94

Back to our immediate family status, By practiced anesthesiology in a thirty-six person group at St. Joseph's Hospital in Eugene, Oregon for almost fifteen years when sadness struck him between the eyes. His first wife decided that she didn't want to be married any longer. She went to Tibet to meditate with the monks.

By met a wonderful nurse, Shirley, who was the OB, Nursery and Infant ICU supervisor, and she quickly, captured his heart. She managed about one hundred and ten hospital employees of all types. She was a very organized and extremely competent person and nurse.

After a whirlwind romance, they were married in By's yard with the birds billing and cooing. This marriage occurred in 1987 just before I retired. Mary and I were at a meeting in San Francisco when this great event occurred. We were informed after the fact of this event.

After her retirement from the hospital, Shirley handled the County immunization program for 13 years. She did a magnificent job until they moved to Bend, Oregon; then, she gave up this position. By and Shirley spent much time and energy raising money to furnish one hundred indigent children with a new bike. This was a very worthwhile cause and brought much happiness to many children. This venture had to be discontinued due to worrisome legal implications. Their next venture was to organize the De Chutes Bicycle Ride to raise money for the Lance Armstrong Foundation and the local Cancer Survival Program. Over a thousand bike riders participated in this annual fund raiser. Donors gave over $50,000, and the entry fee for each biker was $40 which raised another $40,000. This immense organizing task requires about a year of preparation and has been very successful for the past several years. Wow!

By retired from the field of anesthesiology and moved to Bend, Oregon. He wanted to smell the roses, and enjoy life doing activities that he liked best. On my part, I suspect he retired early because of burn out due to high pressure heart operations with the extra long eight and ten hours in the operating room. The frequent damp and rainy days so prevalent in Eugene added to his incentive to seek a drier living location.

We had traveled to Oregon almost every year for a long time. I have photographed most of the beautiful Oregon coast and much of the state itself. On one trip, we stayed at a five star resort, "Sun River" where By and I played golf and canoed on the De Chutes River. On another occasion, By and his wife drove us to the northern border of Oregon to the "Timberline Lodge" which has been famous in that region since the 1930's. We drove down the Columbia River Gorge to Portland. We have seen the High Desert Museum and many other Oregon sights.

The year after I retired in 1989, By called and invited me to be his guest for a week of observing Elk in the Yellowstone part of Montana. The Elk were magnificent animals. We packed in with horses with a supplier, who set up our camp and left us on our own. We had a wonderful time hiking up and down the mountains. I discovered that my physical conditioning left a lot to be desired in the mountain air. Oh well! "Live and learn", I always say.

Early in the mornings, we would walk to a nearby mountain meadow and observe a herd of at least 100 Elk coming out of the woods to eat. This sight was breathtaking. At night, By would give me an astronomy lesson on the stars. Speaking of teaching, this was a "Turn about is fair play" episode with him teaching me rather than vice versa. This trip was filled with many wonderful memories.

When the packers came to bring us back to civilization, they brought word to me that my Mother, who was 102 years old, had passed away. This was a very sad moment for me. I was glad that By was with me.

By loves the outdoors. He hunts and camps each fall. It used to be with a rifle, but the Bow and Arrow has replaced the rifle. He has garnered elk, moose, caribou, and a mountain goat with the bow and arrow. Cross country skiing is his main physical activity of interest during the winter season. During the summer time, it is nothing for him to hop onto his bike and peddle 100 miles and not be worn to a frazzle or to paddle his kayak on the De Chutes River. After retirement, he built a home in Bend, Oregon on a golf course. It is a fifteen minute drive from his house to the groomed cross country ski trails.

He swims every morning and hiking is a frequent activity. He keeps himself in great physical condition for being 60 years old. His existence must be a terrible lifestyle to endure. Ha! Just thinking about all of the exertion he has expended has worn me out and made me want to go and take a nap.

Chapter 95

The book written by John M. Long and myself, "Computers in Private Practice Management" was an outgrowth of my philosophy and experiences in Office Practice Management. This book, in contrast to the other two, was mildly successful and reasonably utilized. We each made a few dollars on this venture. Over time, many readers had notified me of their pleasure and the help that they had obtained from this book. The contents of this tome had provided the outline for part of the 1980 Long Range Plan. This new Plan, itself, was written with the following Divisions and the contained the following subjects:

1. Mission Statement – where the major description of what we intended to accomplish in our business was stated in broad terms.

2. Key Objectives – each Key Objective defined some aspect of the Mission Statement.

3. Critical Objectives - these Critical Objectives defined the situations and enhanced the parameters of the individual Key Objectives.

4. Management by Omission or Exception – covered those situations which seemed to be outside the general parameters of the Long Range Plan. Within this particular time period, it seems to me that now is an opportune moment to recap and to integrate the 1980 OCCPC's ten year Long Range plan segments within my eight Medical Office Management Divisions:

1. Four Divisions relate to the business side of the practice
2. Four Divisions relate to the patient side of the practice

Four Business Management Areas

Administrative Management

This is the area where important decisions are made

My mentor, Jim Canedy always emphasized that before any decision, large or small, was made detailed facts, figures, thoughts, and serious discussions both pro and con needed to precede the decision making process. Using this approach, many serious errors could be eliminated. If, after making a decision, the results do not turn out as anticipated or desired; a new decision can readily be made based upon the fore gathered data and utilizing the information gained from the experiences of the unacceptable outcome.

1. The OCCPC physicians would meet at my house once per month and discuss the agenda items which had been prepared by me.
2. We would meet with our accountant every six months and review the financial and collection aspects of the practice.
3. We would meet with our attorneys once a year unless there was some new major area in the Labor Laws which impacted the practice workers and had to be addressed.
4. All actions affecting the practice were discussed in detail including the hiring's and firings.
5. If something was needed to be purchased, Dr. Jim Wax would be the point person as he had many contacts for discounts.
6. If there was a major monetary situation to consider in order paying for something, Dr. Phil Itkin would take the lead. He would lean back, close his eyes, and visualized the necessary calculations. He would quickly be able to give many different pros and cons as to where the money should come from or go to. He was uncanny in his thought processes. After his input, the decision would be made in favor or more often than not against the proposal's costs because of Phil's postulations.

7. Finally, if all strategic decisions met our long standing criteria, we would proceed to the next level of decision making:

   7.1. Is it good for the Practice?

   7.2. Is it good for the Patient?

   7.3. Is it good for the Person proposing the idea?

8. All Legal and Ethical issues relating to the practice and computers and other situations were handled here.

9. All practice statistics were examined monthly in detail complete with graphs and charts which were supplied by me.

10. Inventory control was critically reviewed to assure adequate supplies without having too many funds tied up with materials on the shelves or in the refrigerator.

Accounting Management
This is the area that makes the practice wheels go round

2.1. Revenue Accounting – The income source – Accounts Receivable - Cost Centers were essential as all revenue and any costs must be posted to some specific location.

2.2. The value of money on the books decreases every day and reaches 50 % of its original value by 60 days. This fact of life makes the collection process one of the top priorities for the practice.

2.3. We started charging interest after 60 days which greatly aided collections and irritated some patients.

2.4. We found out that many patients paid the accounts charging interest first and the other bills second, if there was money still available to do so.

2.5. Our Practice decided not to be a Loan Agency any longer.

   2.5.1. It seemed to me that we were giving courtesy discounts to almost anyone including the dogcatcher.

   2.5.2. We determined that we were giving too many discounted dollars to various people. The amount of money, which we gave away, ended up being the equivalent to our monthly rent; so this procedure had to be greatly curtailed.

2.5.3. Our collection procedures were fairly effective.

2.6. When using a collection agency, less than 25 % of the paper value of the debt is recovered when turned over to a particular agency by the practice – maybe even a lesser amount - and much ill will can be generated from the constant dunning.

2.7. At Christmas time, the bookkeeper would give each doctor a short list of his/her patients, who through no fault of their own, were having a beast of time trying to make ends meet. We would send to the family a letter stating their outstanding charges had been cancelled and "Have a Merry Christmas". These actions made us feel good and created much good will amidst the public as the word of this generosity spread.

2.8. Because of the increased paper work from Insurance Forms and Welfare Documentations, we needed an additional clerk to handle the insurance forms and another one for the welfare charges. These positions added much to our overhead costs.

2.9. Each of these clerks kept a log as to the reason that a claim was rejected and with which person she had spoken to about the claim, what was recommended, and how the claim was finally resolved. In this manner, she would know the most advantageous method to resolve the same type of situation at the next claim rejection. As sure as the sun would rise the next day, there would be another similar claim rejection. It was almost impossible to speak with the same claim clerk twice in a row about any claim.

3.0 We instituted a Cost Center Concept where each physician was a Center and income and expenses were allocated to the appropriate Center. This concept avoided many headaches.

3. I. I instituted a $10 charge for my medication phone calls because these phone calls required much time and Chart handling.

Disbursement Accounting

Accounts payable - This is where the money goes

1. Salaries - the payroll for all members of the practice, doctors and staff.
2. Standard monthly Fixed Costs - such as Rent, Electricity, etc.
3. Variable Costs – which amount would change from month to month such as the Telephone Bill, Medical Supplies, etc?
4. Incidental expenses which occur sporadically.

Time Management
Time – A Forgotten Resource

Wasted time is lost revenue which is non recoverable. This fact is a very difficult concept for most physicians to grasp. Many physicians enjoy standing around gossiping or visiting in the doctors lounge while at the hospital or in the office halls.

1. Time Motion Studies were done.
2. Telephone time was studied, the system was changed, and calls were diminished.
3. Out of office time was reviewed:

    3.1. Hospital rounds.

    3.2. Vacations and days off.

    3.3. Medical meeting trips.
4. In office time was considered:

    4.1. Patient Time.

    4.2. Charting Time.

    4.3. Appointment scheduling – is it efficient?

Marketing Management

4.0 Marketing Management – A new field for thinking progressively in medicine and addressing the competition.

    4.1. There is a great need for patient profiles – office database management helps here.

    4.2. There is a need for a practice analysis.

    4.3. Market research is vital – surveys/focus groups etc.

    4.4. Determine positioning as to what market penetration is desired and into what areas/niches.

    4.5. Review of the Various Marketing Techniques that had we already utilized as to their effectiveness.

Some of the marketing techniques OCCPC instituted:

1. The Marketing Nurse – Use of the Welcome Wagon.
2. The Home Visit Nurse.
3. The Newborn Visit Nurse.
4. A classy multicolored Office Information Brochure about office procedures, hours, doctor's profiles and pictures, and similar information.
5. Inserting flyers in newspapers in specific targeted zip code areas concerning our practice features.
6. Establishing a Patient Advocate:

    Axiom - One satisfied Patient tells four to five other potential patients about the feelings of satisfaction.

    Corollary - One unhappy Patient tells eight to ten other people how unhappy they were.

7. Establishing the "Drop in Hours" am and pm.
8. One doctor saw sick patients on Saturday Mornings while the others saw regularly scheduled patients.
9. Establishing a Sunday Nurse to screen calls and arrange for those patients, who need to be seen by the doctor, to come to the office around 2:00 pm. This adjunct situation was

almost as pleasing as the "Drop in Hours" and saved many a trip to the expensive ER on the weekends.

10. Family and Referring Physician communications and prompt reports.
11. Letters to parents after a middle to late teenager visit.
12. The Consultation visits to Denison and Harlan, Iowa.

    I am sure there were others that do not come to mind at this point in time.

13. Detailed monthly analysis of the various Practice Statistics

Four Medical Care Management Areas
Patient Care Management

Utilizing a Full Service Bank Concept for patient convenience

1. Having a part time nutritionist.
2. Having a part time educational psychologist.
3. Enhanced laboratory testing including many chemistry tests performed with a Level 1 Certified Lab Technician.
4. Having X-ray capabilities with a Certified X-ray Technician and an additional reading of the X-rays by a paid Radiologist.
5. Using the Problem Oriented Medical Record with the SOAP Format.

    5.1. Enhancing the evolution of a computer ready manual of Medical History Forms through age twenty using a "YES/No" Format for future optical scanning

6. Incorporating a very sophisticated "Guided Growth Program" from the well child years through the adult years including the physical and educational programs.
7. Having a completely equipped Emergency Room, which doubled as a GYN Examining Room?
8. Utilizing the AAP Guidelines for healthcare which were incorporated into the "Guided Growth" program.

9. Creating a defined and detailed long range medical plan for teaching and supporting the patient who had had a major medical problem which was more than just an individual acute episodic illness situation.
10. Monitoring the long term use of medications by patients through telephone calls and office visits.
11. Establishing a manual method for a random technical audit of some patient charts by an individual physician to be sure all aspects of the Chart has been completed.

Physician Management
Physician Management –Quality Management of all types

1. Having each physician earning the AMA Physician's Recognition Award every three years.
2. Having the OCCPC Physicians reading the X-rays with an over reading by a contract Radiologist.
3. Using the detailed analysis of the American College of Pathologists' Laboratory Control Program.
4. Expecting each physician to go a medical meeting outside of Omaha twice per year and reporting significant advances cited at the monthly corporation meeting.
   4.1. Each doctor was to have a defined self Continuing Medical Education Program
5. Having frequent Employee, in situ, training sessions and details.
6. Having practical quality control on patient care.
7. Defining parent-child/teen responsibilities relating to their health maintenance
8. Obtaining and reviewing annually the adequacy of malpractice insurance coverage.
9. Determining computer data policies.
10. Determining and instituting any changes in legal responsibilities.

11. Holding a monthly office staff meeting to enhance office communications and decisions.

Hospital Management
Hospital Management: The efficient use of resources

1. The Hospital Admission history, physical exam, appropriate lab tests and x-rays, and preliminary orders were to be submitted simultaneously with the admission of the patient.
2. Physicians would check with the hospital laboratory for the early results on tests before seeing their own patients in order to inform the patient and make any necessary treatment changes.
3. The physicians would check with the Radiologist for the early readings on the x-rays before seeing their own patients in order to inform the patient and make any necessary treatment changes.
4. Physicians would spend less time in the Doctors Lounge.
5. A copy of the Hospital Discharge Summary would be sent to the referring physician and another copy to the parents.
6. Doctors would post their hospital charges daily to avoid missing any charges rather than waiting and posting charges on the day of discharge. Income was lost using this latter approach because of the forgetful mind.
7. The physicians should pay close attention to the Hospital Algorithms for Length of Stay criteria and other required hospital criteria.
8. Expedient completion of the hospital discharge summary with the diagnoses being compatible with the appropriate ICD and CPT Coding Systems within one week's time.

Medical Information Management – coping with the Volume of data

In today's world, it is imperative that the physician continually add to his/her medical knowledge and the understanding of various disease processes.

1. Frequent Use of the National Library of Medicine via the computer.
2. Use of the AMA Disease Information Database at the office and at home.
3. Use of the AMA Drug-Drug Interaction Program whenever indicated.
4. Read specific medical journals in the areas of personal interest and medical books of choice.
5. Use of the free Phycom, Physicians-on-Line, now Web MD for physician to physician communications.
6. Use of the Electronic E-Mail.
7. Use of Journal study clubs.
8. Use of audiovisual tapes.
9. Use of audio tapes.

This review is a short synopsis how the OCCPC endeavored to conduct its pediatric practice and to care for its patients.

Chapter 96

After I met with my accountant and decided to retire in 1988, I told my partners of my plans. They were told not to plan a big fancy retirement party as I just wanted to quietly ride off into the sunset with no muss or fuss. They had a small office goodbye gathering with the office personnel for me instead. They gave me a beautiful briefcase as a parting gift. I laid my keys on the manager's desk and walked out the door never to look back or to return. This door was closed on my past. There was an exciting future in front of me. At long last, there would plenty of time to spend with my beloved Mary.

An interesting point, my old office is still going strong with Drs. Ellison and Itkin and two younger pediatricians. The office has stood the test of time from 1946 to 2010. These years established a pretty good record and evidence for a practice to have achieved this longevity. The planning and execution must have provided for a solid foundation to survive so many years, changes in personnel, and innumerable crises.

My passion for medicine never had waned or tired but took different roads and pathways over time. Towards the end of my practice, I really loved and enjoyed as patients the high school, college, and early adult years the most. It was so pleasurable to work with so many interesting and exciting young people. I learned as much from them as I did from my parents over the years. It was a constant battle to keep the wall solid between medicine and my family life.

In my early years, I would have fun with the three to six year olds when I would examine the ears, I would say, "I see a little brownie in this ear with a red nose, green ears, and purple shoes. The brownie helps you to remember what your mother says". My! Their eyes would get as big as saucers. Years later, I heard that when several of my old patients, now well aged into adulthood, would be together, a topic of conversation would be my old brownie stories. How great!

In retrospect and as I look back over these Golden Years in medicine, I can recall with amazement how the antibiotics changed the treatment of acute infectious diseases, the wonderful prevention of many major devastating diseases by immunizations, the evolution of laboratory tests both in micro technique methods and in the broadened scope of expanded testing of many different body functions, and the many changes in the surreal types of imaging that have become available and are so commonplace today. The ability to sustain people through technological advances such as renal dialysis is remarkable.

Some illnesses have almost became extinct such as diphtheria, measles, whooping cough, three day measles, and small pox, pneumonia with its lung abscesses and empyema, and some of the different meningitis diseases. Many of these entities remain but with a much less serious concern for major complications. To continue to control these diseases, it is imperative that people keep their immunizations up to date. Everyone's protecting depends upon each other being protected. The herd effect is a critical item in public health concepts.

The diagnostic techniques, which were rarely and crudely available way back then, to the modern wonders of the armamentarium which is now available and which lie at the physician's fingertips are an almost a miraculous achievement in and of itself. In the past, surgical operative speed was the desired goal of most procedures so as not to shock the patient too much; whereas, now surgical procedures can last almost all day or night long because of better anesthesia and supportive care.

Strangely enough, I still hear from a few patients and parents after being retired for over twenty years. We must have forged some kind of an alliance. The main item I miss from my medical practice days is the wonderful people I was privileged to care for.

Part VII is to follow
The Years 1988 to 2009

My post practice years and adventures will be described in this next segment.

Part VII

The Years 1988 to 2009
The Retirement Years and
New Adventures
and
New Fields to Conquer

After I left the practice of Pediatrics, I had a great deal of time on my hands. Oh, what should I do with this time? Knowing myself like I do, twiddling my thumbs for very long would not suffice and would not breed feelings of satisfaction. As I mulled the possibilities, my mind kept turning to the computer field.

Looking back over my practice years and the goals which I had envisioned back in the 1950's, the following achievements had occurred:

1. I had not only been a member of a medical organization's National Committee. I had been on 11 Committees in several different medical organizations.
2. I had been on the Board of Directors for the Society of Computer Medicine, on the Physician Advisory Board to Phycom, a member of the Clinical Diagnostic Scientific Advisory Panel for Clinical Diagnosis, on the AAP Task Forces on New Technologies and Privacy in the Adolescent Medical Record, and other important activities.
3. I had published 41 medical articles and authored or co-authored three books.
4. I had given 83 lectures/seminars at the local, state, regional, and national levels.
5. Locally, I had been on most of the various important medical committees at Childrens' Hospital, Methodist Hospital, Clarkson Hospital, and some at Bergan Mercy Hospital.
6. I had served on several committees for the Omaha Metro Medical Society and the Nebraska Medical Society.
7. I was the medical representative to the Omaha-Douglas County Board of Health.
8. I was on the faculty of the University Of Nebraska College Of Medicine from 1951 to 1988 and had been on many important committees. I retired as a Senior Consultant in the Department of Pediatrics.

My medical life had been filled with different and stimulating experiences and activities of all types and descriptions. It had been a very satisfying life. It was time to turn the page in my life's drama to other areas of interests. The siren and enticer "Lady Medicine" was shunted and spurned to a back seat in lieu of the family and new fields to conquer. The protection wall between medicine and family no longer needed to exist.

It had long been my contention that Computer Programmers who worked in the medical field of software development knew very little about the workings of the practice of medicine per Se. This lack of insight made it difficult for a programmer to fully address physicians' needs. These medical requirements could not be completely met by utilizing a common uniform format for most reports. The various output of data items and in what manner the date appeared on many reports left much to be desired as far as a physician was concerned. Here was an opportunity to test this theory.

A great deal of time and thought was invested into my proposal to Medical Computer Management Inc. (MCMI) whose system had been installed in our office in the mid 1980's. An appointment was requested with Phil Kreig, who was the majority stockholder and president of MCMI. My carefully prepared offering was presented to him. My sales pitch was the following:

1. To work two mornings per week – Tuesdays and Wednesdays from 8:00 AM until noon.

2. To print each and every Report that the AMOS System would and could generate.

3. To analyze each report and to classify each one of these reports in the relationship it had to my 8 Practice Management Areas.

4. To segregate these reports into practical working groups with a description of the contents of each report, its usefulness, and its applications.

5. To have an explanation for and a possible specific application for each report.

6. To group each report into two large manuals relating to my concept of the 8 Management Areas with four in each manual.

7. To assist the programmers in developing any new software from the standpoint of how the physician would view the data in these output reports and how these reports would be utilized in his/her practice management.
8. To have a salary of $15,000 per year for my consultative services.
9. To do much of the analytic work at home with no added costs to MCMI. Over time, my work at home averaged about fifteen to twenty hours per week which I thoroughly enjoyed and ensured my usefulness to the company.

The meeting with Phil Kreig went very well. The proposal seemed to be practical and useful to him. He consulted with his four other owner partners. They accepted my proposal. I became the MCMI Medical Advisor from 1988 to 1995 when the company was sold.

Chapter 97

My first year was spent producing the innumerable reports which were generated by the "AMOS" System. Each one had to be studied in detail as to its content and as to its possible applications. This was a far bigger task than I had first envisioned, but it was exciting and very challenging. There were some reports which were filled with useful material, and others that were not worth the trouble of printing them.

It was so rewarding to work with such bright young computer minds. The computer industry was and is a sharp, mentally alert, young person's field. Over time, I became a sort of a personal counselor to several of the MCMI personnel with major problems such as a parent with cancer.

After a while, I was accepted as a real contributing part of the company and not a spot of window dressing. I gave my initial presentation for MCMI at the Annual AMOS User's Group Meeting in Omaha in June of 1989. The presentation was well received.

Subsequently, I gave a Seminar on Practice Management and the AMOS System at the Phoenix, Arizona Childrens' Hospital in November, 1989 and, again, in Omaha, Nebraska in June, 1990. I gave a three day Seminar in Phoenix on the AMOS Reports and how to use them in February, 1990 and again in January, 1991. There was good attendance and I had an excellent reception at both seminars. The accolades were very rewarding.

Medical Societies were being faced with the dilemma of having to personally Credential and Re-Credential their own membership. Until now, this was a daunting intensive hand labor task. Using the Phoenix

Maricopa Medical Society as a laboratory site, MCMI proceeded to develop an automated Credentialing System which worked very well and was received with a great deal of enthusiasm.

Part of my role, in addition to contributing to this development, was to go on demonstrations with the Head of the Sales Department, Rob Mitchell. We addressed various interested Medical Society Groups. This experience produced a real insight into the difficulty of selling a needed product to an unwilling audience. After time passed and the need increased, this slow sales situation became much easier. I traveled to Milwaukee, Wisconsin, Cedar Rapids, Iowa, and other cities where the AMOS System was known and in use.

It is critical to the development of medical software that computer knowledgeable physicians help develop the specifications for any project as to how the data should be displayed; so that it could be used in an intelligent and professional manner. This advisory input needed to be done before the fact and not after a project is underway. Trying to change programmed items after the fact is very costly and frequently self defeating. How the data is presented is critical to its usefulness.

After the first year, I was honored and privileged to be asked to conduct a two day Annual Management Planning Session for the five MCMI partners. I was privy to the intimate aspects of the company. Obviously, my professional integrity was crucial to these sessions. When the sessions were completed, I would compile the many discussions and conclusions into a workable and easy to digest format. Each partner was given a copy of the report. Never did I keep a copy of this report for myself. I conducted these Planning Sessions yearly while I was associated with MCMI.

Naturally, I introduced my old tried and true Management Concepts which were new to them including generating a Mission Statement, Key Objectives, Critical Objectives, Management by Objective, and Management by Omission. These were critical concepts and very necessary if a good review of the business per Se and planning for the near future needs was to take place. These concepts were an intricate part of all of these planning sessions. This approach was very informative, useful, and fruitful for the partners.

Chapter 98

One of my most popular seminars was on "Marketing of the Medical Practice". This one was repeated by request several times.

MCMI began the arduous task of developing an Electronic Medical Record. In the beginning, it was a monumental task to convince the development team as to how the record should be constructed; what the various components of the record should be composed of; why these items were important; and in what order they should be displayed. It was here, in this vista, that my past expertise began to shine. This product proceeded to the stage where the field testing of this electronic record was tried in several different types of medical offices. The initial reports and responses suggested that the MCMI approach was going to be a good and useful success. At long last, my dream would be fulfilled. However sadly, this dream was not to be realized.

One day when I came to work, the general manager of MCMI, Scot Brown, who had a MBA and handled the finances and everyday operations, asked me into his office for a chat as had happened on many previous occasions. Well! Today was a bombshell. MCMI had been sold by the partners to The Credit Union Services Association (CUSA) of Utah in 1995. You could have knocked me over with a feather.

This Credit Union had a number of physician offices for credit accounts. CUSA thought it would be profitable to migrate upward and enter into the Medical Practice Management field which was a totally unfamiliar area to them. Each of the MCMI personnel, including myself, was interviewed for a position with CUSA. My credentials were outstanding; so I was retained. Unfortunately, my role was never really outlined, defined, or utilized. As time passed, it became obvious to me that this new company was in deep over its head and didn't have the slightest clue as to what to do about the tiger it had by the tail.

CUSA bought an Emergency Room Medical History package without any advice from me or anyone else that I knew of. This judgmental error ended up being an expensive disaster for the company in trying to modify a crafted site specific medical history into a useful one for everyday office general practice use. This experience was an unmitigated disaster for this naïve company.

Meanwhile, I was working with a team of delightful CUSA people in North Carolina continuing to develop the former MCMI's Medical Record as a safety net for the CUSA Organization. My computer support person was great and very knowledgeable. Long before the software was readily available on the commercial market, he could manipulate my computer in Omaha from North Carolina. It was amazing to see my cursor responding to his commands. Once again, we had a great start on the much needed medical record, but for no avail.

The company began to change its tune and shifted its interest gears. Personnel were being eliminated in droves. Now, I had to report to someone in the San Diego area. What a mess this venture had become for this poorly prepared and ill informed company. At long last, CUSA acknowledged its mistake of trying to be something that they were not destined to be. CUSA sold off bits and pieces of the MCMI products until it was no more. Gone with the wind forever were my dreams of an Electronic Medical Record.

Chapter 99

After I had been with Medical Computer Management Inc. for about eighteen months, I felt that I was losing some of my insight into patients and medical skills. I did not want the headaches of handling a practice, meeting payrolls, coping with overhead, or any of the other myriad of concerns in a medical practice. I began to check different options of what I could do on a part time basis to enhance my fading skills while still working at MCMI

I answered a newspaper ad which the government had placed wanting to hire a physician to perform routine civil service physical exams. This would be a part time position with very little responsibility and sounded somewhat appealing to me. The salary was $25 per hour for a half a day's work. However, the kicker under the rug was that one had to provide his/her own malpractice insurance, No way! This job was much too expensive for me to consider as the insurance premium would be over $5000 per year for a half day's work once per week. The net income would not begin to cover the premium costs. So no dice to this job!

Perusing the want ads on another day, there in big bold type and hitting me right in the eye was an ad for a physician to perform screening physicals on commercial plasma donors. Malpractice coverage was provided. Well! An answer to the maiden's prayer had just arrived. I applied for the position and was hired after about a two week background investigation and drug check.

This new adventure lasted for almost fifteen years. Initially on a new prospective plasma donor, there was a brief screening medical history, a cursory physical examination, and urine was tested for sugar and protein. This routine was performed on each would be donor. The donor was paid for his/her plasma donation by body weight ranging from $15 to $20 dollars per unit of donated plasma.

Initially, my salary was $25 per hour. Over time, this amount gradually rose to $40. Any post donation reactions were handled by the Center Physician if it was serious and warranted.

When I first started at Plasma Alliance, (the initial name of this company and which title was destined to be changed several times during the time I was employed), there was a nurse who acted as a semi-nurse practitioner. She was without any formal training. I was not too comfortable with her credentials to do this job, but she was all this Center had available. There had not been a physician on the staff for some time. She handled the medical aspects of the business except for the two mornings a week when I worked from 8:00 am until 11:00 am on Mondays and Tuesdays. These were such oppressive hours. I really had to force myself to attend to this arduous task. Ha!

My time at MCMI had decreased to just Wednesday mornings for reasons too numerous to mention. Before long, CUSA had sold off MCMI piecemeal after the unsuccessful endeavor to break into this new field of medicine. CUSA had been without any prior insight into or understanding of the medical field. This fact was especially obvious as to not knowing which end was up in managing a medical practice.

Initially and true to form, I drafted my own goals for the Omaha Plasma Center's Medical staff to upgrade it functions. These guidelines were to be followed by the nurses:

1. To protect the patient from any personal medical problem that could be aggravated by donating Plasma twice per week.

2. To protect the Plasma Products used by the public from any difficulties caused by possible contamination of the donated plasma.

3. To protect the Company from any malpractice exposure caused directly or indirectly by the medical staff.

These goals were approved by the Center Management. The manager seemed to be relieved that he had someone on his staff knowledgeable about corporate needs and workings.

One of the major deficiencies at Centeon, one name of many to come, was the absence of a companywide Medical Director. Each Center acted as a semi-independent unit regarding the interpreting of donor eligibility and deferral criteria. Each center set their own plasma collecting standards and donor acceptance criteria so to speak. The FDA set the underlying basis for the regulations concerning all aspects of plasma collections. Local interpretation of the regulations was the norm permissible within the FDA parameters. This lack of uniformity resulted in chaos at times. There was no defined training curriculum for the Center Nurses and their role or a central person from which to obtain an answer to an immediate pending decision that was needed.

True to my nature, I drafted what I envisioned as an adequate curriculum which was imperative for a skilled nurse to be trained in for this position. The next step was to lobby my Center Manager, Alan Coleman, to allow me to institute this training program in the Omaha Center. He thought it was such a good idea that he brought this curriculum to the central Centeon Corporate Management's awareness. He lobbied to institute this program throughout the Company. With some modifications, this needed action was soon accomplished.

The next order of necessity was the obtaining of a Company-wide Medical Director who would oversee and coordinate the many essential aspects of the medical side of plasma collections. Plasma was a critical medical therapeutic source for the blood clotting agents, RhoGam for rH negative mothers, human rabies vaccine, human tetanus vaccine, and many other medicinal items. It was critical that all Centers work, collectively, with a more united and uniform medical approach to the collection of human plasma.

At long last, a great lady internist, Sandra Fielder M.D., was hired as the Company Medical Director. Within a short time, she developed order out of chaos. When we became better acquainted, I lobbied her for establishing a medical advisory committee composed of several Center Medical Directors to be included as a part of this group. The Center Directors were necessary for grass root input into donor situations, protection, and the myriad of other problems at the grass root level. These entities could arise almost every day within any Center.

With the passage of time, the Aventis Bio-Services Medical Advisory Committee, note the new company name, was instituted in 1998. I was one of the original members of this group along with a Dr. Kim Lawler from the Oklahoma City Center. He was a great fellow with very good ideas. We complemented each other well. Again, it was interesting to note that an unknown pediatrician from the hinterland could affect changes in a large company.

Because I had been given the task of training, in my Center, several newly hired Center Medical Directors; I developed a useful curriculum for their supervisory needs.

Over time, my role as the Center Medical Director shifted gears; and the training of additional nurses to handle this myriad of tasks became the norm. I evolved into a supervisory role over the medical staff which consisted of a part time doctor and three to five nurses. I no longer examined prospective donors.

Most of the cliental were indigent folks who rarely if ever saw any one in the health field. Other groups of donors were women who wanted some extra money for Christmas or for their spring garden plantings. The medical exam at Aventis became more of a brief medical health review including simple suggestions for obtaining improved health conditions relating to hypertension, obesity, self breast exams and testicular exams, mouth hygiene, and similar common medical needs. Fortunately, the Plasma Center Manager seemed to appreciate the improved screening of the donors as this significantly decreased his problems elsewhere in the donation process. It was imperative to endeavor to protect the donor from him/herself. For example, occasionally, a pregnant woman would try to slip by the physical exam only to be caught when there was an unexplained mass in her abdomen. One off chute of this improvement in donor health was that the manager experienced fewer post donation Donor reactions.

Over the years, the Omaha Plasma Center evolved through a number of owners and name changes: Plasma Alliance, Centeon, and Aventis Bioservices. When I left the Center, an Australian Company owned the company.

During my years of employment, I instituted a mandatory monthly medical staff meeting where medical problem areas occurring within the Center were discussed and solved. There were some important additional personnel training accomplished at this meeting. The Center building underwent a remodeling and refurbishing program. I was permitted to design three new donor examining rooms which provided for greater efficiency of operation.

One of the cross checks for adequacy of the physical evaluations was my keeping statistics on the reasons for temporary or permanent deferrals of clients from donating. I ran a tight ship which paid dividends when the Center was inspected by the FDA and Dr. Haag of the German Health Authority. The Center medical department usually received glowing accolades from these inspections which made the Center Manager very pleased. Dr. Haag seemed to like the various methods that I had introduced and passed the word up the chain of command to the Company Management. The Omaha Center was considered one of the best amidst the some 50 Centers that the company controlled.

Because he was such a good manager, it was only a matter of time before Alan Coleman was promoted to become a Division Manager. Mark McKinney, the enthusiastic and resourceful Assistant Manager, was promoted to the Center Manager job. He was the one who interviewed and arranged for my pre-employment evaluation many years before. This action began a long, satisfying, and fruitful association for the next 10 to 12 years. He was a delight to work with and for.

When the Australian Plasma Company bought Aventis, the corporate philosophy changed for the worse towards the donor population. The company thoughts about donor eligibility differed greatly from mine and were not compatible; so I handed in my keys and left the Center. I could not stomach this approach. After making several futile protests to upper management, I laid my Center Keys on the new manager's desk and walked out the door, never to return. This action ended my part time working. It was time to completely retire and smell the roses.

Chapter 100

    Now, to update the family activities which had transpired during my time of retirement since 1989, they consisted of the following:

1. My beloved Mary suffered a serious disaster in the fall season of 1989. We were golfing with our friends, John and Kay Bohrer, at the Omaha Country Club; where they were members. The ladies teed off on hole number four. John and I were standing back on the tee box waiting to tee off as soon as the next green was clear of golfers. Kay was driving the golf cart rather fast towards the next hole which lay over a rise so the hole and greens could not be visualized. However, most golfers were very safe from me hitting the ball too far to injure anyone. It seemed as though any club, bar none, that I used, the ball would only travel about 100 yards or less. This limitation was very frustrating to me to say the least.

    They raced the cart to view the hole and turned sharply back towards us to wave us onward. Well! Mary flew off the golf cart seat like she was shot out of a cannon, rolled over while in the air, and landed with a major thump. We dashed up to her with my heart in my mouth. She was stunned and obviously had injured her left knee. We hurried back to the car parking area and drove to Methodist Hospital. Dr. Bach, a wonderful Orthopedist, examined Mary, had X-rays taken, and determined that she had an impacted fracture of her left Tibial

Plateau of her leg. The next three months were filled with much pain and discomfort for her.

2. By had retired from his anesthesiology position at St. Joseph Hospital in Eugene, Oregon and had built a home in Bend, Oregon on a golf course. Shirley and By are avid cross country skiers. There were excellent groomed trails just 10 minutes from their home near Mount Bachelor. They kept occupied with bicycling, swimming, and traveling. Every fall By goes Elk hunting or for some other big game for two weeks with his bow and arrow.

3. Terry had an apartment in Lincoln, Nebraska from whence he directed a bimonthly Writer's Workshop at the nearby Recreation Center. His group members have given poetry readings at various coffee shops in Lincoln. He walked daily, and swam three times a week. He was and is active in the Lincoln Metro art scene.

4. Matt retired from Mutual of Omaha after twenty-five plus years to become the general business manager for his son, Conor –"Bright Eyes", an Inde Rock popular musician. Matt handles the several streams of Conor's income, disburses funds to the various members of the group, pays the other expenses, and oversees Conor's various properties. He keeps busy.

Matt and Nancy plan to move to the Washington DC area in July 2010 to be near their newest grandson and to be nearer to their oldest son, Matt, who lives in the Raleigh, North Carolina area with their two grandchildren, John and Annabelle.

Matt and Nancy have upgraded their home in various ways. They put a very ultramodern and fancy kitchen. Matt had become a gourmet cook and enjoyed cooking exotic and regular dishes.

For many years, I have heard from many of my old patients. It was so satisfying to be remembered. I still hear from Martha, an early thyroid problem, about every six months. She was the failure to thrive child at one year of age, who, now, is in her 50's decade and fairly self sufficient. In fact, I just have received another detailed letter from Martha bringing me up to date on her activities. Mrs. S. of Scottsdale,

Arizona keeps me informed every Christmas season about her family. It is so gratifying to be remembered after these past twenty plus years of retirement.

Chapter 101

My dear friend and mentor, Jim Canedy, retired from Clarkson Hospital at the age of 70. He was only able to enjoy his retirement for about seven months when he suddenly passed away from a heart attack.

By now, many of the folks who helped me along my life's pathway have passed on. How sad and what a loss for me. How much I owed them? I trust that they are satisfied with their end product and that I have justified their faith in me.

In 1991 while at Myrtle Beach with Jo and Bob Arfmann, we cussed and discussed the probability of a trip to England. Through Bob and Jo's travel agency, we settled for a tour conducted by the Globus Travel Agency. The tour would cover the Southern part of England. We flew to London where we saw the Westminster Abby, where so many greats of history were buried; the Tower of London, where there was a wonderful collection of Medieval Armors plus the Crown Jewels; the Changing of the Guards at Buchingham Palace; Churchill's W War II War Planning Room; Parliament; and many other sights. We traveled to Churchill's grave at Blandon; then, on to Shakespeare's home at Stratford-on-the-Avon. The Roman ruins at the city of Bath were fascinating, and it was very close to prehistoric Stonehenge. We traveled through King Arthur's country to Land's End, which is the furthermost point of western Wales. We stayed at Plymouth where Sir Francis Drake sailed forth to defeat the Spanish Armada. We took a ferry to the Isle of Wight where Queen Victoria had a magnificent home. She elected to live here semi-permanently after her husband, Prince Phillips, died.

One of my favorite sites was the Royal Navy Yards at Portsmouth where Admiral Lord Nelson's ship "HMS Victory" was anchored. I so loved English History from my reading of the one hundred G.A. Henty books, based upon English history that my father had collected over the years. I fell in love with these books when I was fourteen and have read them over and over. They were and still are great stories written in a Horatio Alger motif with the young teenager experiencing the historical events in the story. My beloved Mary says that she can tell when I am concerned over something as I will start reading one of my Henty stories. I can't keep any secrets from this master sleuth, my wife. We went to Canterbury Cathedral on our way back to London. The trip was everything that I had hoped it would be. The tour bus and guide were very efficient and helpful. The hotel accommodations were more than satisfactory. We flew home pleasantly satisfied.

1995 came and with it our 50th Wedding Anniversary. Mary and I agreed that we did not want a big, big party and/or gifts. For a long time, we had wanted to see Rome, the Vatican, the Pope, and ancient history. I talked with our travel agent about our desires. We decided to go a bit early towards the end of May before the official tour season started in order to encounter fewer crowds. We used the Delta Airlines' personalized and individualized tour approach so that we would be on our own while in Rome. We would spend a week in Rome taking different local Greyline Tours; then, we would fly to Athens and take a Greek Island Cruise. My beloved Mary was a great traveler and was always game for a new adventure. However, because of her old left knee fracture, she could not walk too far at any one time.

We arrived in Rome and looked for our previously arranged for driver to be transported to the hotel. Finally, we made connections and lo and behold the transportation was a big, big bus. We were the only passengers on this bus. We are off to a grand start on our adventure. The Hotel Venito was highly recommended by the Delta Tour Agent as having been recently renovated. The hotel was on Venito Avenue in a very quiet part of Rome, which was pleasant. We arrived and found the hotel had a very miniscule lobby. Our room was satisfactory; but small and nothing to write home about. There was to have been a restaurant in the hotel; but recently, it was closed except for a breakfast of rolls and coffee or juice. This was Item Number Two on our disappointment sheet. Would there be more rough waters ahead?

There was a nice sandwich shop up the street on the corner from the hotel. After our morning Greyline tour, I would purchase a ham and cheese sandwich and a beer at this shop. We would eat rest a bit, and get ready for the afternoon tour. Obviously, our Italian adventure was off to a great but somewhat shaky start. There was a lovely restaurant just up the street from our hotel where we had several outstanding meals as part of our tour.

It so happened that the Greyline Office was just two blocks from our hotel, which was very convenient for us. We elected to see Rome via Greyline city tours as it was a great way to see more places in less time. Because of Mary's knobby knee, it was important to limit the amount of walking she did. My favorite tour was "Ancient Rome" with the many ruins including the Coliseum and the Roman Forum. Medieval Rome was filled with many churches and Basilicas. My biggest disappointment was a visit to the Catacombs. I had expected to have a spiritual feeling when there; but nothing of the sort occurred, except blah! Our guide at the Catacombs was a non entity and a real bust.

Before we left Omaha, I had obtained a letter to secure tickets to the Papal Audience which was held on Wednesday mornings. The letter had to be taken to the North American University which was located near the Trevi Fountain. It was the lunch hour when I arrived, and no one was at the University. The lunch hour was known to be at least 2 hours long or more. After wasting some time waiting to no avail, I tried to find my way back to the hotel. As luck would have it, a cab came wandering by; and I quickly grabbed it.

On Wednesday morning we took a cab to St. Peter's Basilica for the Papal Audience. We were admitted to the audience on the strength of the Omaha letter alone. I was holding my breath as we did not have the official tickets. We were early enough to get a good seat. This day was a very special one, especially, for Mary. The Pope came in his Pope Mobile and passed within four rows of where we sat. This day was his birthday. There was a contingent of Polish children seated around us all dressed in yellow for his Polish colors. Mary's father had come from near Warsaw, Poland; so this was a special occasion in more ways than one.

St. Peter's Basilica Rome

The Pope gave his greetings in several different languages as he was a skilled linguist. This morning became an outstanding and memorable day for us. After the audience, we revisited St. Peter's Church which was awesome. It seemed more like a huge art museum than a church. Beneath the main floor of the Basilica, there were many small elaborate burial chapels for several of the Popes. Each chapel was magnificent with its own decor. The mosaic work was awesome. We enjoyed the Vatican Museum, which was very large and contained much more to see than one afternoon could accommodate.

We took an evening tour to see the Rome lights that ended with a five course Italian meal. We met some very interesting people at our table from Israel and Canada. Rome has many, many beautiful fountains. The Palazzo Narvara, where we ate the dinner, had two of the most famous ones.

We took a side trip to Naples and Pompeii. The ruins at Pompeii were fascinating. The upscale living by the wealthy at that time was hard to visualize; and, obviously, they lived in a very opulent manner. While on this tour, we visited a Cameo Factory. It was interesting to see two men hand carving various cameos figures out of abalone sea shells. Any resemblance to one of our assembly line factories was purely coincidental. I bought a set of cuff links for my collection which, now, was up to forty different sets. I had made a hobby of finding interesting and not expensive cuff links wherever we traveled, as a memento.

We took a tour of the Tuscan Hills to Emperor Hadrian's Villa. He was an amazing person having been an architect, emperor, general, engineer, and poet all rolled up into one person. He designed and instituted the first dome which was a new concept from a building architectural standpoint. This estate was remarkable with pools, a theatre, many rooms, hot and cold baths, and other significant features.

From Hadrian's Estate we traveled to the Villa of Cardinal D'Este which was a sight to behold. There were over 100 different types of fountains throughout the gardens. There was one fountain that made actual organ sounds. The early Church Fathers certainly knew how to live.

From Rome, we traveled to Athens, Greece where we stayed overnight at a five star hotel. The next morning we journeyed to the Acropolis and walked up the hill to the ruins. We walked around the beautiful Parthenon. It was magnificent. I could hear Socrates and Aristole philosophizing and making profound statements near me. This was a memorable experience as a fond lover of ancient history.

Later this same afternoon, we boarded the "Stella Solaris" Vessel for the Greek Island cruise. We stopped at Crete where the Minoan Civilization had flourished including where the fable of the Labyrinth and the Minotaur two thousand years ago had originated. The sanitary system was unbelievable for these ancient times. Water was brought several miles through clay pipes. The palace was remarkable and had indoor running water. For an old public health doctor that I was, I was amazed and astounded.

We stopped at the Island of Rhodes where the Knights of St. John's (Knights of the White Cross} withstood a massive assault and invasion by the Turks. This outpost of Europe stood as a bulwark and protector for Southern Europe for a great number of years from invasion by the Turks. This ancient time was one of my favorite periods in history having read about these days from my G.A. Henty books that I had fallen in love with.

The Island of Santorini was beautiful and quite small. It was necessary to take a cable car up the mountain to the city. We decided against the donkey ride up the hill. The city was covered with beautiful flowers everywhere. We stopped here on our way to Ephesus, which in itself was awe inspiring.

Ephesus was the crossroads of the trade routes in ancient times. It was conquered by Alexander the Great and, then, by the Romans. The outdoor toilets were amazing with running water to remove the feces, and another convenient trough of running water for hand washing. The streets had holes for torches for lighting at night. There was a great amphitheatre where St. Paul preached to twenty-five thousand people. Chills went up and down my spine while I stood outside this stadium.

Amphitheatre where St. Paul Preached at Ephesus

The magnificent Library ruins at Ephesus were a sight to behold. Alexander the Great had taken the huge collection of records and books from this library to the library in Alexandria, Egypt. These ancient records were lost in a major fire never to be able to be used by any researchers. How tragic!

After Ephesus, the Vessel returned to Athens where we flew home via Kennedy Airport in New York City. This trip exceeded all of our expectations and then some.

Chapter 102

By and Shirley arranged through their time share membership to obtain two condos at Lake Okaboji in July, 1995 for a small intimate family fiftieth Wedding Anniversary party and family reunion. By, Shirley, Matt, and Nancy shared one condo while Mary and I, Terry, and Karen shared the other one. We visited our old haunts such as Brooks Beach and the Edgewater Cabin where we had stayed so often. We ate at Vern and Coila's excellent restaurant for dinner, and played several rounds of golf. We had an extra special time as a family during these days. We did a considerable amount of reminiscing about our past vacations here including much family foolishness.

In February, 1997, my beloved Mary had an acute abdominal pain which was very severe. As her appendix had been out since she was eighteen, it was not appendicitis. She had had a major attack of duodenitis (small bowel infection) which required a stay in Methodist Hospital.

She received an IV antibiotic, Cipro, which was supposed to be specific for this condition. She was shifted to the oral form when she went home and was to continue on this med for several days. About midnight the first night home, she experienced a horrendous generalized pain and itching. She was in total agony and misery. I took her back to Methodist. As had I suspected, she was having a major anaphylactic reaction to the Cipro. When the dust finally settled, Mary ended up with an autoimmune body reaction resulting in Rheumatoid Arthritis, which disease was to change her way of life hence forth and forever more.

We took a belated trip to Disneyworld after she had recovered from her hospitalization. This trip was big mistake on my part. She did not complain, but her hands hurt so much that it was hard to cut up her food. This sad trip was the end of our travels forever more.

To add salt to her wounds, we were visiting the home one evening of my dear old grade school friend of many, many years, Bill Shook, when Mary stumbled on their backyard deck. She wrenched her back, sustained several thoracic and lumbar impacted and compressed vertebral fractures. She was in intense back pain. The back pain has been with her ever since. Even, the slight jarring from bumps while riding in the car could precipitate a flare up of back pain. I changed several cars seeking a much softer ride for my darling.

This pain has changed her world and has severely limited her physical ability to do much of anything. She had to see so many physicians, internists, orthopedists, and rheumatologists that she refused to see any more doctors for a long period of time. Who can blame her for this attitude?

I had turned seventy-five so I thought that it was time for this not so old man to stop water skiing. I gave the motor boat to Matt along with the Snipe Sail Boat. From now on out, a poor game of golf was my cup of tea. For a number of years, I played with several members of the Lakeshore Country Club until they dropped one by one along the wayside.

Mary and Obie on Backyard Patio South 93rd Street

Chapter 103

The 2000's arrived and with it there came another major change in our lifestyle. My wonderful Mary had a fainting spell and fell in the kitchen. She sustained three pelvic fractures including one closely adjacent to her right hip socket. She spent about six weeks in Methodist Hospital. She was not able to put any weight on her right leg for another three plus months.

To me, the writing was on the wall that we were faced with a change from our present living conditions to a different lifestyle. It became impossible to handle Mary's needs, the house, the yard, and the part time job at Aventis. I began cleaning out the basement and, then, did one room at a time for the next six months. This was a monumental job due to 40 years of accumulated material including much camping and sports equipment from the "Old Days". Mary was extremely adamant against leaving her wonderful home and "precious junk". Our sons were consulted and agreed that a change was necessary.

I investigated several places to live, but each time the Regency Lakeside Apartments came to the top of the list. At last, it was time to gather some data about rent and related expenses. I re-evaluated our financial situation with our accountant and the pending move to see if it would be feasible. The move would be alright and well within our budget.

I learned an interesting bit of information about our Long Term Health Insurance while utilizing the home care provisions that it provided. It was necessary to have an aid be with Mary on Monday and Tuesday Mornings from 7:00 am to 1:00 pm while I was at the

Aventis Plasma Center. The aid's cost was $30 per hour times five hours which equaled $150 per day. Jessica was needed for two days per week which totaled $300. My monetary reimbursement sum from the insurance company barely touched the total expense outlay as the insurance reimbursed me $25 per day which equaled $50 total for the two days. This insignificant amount was a minuscule item in the overall course of events. We needed Jessica for about three months; then we did a makeshift arrangement on our own with Mary's sister, Jenny, helping at times.

We planned to move to the Regency Apartments on November 1, 2001. This move was accomplished with a minimum of headaches. It took Mary several years (not months) before she stopped grieving over the loss of her beautiful home and feeling like a displaced person. We had plenty of room for most of our furniture and any surplus was stored in a commercial space. It was eight years before this excess was disposed of.

Mary, as always, turned our apartment of fifteen hundred square feet into a beautiful home. We were very comfortable with no yard to manage, snow to remove, no need for new windows and/or new roof to install. I enjoyed parking our car in the basement garage out of the weather. This location was handy for all of our needs; so the move had been worthwhile for all concerned.

Our lovely and beautiful home is lovely no more. I, once, visited the people who bought it. The basement had been gutted including the one half bath, the darkroom, the train room and trains, the work shop, and several other items. The attractive wood paneling in the recreation area of the basement was painted white. Ugh! The outside landscaping was depleted in the same manner. All the bushes and many flowering trees had been removed. The house looked like an ugly wart on a grass covered knoll with all of the beautiful landscaping gone with the wind. When attending a graduation function at a former neighbor's house, someone referred to our former home as the house without any landscaping. Oh my!

Our subsequent life has been a quiet one. It has been important that Mary rest every afternoon. Her back looks like an "S" curve in the highway. She has a marked scoliosis and a marked forward curve in her back with a Kyphosis. Her back is very painful at frequent intervals.

She has to be careful not to fall or agitate it. Prolonged car rides with a poor suspension system can create severe back pains which may persist for several days to weeks. The cold weather bothers both her and my osteoarthritis. Finally, Father Time won out and my beloved Mary accepted the need for the apartment after lo those many years.

We read a lot. As the library keeps track of all books checked out, in 2008 I read two hundred and sixty books. I almost equaled that with one hundred and ninety books during 2009. As our life together begins to wind down at the ripe age of eighty-seven, we have had a wonderful and very fruitful time together. Never in my wildest dreams did I expect to have sixty-five unbelievable years with the magic of my wonderful Mary with more years yet to come. God willing! If it were left up to me, I'd like another sixty-five years of being together.

Chapter 104

I received two very important and unexpected honors during 2006. My old alma mater, North High, made me a "Viking of Distinction" which is that school's Hall of Fame. At first, it didn't seem of much importance to me; but as time has passed, it is one of my most appreciated honors. The other surprise honor came via Childrens' Hospital with being chosen as one of the very first inductees into the "Legends in Pediatrics". This was Childrens' newly instituted Hall of Fame. I was honored along with Dr. John Thomas and two of my early bright lady residents who went on to great fame and fortune, Dr. Matilda McIntyre and Dr. Carol Angle. This honor really touched me to the core. After all, I had been out of sight and out of mind for almost twenty years.

Vikings of Distinction Award

Legends in Pediatrics Award

In the fall of 2006, we had a big, big 1946 medical class reunion. We had started with one hundred and six students in March of 1943 and graduated eighty-six in March of 1946. Now there were less than twenty of us still around in one form or another. Five showed up for our fiftieth reunion. Ed Malashock, a Urologist, I took care of his family and went to Saratoga Grade School with his wife, Sally Gross, Jack Latenser, a General Surgeon, Roger Boulden and his wife, Betty, a General Practitioner in Lenox, Iowa where he referred me many patients, and Jack Filkins, an Ophthalmologist. We had an enjoyable time gossiping and visiting about old and new times.

Part VIII to follow

A major catastrophe occurred which changed our lifestyle once again.

Part VIII

Major Changes in 2009
A Catastrophe Happened

An event changing happening occurred on December 6, 2009. Mary had a lab visit at Dr. Palmer's office, her Rheumatologist. All went well. There was ice in the parking lot. I brought the car to her standing on the dry sidewalk. Just as I opened her door, she called out, "Catch me". Before I could react, she fell flat on her face and was unconscious and unresponsive for at least five minutes. Blood was pouring from her forehead. Because of my recent right knee arthroscopic surgery, I could not kneel down to help evaluate the situation. I felt totally helpless and called frantically for help. About six professional people came running from the office. Someone called 911. The Squad arrived within a very short time. This situation occurred about 12:15 pm near noon.

The squad took Mary to Creighton St Joseph Hospital which was the Omaha trauma center on call for that day. I called Matt. He went directly to St. Joseph's Hospital from his home. I left Dr. Palmer's parking lot and drove to the hospital with my heart in my mouth. It took me about forty minutes to fight my way through the noon traffic. Matt met me. We filled out a thousand different papers and answered a million questions.

Meanwhile, at the hospital, X-rays, Cat Scans, and many other important evaluations were taking place in a very efficient matter. Time passed very, very slowly before Mary was returned to the ER cubicle where I could see her. She was really battered from the fall. Both of her eyes were bruised, had turned black and blue; and she looked like a raccoon. She had a large unicorn type lump right in the middle of her forehead. I was told she had a fracture of the neck of the left humerus [upper arm] with no displacement. The ER personnel wanted to admit her, but I elected to transfer her to Methodist Hospital where we both were more at home and comfortable.

Chapter 105

Due to the amount of paper work required both at St Joe and Methodist hospital, finally, Mary was admitted to her room on the acute Orthopedic Floor of Methodist about 8:30 pm. Dr. Cochran was called for her Orthopedic care. Dr. Giitter, her Internist, handled her general Medical care. Over time, it seemed as though there were a hundred different doctors wandering in and out of her room looking wise, and writing notes on her chart. All I could do was answer questions and nod yes. At least my beloved Mary was alive and responsive except for the facts around her fall.

As they evaluated her condition, it was found that she had a broken nose and a left wrist fracture in addition to her left humerus break. Her left eye was swollen shut. She looked a royal mess, but no major serious traumatic injuries or head trauma had happened. Thank God! After the evaluation and observation period was over, Mary was transferred to the Acute Orthopedic Rehab Unit. While at Methodist, she engaged in a vigorous program of physical and occupational therapy. Her left arm and wrist were immobilized by a restraint, not a cast. No surgery was required. Thank heavens!

It became very obvious to Matt and me that our living conditions would need to be shifted from our apartment in Regency to an Assisted Living Facility. The search began.

Chapter 106

The search for an Assisted Living Facility that did not appear to be a Nursing Home per Se was desired. After visiting several facilities which were eliminated either due to odd smells or a tomb like atmosphere, I inadvertently stumbled across the Immanuel Lakeside Village Community and Lighthouse Facilities. This place seemed like a four star residential resort hotel as seen from my introductory tour. Any resemblance to a Nursing Home was purely coincidental. This facility was nestled in large beautiful park like grounds. Detailed discussions entailed. There needed to be a $500 deposit. I went home full of enthusiasm. By the next day, a deposit was made for a two bedroom and two bathrooms Assisted Living Facility. We were placed upon a waiting list behind three others for the seven available units. Waiting, it would seem, would take quite awhile.

After a month, Mary needed to be transferred from the Acute Rehab Unit at Methodist Hospital to a Skilled Nursing Facility. I elected to use the "Lighthouse", which was associated with the Lakeside Village Community Living Apartments and the Assisted Living Units. These facilities had an added Memory Unit for Alzheimer's patients. All of these facilities were conveniently housed under one continuous roof including a Wellness Center and a great heated indoor pool. On January 6, 2010, Mary was transferred to the Lighthouse where her medical, physical therapy and occupational therapy were vigorously continued and enhanced.

Chapter 107

Our experiences with the new facilities exceeded our expectations. It was a comfy and cozy place to live. It was a community rather than a nursing home. The people were friendly, supportive, and nice to be around. They made a pet out of Mary because she was so sweet and so tiny.

She had daily physical therapy by a Kelly F., who was a wonderful PT terror. She made Mary become mentally involved in the PT program with her special needs. The occupational therapist, Maribeth, was as equally persistent. "No" was not a word understood to be in either of their vocabularies. They worked on Mary's walking and her hand use.

At our initial progress conference on January 6, 2010, I was asked if I wanted Mary to walk again or just shuffle her feet and rely on the need of a wheelchair. What could I say?

Because I missed her so much, I would call Mary in the morning before breakfast, before lunch, before supper, and before she went to bed. Her Care Person soon recognized my voice. Within a short time, I joined Mary for supper in the Lighthouse Dining Room. The food was very good and not at all like that of an institution. The workers began to tease us. The nurses said to us,"No playing footsie between you two under the table while at your meals". They seemed to think that we were a couple of "love birds". I wondered why? We have always been very close and supportive of each other. Previously, we had our own "Assisted Living Facility"; I assisted her, and she assisted me.

My original plans were to be sure that Mary was doing well; then have my right knee replaced before Matt and Nancy left for Washington

DC in July. My carefully planned time table went quickly down the drain.

At our second family conference, a bombshell went off. The various therapy workers and nurses said Mary needed many more weeks of therapy before she would be able to be semi-independent and move into our apartment on her own. Well!!! This news changed the landscape totally. Matt looked at me and implied that my knee had to be done very soon. We visited Kim Hall who handled the Assisted Living and Independent Apartment leasing position. We looked at a two bedroom unit in the Independent Apartment area with two baths. I decided to rent one until an Assisted Living Unit became available. Whenever!!! It probably would occur in this century or maybe in the next one. At least, we will be living in a very supportive community.

I called Dr. Cochran's office and talked with his Mary who handles the surgery scheduling. Luckily, it could be done on January 27, 2010 at 1:00 pm. The Lighthouse personnel suggested that we use Denise, who ran a Senior Moving Services, to move our Regency Apartment items. What a God send she turned out to be! She came to Regency, evaluated our needs including the packing, and arranged for four brawny movers to handle the actual moving of materials. Matt, with much arm twisting by his father, would help her with the supervision of the packing and redeploying of the furniture in our new digs. Ha! He was more than adamant about helping his Mother and secondarily his father.

Talk about pressure and the need to hustle, I quickly began emptying unnecessary clothes, linens, sweaters, and many, many other items to go to the Goodwill. I had my Pre-op visit with Dr. Cochran on Tuesday, January 19 and my Pre-op Physical with Dr. Giitter on January 21. Surgery proceeded on the 27th as planned. The Packers came in on Thursday, January 28. The move occurred on January 29, and the unpacking and reassembling of our apartment occurred on Saturday, January 30. Whew! The Cox TV people hooked up the three TV Sets on that same reassembling Saturday. Matt and Denise had performed a Herculean and miraculous task in those few days. As that modified Churchill quote goes, "Never has so much been accomplished by so few in such a short time".

My surgery went well. My Rehab at Methodist Hospital went on as scheduled until Monday, February 1 when I joined my beloved Mary in her room at the Lighthouse. Her Care-Givers said that she began to sleep better after I joined her. I wonder why?

My Rehab went extremely well with both morning and afternoon sessions. Mary's sessions were at different times from mine. We had a tough little Physical Therapist, Kelly F, whom I called the "Mean Lady". She was terrific. I admired her greatly but teased her unmercifully. At the next family conference on February 11, everyone decided that I could move to our new apartment using a walker on February 16; because I was progressing so well. Mary needed more time with the PT and OT people in the Lighthouse facility. I agreed heartily.

Arrangements were made through the Alegent System Home Care facilities to provide me with Physical Therapy, Occupational Therapy, and RN visits in my apartment. I did not need a bath aide. These experts started on February 22. They felt that my needs would be short lived as I was progressing so well.

By and his wife, Shirley, arrived from Bend, Oregon on February 17 like a whirlwind. Their arrival gave me an added feeling of confidence. This occurrence allowed Matt to devote more time to preparing his house for the housing market. By Friday February 26th, the Home Care folks finalized my care and dismissed me. Now I was on my own, totally, and completely. Hurrah! For me!

Chapter 108

By and Shirley were like a breath of fresh air with their arrival. They scouted the surrounding area banks, shops, and restaurants, and located the various stores useful for me. We made a trip to Bed, Bath, and Beyond and to the Super Target Store to obtain some necessary items for the apartment. All of the necessary stores were at our finger tips with this location even though it was far, far west from our Regency apartment area.

My, how Omaha had changed in developing new areas for housing and stores so far from our former home. Everything was falling into place. In between our needs, By and Shirley helped Matt with his house preparation. Shirley spent a considerable amount of time painting Matt's third floor room while By and Matt hauled stuff here, thither, and yon.

After several trial runs for Mary coming to visit and to explore our apartment, at long last, the "Mean Ladies" determined that she would be able to handle the change from the Lighthouse to the apartment. She joined me on March 6, 2010. What a joyous and momentous occasion this occurrence was for us. The six of us had dinner one night; adjourned to the apartment; and an intense period of moving furniture took place. Mary supervised all of the proposed changes. As an aftermath, the apartment became cozy, warm, and very friendly. Many pictures were hung on the walls. When they left, Mary and I fell into an acute state of mental and physical fatigue. By and Shirley left on Sunday, March 7. They had accomplished a yeoman's job for both Matt and us in a very short space of time.

Chapter 109

Now, we are on our own for better or worse. It was strange having my beloved Mary around all of the time as we had been apart for over three long and lonely months. Having a "Roomie" again took some readjustments by me to accommodate to her needs, likes, and dislikes.

Arrangements had been made for the Alegent Home Care folks to provide for Mary's PT, OT, and RN needs in the apartment. There was even a Bath and Care Aid person included. We seemed overwhelmed with bodies, appointment times, and the like. Someone was always underfoot even though they had the best of intentions. We both had multiple medications to take from before at Regency and more meds after the Lighthouse Skilled Nursing facility. Within a short period of time, we rebelled. The first to go was the unnecessary medications to us. We went back to what we were taking during our Regency days.

The next item of issue was to schedule any PT, OT, or RN visits after 10:30 AM as we wanted to have a leisure breakfast and to be able to read the morning paper. With Mary's permission and relief, I cancelled the Bath Aide; and we eliminated the RN very soon. The next personnel to go was the OT after she OK'd Mary's ability to shower herself, to get in and out of bed alone, and to perform several other essential living needs. We were left with the most important person, the Physical Therapist, for the long haul.

With By's encouragement and after I had completed the time with my PT lady, I visited the Wellness Center to begin a regular routine of planned exercises. I told Penny, another nice but really mean lady, that I wanted muscles like Arnold Schwarzenegger. Ha! Penny had a good laugh at my expense. I had used the "Nu Step" machine in the Skilled Nursing PT and enjoyed it. After three orientation sessions, I was on my own for the Cardiovascular machines, stretching, warm-up, and cool down activities. The machines I worked on Monday, Wednesday, and Friday mornings. The "Nu-Step" I accomplish daily including Tuesday and Thursdays when Mary was doing her exercises. I planned to start some pool activities such as wading and using the kick board. Later on, I want to try to swim again as I haven't been swimming since I stopped water skiing at the tender age of 75.

This regular regime has been very satisfying, and the Supervisors have been great. My new nemesis has been Penny A. She was, at once, a true delight, but a real taskmaster. She will not allow any cutting of corners by me. I played games with her but always got caught. I swear that she has eyes on all four sides of her head. Subtly, she is on to my intentions and keeps one eye peeled in my direction. I had tried the pool once and did not find it very satisfying; so I planned to give it a few more chances to prove itself. Subsequently, it has proven its worth.

Meanwhile, Mary started to go to the Wellness Center with the "Nu-Step" Exercise Machine and some easy range of motion arm and leg exercises. With her regular PT person, whose name was Mary; Dr. Cochran wanted her to begin gentle left arm motions, which exercises have been started.

The evening meal is a special time for us here at the Village. We have renewed our relationships and have eaten with our old friends, John and Dorothy Barmore from med school, internship, Texas, and Japan days, and with several other pleasant residents. We have had many enjoyable new acquaintances and enjoyable conversations with different folks over dinner. Mary is becoming a great visitor, once again, with these many different contacts. She is gaining weight at long last. At this moment in time, we, both, are making good progress.

Mary was rather fragile physically and, initially, had been trying too hard with her exercise program. As a consequence, she would become nauseated when overloaded. Because the Wellness Center was so convenient and enjoyable for both of us, I cancelled the regular PT person. We were almost back to our old Regency living regimes. We have been enjoying living here more and more. Once again, I would describe this place as a very friendly, comfy, and cozy community

I usually have done our grocery shopping for what few items we need and run errands on Monday afternoons. There needed to be two tub loads of personal whites and one of colored clothes washed each week; which I do. The cleaners have picked up and delivered our cleaning at the door. Tracy, the housecleaner, has cleaned and vacuumed the apartment every other week. She even changed the bed sheets, changed the towels, and washed them. Bless her for the help. The newspaper comes at our door each morning. We go to the in-house beauty shop every two weeks for Mary and the barber shop for me monthly. There was a small convenience store near the office to obtain milk and other small items as needed. How much better can it get? This place was much like a small community where everyone is supportive and interested in everyone else.

Chapter 110

Here are some family vignettes to enjoy, especially, the items about the great Fiddler and Diddler from his dim, dark past:

For awhile, I had a bad case of rose bush fever and delved into rose culture with both feet. I had dwarf roses and tree roses covered with the big, red New Yorker blooms and almost everything in between. I didn't like the tree rose as it had to be buried every fall like a body and set upright in the spring. At one time, there were over 100 roses of all types in the yard. Father time took care of this interest because the growth of our trees dimmed the sun; and so the roses shriveled up and one by one went to rose heaven.

Next, I went for something flowering during all 12 months of the year starting with the early bulbs in late January and early February until December. I never ever could get anything to bloom in those last few December weeks of the year. I spent a small fortune on the Helleborus niger- Christmas rose to you, the reader - with a total failure to report. The Christmas rose was guaranteed to bloom in December, but never did it do so in my yard. Bah! Humbug.

I grew geraniums in the basement under lights before the home grow light garden carts came into being. I liked the cinnamon scented geraniums the best. We had twenty different species of trees in the yard. I never knew how tender trees were. I thought that you stuck a tree in the ground; and, then, it was on its own. HA HA! The maintenance of trees is a very expensive proposition. They are subject to many different diseases like wilt, beetles, borers, and a thousand other things. Trees have to be sprayed, injected with iron, regularly pruned, and a real must is that they need to be talked to and praised so that their blooms will look beautiful. I really wanted to find a hale and hearty old Oak Tree which could stand on its own roots and thrive for years on end without any pampering. The finding of a truly hearty tree was never to happen.

Before the trees, we had a big flower garden across the back of the back yard which was ten feet deep and thirty feet long. The trees and lack of sun did this garden in. Mary had cut flowers for a long time. I tried to play landscaper and wanted to have a sunken pond near the backyard patio; but after several uninspiring attempts, this wild hair went down the tube along with many other foolish ideas too numerous to mention.

Our boys and their early interests:

We entered the tropical fish hobby with both feet getting wet. A small ten gallon tank led to a bigger one and so on until we had a one hundred and a couple of fifty gallon tanks. My favorite tropical fish were the Neon tetras and Angel fish for beauty and the Zebra Fish for constant activity. This hobby stuck with our son, By, through high school until he moved to Milwaukee for his pre-med schooling at Marquette University.

I looked out the front window one day to see how Matt was coming along with his chores. Well!! There he was lying on the ground, watching the fleecy clouds float by with old "Duke", the family dog, lying with his head on Matt's chest. What a wonderful picture of contentment.

Terry had a great big heart. He would go to the grocery store with Mary in order to fleece her out of another youth book in the current series being offered. When he returned home, he would walk all over the neighborhood looking for his brothers to give them their "Twinkies"; before he would eat his own.

During the summer on Saturdays, I would make rounds in the yard and make a list of chores for each boy to perform during the following week. Later, I checked on how well the work was done. They did a good job. I think Terry was the most conscientious worker. The boys learned in detail how to care for a yard as evidenced today with their own yards.

The grandsons, each in turn, came on Saturdays to do the same type of yard tasks for a small wage and to learn about yard care. One day, our

Matt asked one of his boys, "Does Grandpa still make out those work lists"? When he received an affirmative answer, he replied, "Oh, how I hated those lists." Ha Ha!

Grandson, Justin, was sort of sneaky in that after he arrived, he would go to visit with Grandma, have breakfast, and while away valuable work time visiting. The irony of it was that he felt that he should get a better wage. No way Jose!

Old "Duke" was a faithful friend for over fourteen years. Everywhere the boys went, there was old Duke. After fourteen years, he became old and decrepit and had to be put to sleep. While Mary was at the beauty shop, Matt and I did this dastardly deed and took him to the Vet. How we all cried and cried when it was over. We got a new dog and argued over names. When it was suggested that he be called "Duke", By vetoed that name very quickly. He said, "There is only one Duke". Another name was found – "Beric".

Sometimes undesirable outcomes occur when they are least expected. By was to trim the bushes along the backyard fence, which he did. The problem was that he not only trimmed the bushes but he mangled our beautiful Magnolia tree in his zeal with the process of trimming. As a consequence, our neighbors had lovely blossoms to observe over the fence in the spring in their back yard while we looked at some bare spots where limbs used to be. Grrr! Oh, well it is only a tree.

Whenever Mary becomes nostalgic about her home of long ago, I remind her that her house is still taking good care of us as the investments made from the house sale are caring for us now. How true this fact is! Our home was and is still sheltering us.

It is time to close this saga on our past, present, and future. It has been a fruitful and enjoyable journey through time and memories. I am eighty-seven, and Mary was so this May. We are in the sixty-fifth year of our wonderful marriage. The marriage is going strong, and hopefully, will be for many, many years to come. Goodbye and God bless you. I hope that you have enjoyed this journey through time with me. B. B. Oberst M.D, FAAP

The Epilogue to Follow

Epilogue

As I stand here looking in retrospect having completed this saga in these waning years of our life together, Mary and I have had a long and fruitful romantic existence filled with many wonderful memories and a few major sad ones. The magic is still very present whenever I hold Mary's hand and that has never changed since our first date at Peony Park sixty-five years ago. It is apparent to our family and to us that we are in a lovely place to live and reside. We have good meals and socialize with many different people from all walks of life. I have encountered several individuals whose children I was privileged to care for, and others who knew of me from the dim dark past.

We can indulge in physical exercise in the Wellness Center at our convenience. I am amazed how many folks here are in their 90's and going strong. There is one lady, Mrs. C., who is 98 and does her cardiovascular exercises along with the "Nu Step" Machine every day. Next, she will whisk into the computer room to access her E-mails from her relatives She is able to do needle point and embroidery without glasses. Wow! Mary and I are mere children compared to some of these active folks living here.

Stores and banks are close at hand and within five minutes by car. The newspaper is at our door, a coffee shop and small store, and mail is just down on the first floor.

The Lakeside Village provides transportation for our doctor appointments. The grounds are beautiful. I have another lake with fountains to walk beside with a quiet place to sit and meditate. We have our religious Mass on site each Thursday afternoon or the "Shut-In" TV Mass on Sundays.

As time passes, if we have need of more detailed care, it is available. The place is not cheap but within our means. Our children are very content because we are in such a nice, friendly, and safe facility. We are looked after by many compassionate people. What more could we desire. As I said before, "Our former beautiful home is still financially taking care of us." Our twilight years are very pleasant.

Many people have asked me about contrasting the old and new delivery of medicine today and what are my feelings about the modern aspects of medicine. The miracles of all types of imaging, organ transplants, and the many other advances cannot be denied, are mind boggling, and border on the miraculous; however, I find some important medical elements have been lost or gone missing over the years.

I find that personal relationships with the medical profession leave much to be desired. I tend to resent being called by my first name when I first come to a medical office without my permission, or until I have had a significant association over a good period of time. This familiarity denotes a relationship that does not exist. This approach to me is a bit too familiar for me early in any medical relationship. I would have hesitated to call any of my former mother's by their first name when I was in practice. To me, this assumed familiarity is almost a point of disrespect. Where did the "Bedside Manner" go? I believe it will seldom, if ever, be able to be resurrected due to the training medical students and residents now receive. With our many trips to many different doctors' offices, the greetings and atmospheres leave much, much to be desired. There is so much waiting and waiting with much inefficiency being readily apparent until the appointment is finally underway.

I shudder at the frivolous pretended use of the stethoscope which hangs around the professional neck like a badge of honor along with the coffee cup in hand. This persona seems to be the badge of the day by many so called professionals. Who could hear and interpret any breath sounds by the stethoscope through many layers of clothing as is so often the case when the lungs are being examined or the blood pressure is being taken in a doctor's office?

Can true lung breath sounds be identified through the layers of clothing as to whether the sounds are vesicular, bronchovesicular, or bronchial and/or are there rales or rhonchi present? The listener cannot have the slightest clue as to what is being heard unless the stethoscope is placed on the bare skin. The same travesty occurs when one is supposedly listening to the heart tones. How can heart murmurs and other sounds be heard? Having taught physical diagnosis to students for years, this current approach is beyond my comprehension and is very irritating to me. Obviously, this cavalier attitude of pseudo examination is a pain in my "you know where". In lieu of actually listening and interpreting breath and/or heart sounds, an expensive x-ray is taken instead.

Personal appearance is another item that seems to have gone by the boards, and this unprofessional attitude really irritates me. Jeans, open collared shirts, casual wear, poorly trimmed beards, and tennis shoes are all too apparent. Where did the professional appearance go? The modern attitude and dress does very little to instill confidence at the time of the first impression on an initial office visit. I admit to being very prejudice towards wanting my personal physician to look like a real live practicing doctor not someone who appears as though he/she just came in from the garden or south forty acreage without changing clothes, washing the hands, or cleaning up. Oh! How the mighty have fallen from their lofty pedestal.

With the growth of the mega medical conglomerates, doctors are owned and employed by someone from someplace and somewhere. It seems to me that "Body Count" numbers of patients seen per day drive the day for most physicians. I well remember what Dr. Kennedy of the Mayo Clinic told me, "Oberst, you are not seeing patients. You are only seeing bodies". It seems to me that we are getting very close to that reality and fact of life.

Soon, unless you only have an acute episodic illness like a cold, there is not going to be much professional time available to really have a true medical visit due to the corporation requiring body counts.

When I returned to Omaha, I was the twenty-second pediatrician practicing; now there is over one hundred, and they are all owned by somebody; except for my old office and one other solo lady pediatrician. Instead of talking about patients, many times people are referred to as "THAT" case of pneumonia, kidney problem, or some other derogatory designation rather the using the patient's name. Why should the physician of today try to demonstrate a professional attitude when he/she is guaranteed a salary? With just so many defined working hours required, why work anymore than is barely needed.

I guess these remarks sums up my thoughts about the present and near future of current medicine. With the institution of the new Health Care Legislation, heaven help us in the future! The unpleasant attitudes of now will become ugly feelings later on with rationing of care due to the paucity of first line physicians.

Best wishes to all of you who took this journey into the past with me. God bless you and yours. Amen B B Oberst M.D., FAAP

CURRICULUM VITAE

BYRON B. OBERST, M.D., F.A.A.P.
(Fellow of the American Academy of Pediatrics)

EDUCATIONAL BACKGROUND

Grade Level Year School Degree Location

1. Elementary 1937 Saratoga Omaha, Nebraska

2. Secondary: 1940 North High Omaha, Nebraska

3. College: 1944 University of Omaha BA Omaha, Nebraska

4. Graduate: 1946 University of Nebraska, College of Medicine MD Omaha, Nebraska

5. Internship: 1947 University of Nebraska Hospital Omaha, Nebraska

6. Residency: 1948 University of Nebraska Hospital Level 2 Omaha, Nebraska

7. US Army: 1949 Post Pediatrician Fort Dix, N.J.

8. US Army: 1950 172nd Station Hospital Sendai, Japan

9. Residency: 1951 Henry Ford Hospital Detroit, Michigan Level 3

10. Private Practice: 1951-88 Omaha Childrens' Clinic PC Omaha, Nebraska

11. American Board of Pediatrics Certificate #4126 October 26, 1952

MEMBER OF THE FOLLOWING SOCIETIES

1. American Academy of Pediatrics, 1951 to date

2. Northwest Pediatric Society, 1951 to 1961

3 Nebraska Pediatric Society (including Presidency in 1958) 1951 to 1988

4. Midwest Clinical Society (including Chairman of Section of Pediatrics in 1957), 1951 to 1976

5. Omaha-Douglas County Medical Society, 1951 to date

6. Nebraska State Medical Society, 1951 to date

7. American Medical Association, 1951 to date

8. Nebraska Heart Association, 1951 to 1970

9. Catholic Physician Guild, 1951 to 1960

10. Pan American Medical Society - Pediatric Section, 1965-1983

11. Fellow, Section of American Academy of Pediatrics on Child Development, 1963 to 1987

12. Charter Member of the Society for Adolescent Medicine, 1968 to 1983

13. Fellow of School Health Physicians, 1970 to 1973

14. Fellow, Section on Community Pediatrics, American Academy of Pediatrics, 1972 to 1987

15. Society for Computer Medicine, 1973 to 1982

16. Great Plains Organization for Perinatal Health Care, 1976 to 1977

17. Charter Member of the Sports Safety and Health Care Society, 1977 to 1988

18. Nebraska Chapter, American Academy of Pediatrics, 1951 to 1988 (including Chapter Chairmanship, 1976 to 1979)

19. American Association of Medical Systems and Informatics, 1982 to 1990

20. American Association of Mental Deficiency, 1984 to 1986

21. Fellow, Section on Adolescence, American Academy of Pediatrics, 1982 to 1987

22. Fellow, Section on Computers and Other Technology, American Academy of Pediatrics, 1984 to 2010

23. Affiliate, Medical Group Management Association, 1988-1989

ACTIVITIES

1. Instructor in Pediatrics at Wayne University School of Medicine, Detroit, Michigan, 1950-1951

2. Instructor in Pediatrics at Henry Ford Hospital School of Nursing,

3. Director of Residency Program University Nebraska College of Medicine and the House Staff at Children's Memorial Hospital, 1951-1954

4. Instructor in Pediatrics at the University of Nebraska College of Medicine, 1951-1954 and Associate 1954-1959

5. Instructor in Pediatrics at Creighton College of Medicine, 1951-1954

6. Vice-President of Catholic Physician's Guild, 1959 (Member, 1951 to 1960

7. Instructor in Pediatrics at St. Catherine's School of Nursing, 1952-1955

8. Secretary of Staff of Children's Memorial Hospital, 1952-55

9. Lecturer for Foundation for Understanding, Inc., 1952-1954

10. Assistant Clinician for Heart Diseases for Services for Crippled Children, State of Nebraska, 1953-1960

11. Clinician in Charge of Nursery at Nebraska Methodist Hospital, 1957-1960

12. Member of Infection Control Committee at Nebraska Methodist Hospital, 1957-1960

13. Treasurer of Staff at Children's Memorial Hospital, 1958

14. Assistant Professor of Pediatrics, University of Nebraska College of Medicine, 1959-1969

15. President of Catholic Physician's Guild of Omaha, 1960

16. Director of Adolescent Clinic, University of Nebraska College of Medicine, 1960-1963

17. Pediatrician-in-Charge of Pediatrics and Newborns, Bishop Clarkson Memorial Hospital, 1963-1976

18. Pediatrician-in-Chief, Archbishop Bergan Mercy Hospital, 1965-1966

19. Adjunct Professor, Psychology, Bellevue College, Bellevue, Nebraska, 1966-1968

20. Vice-President, Medical Staff of Children's Memorial Hospital, 1966-1968

21. Director of Adolescent Clinic, Children's Memorial Hospital, Omaha, Nebraska, 1967-1970

22. Chairman of Youth Committee, Nebraska Chapter of American Academy of Pediatrics, 1976-1981

23. Board of Directors, Operation Bridge, Suburban Youth Guide-line Counseling Service, 1968-1973

24. President, Staff of Children's Memorial Hospital, 1968-1970

25. Associate Professor of Pediatrics, University of Nebraska College of Medicine, 1969-1977

26. A.M.A. Physician's Recognition Award, July 1, 1969, 1973, 1976, 1979, 1983. 1985

27. Nebraska State Medical Association, Committee on Mental Health, 1971

28. Omaha-Douglas County Medical Society, Committee on Education 1971

29. Society for Adolescent Medicine, Member of Committee on Private Practice, 1971-1978; Chairman of Subcommittee on Insurance and Other Third Party Payees, 1976-1978

30. Nebraska Chapter, American Academy of Pediatrics, Chairman, Committee on Medical Practice, 1971-1976

31. Nebraska Chapter, American Academy of Pediatrics, Alternate Chapter Chairman, 1974-1976

32. Member, Committee on Standards, Society for Computer Medicine, 1974-1978

33. Chairman, Committee on Standards, Society for Computer Medicine, 1974-1977

34. Member, Committee on Child and Youth Health Care Standards, American Academy of Pediatrics, 1976-1979

35. Chairman, Nebraska Chapter, American Academy of Pediatrics, 1976-1979

36. Member, Board of Directors, Society for Computer Medicine, 1976 to 1977

37. Professor of Clinical Pediatrics, University of Nebraska College of Medicine, 1977 to 1988

38. Nebraska State Medical Association, Committee on Medical Ethics, 1977

39. Alternate Chairman, District VI, American Academy of Pediatrics, 1979-1983

40. Appointment to Committee on Practice and Ambulatory Medicine, American Academy of Pediatrics, 1979-1980

41. Member, Committee on Legislative Issues, American Academy of Pediatrics, October 1979 to July 1980

42. Chairman, Chapter Chairmen's Forum Committee, American Academy of Pediatrics, 1978-1979, Consultant to the Committee, 1980

43. Member, Committee on Medical Education, American Academy of Pediatrics, 1980

44. Chairman, Committee on Standards, Society for Computer Medicine, 1980-1982

45. Member, Credentials Committee, Children's Memorial Hospital, 1981-1984

46. Member, Committee on Scientific Programs, American Academy of Pediatrics, 1981-1982

47. Member, Long-Range Planning Committee, Children's Memorial Hospital, 1981 to 1985

48. Member, Nominating Committee, Children's Memorial Hospital 1981-1984

49. Chairman, Committee on Standards, American Association of Medical Systems and Informatics, 1982-1985

50. Chairman of the Automated Pediatric Special Interest Group, American Association of Medical Systems and Informatics, 1983-1985

51. American Academy of Pediatrics Representative to the AMA Advisory Council for CPT4, 1983-1986

52. Liaison Member for the Omaha Metropolitan Medical Society Executive Committee to the Omaha Douglas County Board of Health, 1982-1984

53. Chairman, Section on Computers and Other Technology, American Academy of Pediatrics 1984 to October 1988

54. Member, Council on Sections, American Academy of Pediatrics, 1985-1986

55. Member, Physician Advisory Board to Phycom, Fisher-Stevens Co. Physician Communication Network, 1984 to 1986

56. Member, Clinical Diagnostic Scientific Advisory Panel, Clinical Diagnostic, Inc., 1985 to 1987

57. Chairman, Children's Memorial Hospital Computer Committee, 1984-85

58. Chairman, Region VIII Medicine Division of Ombrea Association on Mental Deficiency

59. Member, Clarkson Hospital New Medical Records Committee, 1984-85

60. Member, Clarkson Hospital Medical Record Committee, 1985 to 1987

61. American Academy of Pediatrics Task Force on New Technologies, 1984

62. Senior Consultant, University of Nebraska Medical Center, 1988 to 2010

63. Medical Advisor, Medical Computer Management, Inc, 1988 to 1992

64. Chairman Subcommittee on Practice Management of Retired Physicians for the Metro Omaha Medical Society, 1989-1994

65. Medical Consultant and Advisor, Healthcare Business Solutions, Inc. 1991-1995

66. Medical Director, Omaha Division, Plasma Alliance December 1992-2008

CIVIC DUTIES

1. Member of Omaha Exchange Club, 1952-54

2. Guest Lecturer for PTA at many Omaha Schools, Public and Parochial

3. American Academy of Pediatrics Representative to the National PTA Convention in Omaha, 1957

4. Boy Scout Activities: Public Health Merit Badge Examiner, 1952-60; Committee Member of Cub Scout Pack at Christ the King School 1957-58; Committee Member of Boy Scout Troop at Christ the King School, 1959; Scout Master, Troop #370, Christ the King School 1960-1967

5. Guest Lecturer for YMCA Family Retreat Camps

6. Guest Lecturer for many various church young people groups

7. Guest Lecturer for various school teacher groups

8. Founder and Member of Board of Directors, Omaha STAAR Program for School Learning Disabilities, 1968-1978

9. Member, Committee on Health Planning of the Health Planning Council of the Midlands, 1976--1978l

10. Member, Omaha Douglas County Board of Health, 1982 to 1984

PUBLICATIONS

1. Acute Nicotine Poisoning: Case Report, Byron B. Oberst, M.D. and Ross A. McIntyre, M.D., Pediatrics, Vol. II, No. 4, p. 338, April 1953

2. Circulation Time in the Newborn Infant, Using the Fluorescein Dye Method: Byron B. Oberst, M.D., and Fritz LaRoche M.D.: Journal of Pediatrics, Vol. 45, p. 581, 1954 Pediatrics, Vol. 45, p. 581, 1954

3. Pseudohypoparathyroidism: Report of Case, Byron B. Oberst, M.D., and Charles A. Tompkins, M.D.: AM. J. of Dis. of Children, Vol. 90, No. 2, p. 205, August 1955

4. Congenital Anomalies of the G.I. Tract: Byron B. Oberst, M.D. and Lucy Radicia, M.D.: Nebraska State Med. Jr., February 1955

5. Preventive Care of Infants and Children, IV Influence of "Guided Growth" on Feeding and Sleeping Patterns of Children Clinical Applications, Charles A. Tompkins M.D., Byron B. Oberst M.D., V. Jeanette Peterson Hamlin B.S., Nebraska State Med Jr.,Vol. 38, p 435, December 1953 Jeanette Peterson Hamlin, B.S.; Nebraska State Med. Jr., Vol. 38, p.435, December 1953

6. Preventive Care of Infants and Children, V Infant Feeding and Colic: Charles A. Tompkins, M.D., Byron B. Oberst, M.D. and John L. Gedgoud, M.D., Nebraska State Med. Jr., Vol. 40, p. 128, April 1955

7. Paroxysmal Tachycardia with Cerebral Embolis: Case Report: Byron B. Oberst M.D., Journal of Pediatrics Vol. 44p.203-204, February 1954

8. Colorimetric Determination of Blood pH; Willis F. Stanage, M.D., Byron B. Oberst, M.D. and John N. Brown, M.D.: Jr. of Pediatrics, Vol. 47, p. 571-575, November 1955

9. Exchange Transfusion Technique and Use of Aqueous Adrenal Cortical Extract as an Adjunct to Treatment, Byron B. Oberst M.D.: Ne St. Med. Jr., June 1956

10. Chalasia and Achalasis: Children's Memorial Hospital Staff Conference: Byron B. Oberst, M.D., Ralph C. Moore, M.D., Carol R. Angle, M.D.; Nebraska State Med Jr., p. 251, May 1957

11. Participation in Modern Medicine Forum with L. Diamond, W. Zuelzer, Byron B. Oberst, M.D.: Comments on Exchange Transfusion with Packed Red Cells, June 1958

12. Treatment of rH and Related Blood Problems: Clarkson Hospital Staff Bulletin, October 1959, Byron B. Oberst, M.D.

13. Preventive Care of Infants and Children VI: School Adjustment Problems and Their Relationship to "Guided Growth"; The Journal Lancet, July 1966, Vol. 86, p. 331, Byron B. Oberst, M.D.

14. Preventive Care of Infants and Children VII, A Perspective on Adolescence in General, Ne State Med Jr., June- July- October 1969 1969, Byron B. Oberst, M.D.

15. Preventive Care of Infants and Children VIII, Adolescents and Some of Their Social Problems, Including Parenthood: Nebr. State Med. Jr., Byron B. Oberst, M.D., Sept. and Oct. 1970

16. Preventive Care of Infants and Children IX, Unlock the Door on Youth Problems: Nebr. State Med. Jr., July-August 1971, Byron B. Oberst, M.D.

17. Preventive Care of Infants and Children X, An Anticipatory Guidance Program for General Pediatric and Adolescent Office Practice: Clinical Pediatrics November 1971, Byron B. Oberst, M.D.

18. When is a Child Really Ready for School?: Medical Times, June 1972, Byron B. Oberst, M.D.

19. Book: Practical Guidelines for General Pediatric and Adolescent Office Practice: Charles C. Thomas, Publisher, January 1973, Byron B. Oberst, M.D.

20. A Community Approach to Specific School Learning Disabilities: The Omaha STAAR Project: Journal of Learning Disabilities. Aug.-Sept. 1973, Byron B. Oberst, M.D.

21. The Development of Norms and Guidelines for Office and Hospital Medical Care and Clinical Medicine and the Computer: Proceedings of the Fourth Annual Conference of the Society for Computer Medicine, 1974, Byron B. Oberst, M.D

22. A Total Health Care System as Viewed by a Private Practitioner: Part I, A Composite Overview; Pediatrician 4: 176-189, Byron B. Oberst, M.D., 1975

23. A Total Health Care System as Viewed by a Private Practitioner: Part II, A Conceptual Design; Pediatrician, 4:372, Byron B. Oberst, M.D., 1975

24. A Total Health Care System as Viewed by a Private Practitioner: Part III, Progress Report: Pediatrician, 4: 383, Byron B. Oberst, M.D., 1975

25. A Private Practice System Utilizing the Computer and the Problem Oriented Medical Record: Computer Medicine, October 1975, Byron B. Oberst, M.D

26. Current Status of the Language System in Clinical Medicine, Proceedings of the Fifth Annual Conference for Society for Computer Medicine, 1975, Byron B. Oberst, M.D.

27. Language System for Patient Care -- Patient Centered Health System: Proceedings of the Fifth Annual Conference of the Society for Computer Medicine, 1975, Byron B. Oberst, M.D.

28. The Need for a Commonality of Purpose, Design and Application of Computers Within the Medical Specialty Organizations, Jr. of Clinical Computing, Vol. 5, No. 2, 1976, Byron B. Oberst, M.D.

29. Society for Computer Medicine, Committee on Standards Progress Report and Workshop: Proceedings of the Sixth Annual Conference of the Society for Computer Medicine, November 1976, Byron B. Oberst, M.D.

30. Common Goals: Working Together: Proceedings of the Sixth Annual Conference for the Society of Computer Medicine, 1976, Byron B. Oberst M.D.

31. Why There is a Need to Determine School Readiness: A Philosophical Discussion Based Upon Long- Term Experiences: Byron B. Oberst, M.D., Pediatrician, 8:133-139, 1979

32. What Constitutes a School Readiness Examination? The Component Parts, Byron B. Oberst M.D., Pediatrician 7: 305-310 ; 1978

33. The Administrative Anatomy of the Pediatric Practice of the Future: Byron B. Oberst, M.D., Pediatrics, 18:1, p. 9-11, January 1979

34. The Parents Guide to Child Raising: Glen Austin, M.D., Julia Stone, Olive and John C. Richards, Spectrum Books, Prentice- Hall, Inc., 1978, Contributing Author. Byron B. Oberst M.D.

35. Book: Computer Applications to Private Practice - A Primer: Co-editor, Byron B. Oberst, M.D.; R. Reid, M.D., April 1984 Springer-Verlag

36. Computers in the Modern Medical Office: Update: Computers in Medicine, November-December 1984, Vol. II: No. 6

37. Guidelines for User Access to Computerized Medical Records, Jelovsek, F.R.; Bolinger, R.E.; Davis, R.E.; Long J.M.; Oberst B.B., Reid, R.A., Zimmer J., Journal of Medical Systems, Vol. II, No. 3, 1978

38. Medical Record Linkage - Panel Discussion; Smith, M.E.; Wendl, H.F.; Jelovsek, F.R.; Oberst, B.B.; Journal of Clinical Computing, Vol. 13, No. 2 & 3, 1984

39. Book: Computer Application to Private Practice: 2nd Edition Oberst BB, Long J., Springer-Verlag, 1988

40. Clinical Benefits of a Life Long Medical Record, Oberst, B.B.; Medical Documentation Update, Institute for Medical Record Economics, Inc., V.6, N.3, August/September 1988

41. Oberst, B.B.; Chapter: Doctor Office Systems: Standalone and Linked; Healthcare Information Management Systems: A Practical Guide; Edited by Marion J. Ball; Judith V. Douglas; James W. Albright; and Robert I O'Desky; Springer-Verlag; 1990

PAPERS PRESENTED TO VARIOUS AUDIENCES

1. Northwest Pediatric Society: Exchange Transfusion Technique, Bay Port, Minnesota, 1956

2. Regional Meeting of American College of Surgeons, Omaha, Nebraska, Erythroblastosis and Related Studies, 1957

3. Midwest Clinical Society: 1. Exchange Transfusion, 2. Poisoning Symposium, 1957

4. Nebraska Heart Association: Congenital Heart Disease, Panel Discussion with Doctor Coburn, 1958

5. Midwest Clinical Society, Resuscitation in the Newborn, November, 1959

6. Midwest Clinical Society, Infections in the Newborn Nursery, November 1961

7. Midwest Clinical Society: Panel Discussion, What's New in Pediatrics?, School Adjustment Problems and Phenylketonuria, November 1962

8. Iowa League of Nurses, Annual Meeting, Adolescence, Spring 1962

9. Iowa League of Nurses, Western Division, Adolescent Motherhood, November 1962

10. Sioux Falls Medical Society, October 1964, Problems in Adolescence

11. Adolescence in General, Sioux Falls, South Dakota, South Dakota Medical Society, March 1966

12. Nebraska Obstetrical Society, Las Vegas, Nevada, Erythroblastosis, New Developments, December 1966

13. District II Nebraska State Teacher's Convention, Omaha, Nebraska, The Trying Years (12-16) of Adolescence, November 1967

14. District 2 and District 7, OB-GYN Nurses Convention, Adolescents and Their Problems, Including Parenthood, 1967

15. Panel, Member Sex Education in the Schools, Annual Meeting Nebraska Association of School Administrators, November 1967

16. Midwest Section of OB-GYN Society, November 1967, Problems in Adolescence

17. Dodge County Medical Society, Des Moines, Iowa, March 1968, Problems in Adolescence

18. Teacher's Workshop, Fremont, Nebraska, The Trying Years in Adolescence, January 1968

19. The Pediatrician Looks at Adolescence, Omaha Midwest Clinical Society, October 1968

20. Panel on School Learning Disabilities, Omaha Midwest Clinical Society, October 1968

21. Iowa League of Nursing, Symposium on the Adolescent Years, (Early-Middle-Late), October 1969

22. District 9 Teacher's Convention, Kearney, Nebraska, Junior High Section, The Changing Adolescent, October 1969

23. Panel on Counseling the Adolescent, Omaha Midwest Clinical Society, November 1969

24. Round Table on Anticipatory Guidance, American Academy of Pediatrics, Byron B. Oberst, M.D., Co-Leader with Charles A. Tompkins, M.D. of Tucson, Arizona, Annual Meeting, San Francisco. California, October 1970

25. Guest Lecturer, Tri-County Family Practice Postgraduate Course, Denison, Iowa, May 1972: 1. Continuum of Growth, 2. Preventive Counseling of Teenagers

26. Guest Lecturer, Fourteenth Annual Seminar for Pharmacists, October1973, Omaha, Nebraska; Discussion of the Role of Medications in the Minimal Brain Dysfunction Syndrome

27. Panel Member, Omaha Midwest Clinical Society, October 1973, The Pediatrician's Role in Evaluating and Handling Children With Learning Problems

28. Adolescent Nursing Seminar, Children's Memorial Hospital, Omaha, Nebraska, Processes of Growth and Development, April 1973

29. Helpful Guidelines in Understanding Adolescent Behavior, School Nurse Lecture Series, Omaha, Nebraska, May 1974

30. Round Table, Minnesota Chapter AAP, The Relative Value Scale and Its Application, May 1974

31. Panel on Learning Disabilities, Omaha, Nebraska; State Convention Nebraska A.C.L.D., April 1974,

32. Round Table on "Anticipatory Guidance", American Academy of Pediatrics Spring Meeting, Denver, Colorado, April 1974

33. Panel on Recertification, American Academy of Pediatrics Spring Meeting, Denver, Colorado, April 1974

34. Methods of Health Care Audit in Private Practice, Society for Computer Medicine, New Orleans, Louisiana, November 1974

35. A Total Health Care System: Seminar on Health Care Delivery Systems, Sponsored by the University of Miami, Miami, Florida, November 1974

36. Adolescent Masturbation, Nurses' Association, American College of Obstetrics and Gynecology, Nebraska Section, April 29, 1976

37. Patient Education, Committee on Standards, American Academy of October 1976 Pediatrics Workshop, Annual Meeting, Chicago, October 1976

38. Workshop on Medical Records and Related Data, Committee on Standards, Society for Computer Medicine, Annual Meeting Boston, November 1976

39. The Effective Use of Time - Office Management, American Academy of Pediatrics, Course on Continuing Education, Monterey, California, December 1976

40. Management Planning and Techniques for Quality Control – Office Management, American Academy of Pediatrics, Course of Continuing Education, Monterey, California, December 1976

41. Cost Accounting, Budgets and Overhead Components – Office Management, American Academy of Pediatrics, Course on Continuing Education, Monterey, California, December 1976

42. Workshop-Office Management , American Academy of Pediatrics. Course on Continuing Education, Monterey, California, 1976

43. Round Table, Minimal Brain Dysfunction, American Academy of Pediatrics Spring Meeting, New Orleans, Louisiana, April 1977

44. Round Table, Modern Office Practice, Department of Health, Education and Welfare, Institute for Medicaid Management, Orlando, Florida, December 1977

45. Seminar: Practice Management, North Dakota Chapter of the American Academy of Pediatrics, Fargo, North Dakota, April 1978

46. Anticipatory Guidance Program for General Practice, Summer Meeting of the Iowa Association of Family Practitioners Okaboji, Iowa, July 1978

47. Problems in Adolescence, Summer Meeting of the Iowa Assoc. of Family Practitioners, Okaboji, Iowa, June 1978

48. Course of Medical Economics to the Freshman Class of the University of Nebraska College of Medicine in Conjunction with Dr.

Roger Mason, Medical Director and Vice-President of Nebraska Blue Mason, Medical Director and Vice-President of Nebraska Blue Cross and Blue Shield, April 1978

49. The Anatomy of a Modern Pediatric Practice Workshop, Society for Computer Medicine, Minneapolis, Minnesota, October 1978

50. Straub Clinic, Honolulu, Hawaii, Modern Pediatric Practice, March 1980

51. Children's Hospital, Honolulu, Hawaii, Practice Management, March 1980

52. Children's Hospital, Denver, Colorado, 1. Computer Networking, 2. Computer Applications to Office Practice, November 1982

53. University of Southern California, Los Angeles, March 1983, 1. Postgraduate Course on Computers, Keynote Address: Computers, Computers, Computers; 2. Computer Applications to Office Practice

54. Workshop on the Handicapped Child - Teacher-In-Service, Red Oak, Iowa, March 1983

55, Section on Computers, American Academy of Pediatrics, A Personalized Medical Textbook Utilizing the Computer, Fall Meeting AAP Chicago, September 1984, and Spring Meeting, Atlanta, Georgia April 1985

56. Pediatric Section, American Association Medical System and Informatics Fall Meeting, Washington, D.C., Personalized Medical Textbook Utilizing the Computer, 1985

57. Determination of Wellness-Fitness: Computer Assisted, First National Symposium on Fitness, Las Vegas, February 1985

58. University of Southern California: Third Annual Symposium on Computers, Las*Vegas, Nevada, April 1985
    1. Introduction to Accounting
    2. Introduction to Word Processing
    3. Hidden Office Costs
    4. Personal Finances and Other Computer Applications.

59. American Academy of Pediatrics, Continuing Medical Education Course on Computers in Pediatric Medicine Course Coordinator
   1. Computers, Computers
   2. Introduction to Networking
   3. Hidden Office Costs
   4. Personalized Medical Textbook Utilizing Computers
   5. Vendors and Their Problems
   New York City, September 1985

60. Mental Retardation: A Medical Viewpoint, American Association Mental Deficiencies, Region 8, Omaha, Nebraska, October 1984

61. Adolescence: Talk to Junior High Teachers, Fremont, Nebraska August 1984

62. Section on Computers and Other Technology, American Academy of Pediatrics, Computers and Practice Analysis, Pediatrics, Computers and Practice Analysis, San Antonio, 1986

63. National Conference on Computers, 8 Management Areas of Office Practice, Chicago, 1987

64. SCAMC Annual Meeting, Tutorial with John Long PhD on Computers in the 4 Areas of Health Care Delivery, the 4 Areas of Health Care Delivery, Washington D.C.; 1987

65. Clinical Benefits of a Life Long Medical Record; 4th Annual Meeting of the Institute on Medical Records; New York, April 1988

66. Computers in Private Practice Management, World Med 1988; Minneapolis, Minn.; June 1988

67. The AMOS System and Practice Management, Annual Users Group, MCMI Omaha, Ne June 1988

68. AMOS, Can a System really be that Good?, Iowa Medical Association, Des Moines, September 1988

69. Graphics and Spread Sheets in the Analysis of a Medical Practice; Annual Meeting, American Academy of Pediatrics; Section on Computers and Other Technology; San Francisco, October 1988

70. Computers and the AMOS System in Medical Practice Management; Grand Rounds, Phoenix Children's Hospital November 1988

73. Where in AMOS Do You Find?; Annual AMOS Group; MCMI; Omaha, Nebr.; June 1989

74. Practice Management Seminar Utilizing the AMOS System; Phoenix, Arizona, February 1990

75. MCMI Centralized Credentialing System; Iowa Medical Association Services and the Iowa Hospital Association; Des Moines, Iowa; March 1990

76. MCMI Centralized Credentialing System; Milwaukee Medical Society, Milwaukee, Wisconsin; May 1990

77. 7 MCMI Executive Support Services for Physicians and Administrators; Annual MCMI Users Group; Omaha Nebraska; June 1990

78. Practice Management Seminar Utilizing the AMOS System; Phoenix, Arizona; January 1991

79. Management "Beyond Billing": Future Trends in the Automation of Practice Management; Iowa Medical Services, a Division of the Iowa Medical Association; Des Moines, Iowa; June 1991

80. Seminar on AMOS Reports: What Are They and How to Use Them?; Annual MCMI Users Group Meeting; Omaha, Nebraska; June 1991

81. A Computerized Patient Health Record; Iowa Medical Services, a Division of the Iowa Medical Association; Des Moines, Iowa, October 1991

82. Seminar: How to Save Money Through Better Efficiency and Quality Control of the Functions of Your Medical Practice; Omaha, Nebraska; February 1992; Sponsored by Medical Computer Nebraska and Healthcare Business Solutions, Inc.

83. Seminar: The Impact of Living Wills, ADA, and CLIA'88 on the Medical Practice; March 1992; Sponsored by the Lutheran Medical

Center of Wheatridge, Colorado and Healthcare Business Solutions Inc.,

84. Seminar: How to Promote (Market) Your Medical Practice; Annual MCMI Users Group Meeting; Omaha, Nebraska; June 1992

85. Seminar: CLIA'88-An Update-- Are You in Compliance? Sponsored by the Lutheran Medical Center of Wheatridge, Colorado and Healthcare Business Solutions, Inc.; and Healthcare Business Solutions, Inc.; November 1992

HONORS RECEIVED

1. Who's Who in America Universities and Colleges, 1943 and 1944

2. Recipient of Honorary Lifetime Membership PTA, 1970

3. Recipient of Honorary Lifetime Membership National Association of Childrens' Learning Disabilities, 1974

4. Recognition Dinner, Children's Memorial Hospital - Twenty- Five Year's Service, November 1976

5. Recognition Dinner, Nebraska Methodist Hospital - Twenty- Five Year's Service, 1976

6. Who's Who in Nebraska 1976-77, Bicentennial Edition, Merit Publishers, Inc., Omaha, Nebraska

7. Who's Who in the Midwest Edition, Marquis, 1978-79, Who's Who 's Who Inc., Chicago, Illinois

8. Wyeth Award for Outstanding Small Chapter, American Academy of Pediatrics, October 1977, New York

9. Recognition Dinner, Bishop Clarkson Memorial Hospital - Twenty Five Year's Service

10. Special Recognition Award - American Academy of Pediatrics, District VI Meeting, New York, N.Y., October 24, 1982

11. Men of Achievement, Vol. 10, International Biographical Centre Cambridge, England, 1984

12. Who's Who of Intellectuals, Vol. 6, International Biographical Centre, Cambridge, England, 1985

13. Who's Who In Omaha, 1986 Edition

14. Senior Consultant Status, Department of Pediatrics, University of Nebraska Medical Center, 1988

15. The American Academy of Pediatrics established "The Byron B. Oberst Award" for excellence in computer applications in Pediatrics; 1989

16 The North High School "Vikings of Distinction: Award 2006 Hall of Fame

17. Omaha Childrens' Hospital "Legends in Pediatrics: Award 2006 Hall of Fame

CPSIA information can be obtained at www.ICGtesting.com
Printed in the USA
LVOW130123090513

332975LV00001B/231/P